W9-ASI-191

JEAN TOOMER

CANE

AN AUTHORITATIVE TEXT
BACKGROUNDS
CRITICISM

Edited by

DARWIN T. TURNER

UNIVERSITY FOUNDATION PROFESSOR OF ENGLISH
AND AFRO-AMERICAN STUDIES
UNIVERSITY OF IOWA

Oracular.
Redolent of fermenting syrup,
Purple of the dusk,
Deep-rooted cane.

≫ ≪

W · W · NORTON & COMPANY

New York · London

To my grandmother . . .

CANE by Jean Toomer is here reprinted by permission of
Liveright Publishing Corporation. Copyright 1923 by
Boni & Liveright. Copyright renewed 1951
by Jean Toomer. "Introduction" Copyright © 1975
by Darwin T. Turner.

Library of Congress Cataloging-in-Publication Data

Toomer, Jean, 1894–1967.
    Cane.

    (A Norton critical edition)
    Bibliography: p. 245
    1. Toomer, Jean, 1894–1967. Cane.   2. Afro-Americans
in literature.   I. Turner, Darwin T., 1931–
II. Title.
PS3539.0478C3   1987   813'.52   86-23635

ISBN 0-393-95600-8

W. W. Norton & Company, Inc., 500 Fifth Avenue, New York, N.Y. 10110
W. W. Norton & Company Ltd., 10 Coptic Street, London WC1A 1PU

6 7 8 9 0

Contents

sibility that he continued to revise "Kabnis" in the hope that it would be produced as a drama, there is no clear evidence that he revised any work once it had appeared in the 1923 edition of *Cane*.

The few questions that an editor might want to ask about the text seem impossible to answer. For example, in a manuscript typed several years after *Cane* had been published, Toomer identifies the work as "Cain." Does this spelling reflect an error by a typist who, ignorant of Toomer's book, thoughtlessly typed a more familiar reference? Is the spelling a suggestive error by Toomer himself? Or does it imply that Toomer originally titled *Cane* with intentional ambiguity?—a speculation that has motivated Charles Scruggs's analysis of the work in "The Mark of Cain and the Redemption of Art." Toomer's widow, Marjorie Content Toomer, who typed some of his manuscripts and read others, could not answer those questions. One can merely infer a hypothesis from the fact that this controversial manuscript seems to be the only one among the Toomer papers in which the book's title is not spelled C-A-N-E. A similarly unresolvable question concerns Toomer's practice of omitting apostrophes from contractions. Was this a stylistic device intended to speed the eye through lyric passages, or was it merely a convenience for a typist? Without some statement from Toomer, it is difficult to answer the question. In a handwritten manuscript that possibly predates *Cane*, Toomer used apostrophes in contractions; in a typed manuscript probably prepared about the time of *Cane*, he did not; in later unpublished, typed manuscripts, he did.

Because the textual problems have seemed slight, most scholarly commentary on *Cane* has concentrated on interpretation and analysis. This is the pattern that I have emphasized in the Backgrounds and Criticism sections.

In the Backgrounds section, I have included materials concerning Toomer's life and times, influences on his style and thought prior to the publication of *Cane*, and the printing history of *Cane*. Some of these selections also include criticism of literary materials that later appeared in *Cane*. Because of my emphasis, I have not tried to include in Backgrounds any discussion of Toomer's life after *Cane*. Some readers may question the relevance of the discussions of "Natalie Mann" in Waldo Frank's letter of April 25, 1922, and in my essay. I believe, however, that it is useful to permit readers to discern the context for which "Karintha" was originally prepared: In a drama emphasizing the need for Afro-American women to liberate themselves from repressive, middle-class, Anglo-Saxon morality, "Karintha" is intended to illustrate the artistry and thought of the messianic poet who guides Natalie's development. Careful readers may also wonder about the form of "Kabnis" described in Frank's letters; the letter refers to a version of "Kabnis" as a drama rather than to the revised form in which it appears in *Cane*.

The Criticism section constitutes the major portion of the commentary in this edition. I have arranged these essays in chronological order. Under

Preface

Jean Toomer's *Cane* was published in a small edition in 1923 by
Boni and Liveright publishing company. Despite favorable reviews, it
was not reprinted until 1927, when Boni and Liveright brought o.
limited quantity. For the next forty years, *Cane* remained out of pr.
and knowledge of Toomer's artistry faded into a secret shared primari
by students and scholars of Afro-American literature, friends of Toomei
and the fortunate few who accidentally discovered *Cane* in a library.
Even the high praise of Robert Bone in *The Negro Novel in America*
(1958, 1965) failed to restore *Cane* to print. As late as 1966, an official
of one New York publishing company declared—to his subsequent dis-
comfort—that *Cane* was too insubstantial to reprint unless it could be
expanded by adding other writings by Toomer. But, just as *Cane* had
first appeared during a period that some scholars name "The Harlem
Renaissance" because of the interest in and encouragement of Afro-
American culture, so it reappeared appropriately during a period that
some scholars call "The Second Renaissance" of Afro-American culture.
Reprinted in hardcover in 1967 and in paperback editions with new
introductions in 1969 and 1975, *Cane* created a new generation of
admirers, who, like those of the earlier generation, praised the book but
were sometimes puzzled by it. This present critical edition is an effort
to make the work more accessible to readers by providing notes, background information, and criticism that may further an understanding.

Editing the unpublished writings of Jean Toomer sometimes poses
major problems because he generally failed to date his manuscripts.
Consequently, one is frequently uncertain which version Toomer intended as his final revision. Even the appearance of a work in print does
not resolve all the confusion about Toomer's intentions. For example,
Toomer's "The Blue Meridian" was published in 1936; but, because
there are at least two significantly different versions of the poem in
undated manuscripts, one is forced to wonder whether the 1936 publication actually represents Toomer's final intention.

Cane, however, does not seem to pose such textual problems. There
is clear evidence that, when he prepared *Cane,* Toomer modified some
works that he had written earlier. For example, he culled "Karintha"
from its original context as part of a then-unpublished drama, "Natalie
Mann"; he created a new title, "Calling Jesus," for a piece he had
previously published as "Nora" in *The Double Dealer*; and, probably
following a suggestion by Waldo Frank, he revised "Kabnis" from a
drama into a hybrid of narrative and dialogue. But, except for the pos-

ordinary circumstances, I would have preferred publishing each critical essay in entirety to verify a faithful rendering of its content and tone. Because of space limitations, however, I have made deletions, which I have indicated by asterisks. In general, I have omitted materials that are less relevant to a discussion of Toomer or that repeat facts and conclusions stated elsewhere in this book. In other instances, I have cut the essays in such a way as to select those parts that seem to offer the most significant interpretations of *Cane*. Although I might wish to have been able to include additional essays, I believe that the present collection offers a representative sampling of works that are the most effective in helping readers to understand *Cane* and to appraise Toomer's artistry. I have felt no need to provide examples of essays by authors who have misread the work or negative essays by authors who have disliked *Cane* because they could not understand it. And I have not included some criticism that has interpreted *Cane* solely from the perspective of the 1960's by viewing it *only* as an Afro-American's despair at the loss of Black self to an oppressive and repressive white world. Such a theme was very popular in Afro-American literature of the 1960's and 1970's, when *Cane* reemerged, and such a theme is reflected somewhat in—or can be inferred from—Toomer's work. I believe, however, that an exaggerated emphasis on this theme severely distorts a reader's vision of *Cane* and of Toomer. Needless to say, my choices may be suspected of a slight bias because they are governed by my own perception of *Cane*. But I hasten to add that I have included some essays that I consider useful even though I do not agree entirely with the interpretations that they offer. Careful readers of this volume will discern the differences in the interpretations and analyses; perhaps, as a result, they will learn a ltitle more about literary interpretation and criticism. It is neither a recitation of indisputable fact nor an arbitrary proclamation of individual whimsy; instead, it is, at its best, a conscientious effort to use scholarly information and worldly insight to discern meaning and pattern in the ambiguities that constitute part of the appeal of works as complex as *Cane*.

I wish to thank Jay Berry and Evonnie Terry Gbadebo for valuable assistance in collecting materials for the Criticism section. Completion of this book was made possible by a developmental leave from the University of Iowa, by the support services provided by University House of the University of Iowa while I was a University House Scholar, and by the assistance I received during a month at the National Humanities Center in Research Triangle Park, North Carolina.

DARWIN T. TURNER

A Note on the Text

The text is the 1975 edition published by Boni and Liveright. As is noted elsewhere in this volume (p. 227), the original edition in 1923 printed a single arc on a page preceding the first page of "Karintha." That design appears in this edition.

The Text of
Cane

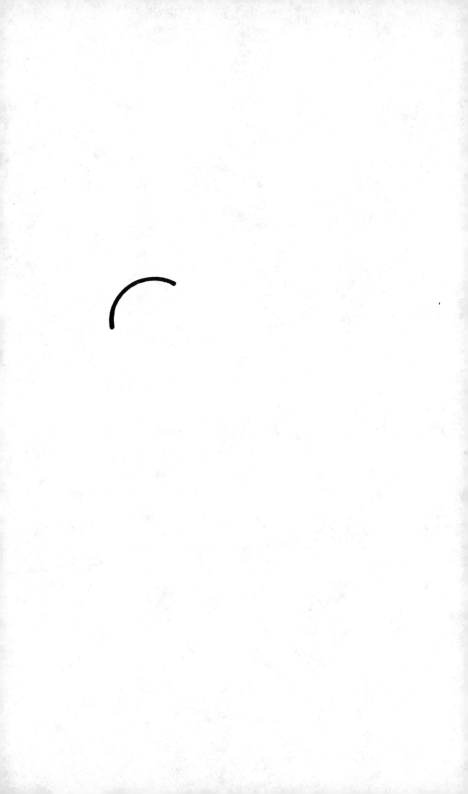

Karintha[1]

> Her skin is like dusk on the eastern horizon,[2]
> O cant[3] you see it, O cant you see it,
> Her skin is like dusk on the eastern horizon
> . . . When the sun goes down.[4]

Men had always wanted her, this Karintha, even as a child, Karintha carrying beauty, perfect as dusk when the sun goes down. Old men rode her hobby-horse upon their knees. Young men danced with her at frolics when they should have been dancing with their grown-up girls. God grant us youth, secretly prayed the old men. The young fellows counted the time to pass before she would be old enough to mate with them. This interest of the male, who wishes to ripen a growing thing too soon, could mean no good to her.

Karintha, at twelve, was a wild flash that told the other folks just what it was to live. At sunset, when there was no wind, and the pine-smoke from over by the sawmill hugged the earth, and you couldnt see more than a few feet in front, her sudden darting past you was a bit of vivid color, like a black bird that flashes in light. With the other children one could hear, some distance off, their feet flopping in the two-inch dust. Karintha's running was a whir. It had the sound of the red dust that sometimes makes a spiral in the road. At dusk, during the hush just after the sawmill had closed down, and before any of the women had started their supper-getting-ready songs, her voice, high-pitched, shrill, would put one's ears to itching. But no one ever thought to make her stop because of it. She stoned the cows, and beat her dog, and fought the other children. . . Even the preacher, who caught her at mischief, told himself that she was as innocently lovely as a November cotton flower. Already, rumors were out about her. Homes in Georgia are most often built on the two-room plan. In one, you cook and eat, in the

1. Originally included in "Natalie Mann," a drama by Toomer, this piece was intended to illustrate the style and the thought of the literature written by Nathan Merilh, one of the major characters in the drama. Never published in Toomer's lifetime, "Natalie Mann" has now been published in *The Wayward and the Seeking: A Collection of Writings by Jean Toomer*, ed. Darwin T. Turner (Washington, D.C.: Howard UP, 1980). When "Karintha" was first published (*Broom* 4 [January 1923]: 83–85), a note instructed readers of the piece: "To be read, accompanied by the humming of a Negro folk-song."

2. Especially in the first section of *Cane*, Toomer contrasts the coloring of Southern Afro-American women. Fern's face is cream-colored, and her upper lip is creamy brown. Esther's face is chalk-white. Louisa ("Blood-Burning Moon") is "the color of oak leaves on young trees in fall." Notice that Karintha is compared with dusk on the *eastern*, not western horizon; consider the color of the eastern horizon at dusk.

3. Throughout *Cane*, apostrophes are generally omitted from contractions. When "Karintha" was published in *Broom*, however, this word was printed as "can't."

4. Throughout *Cane*, Toomer uses two or three periods to indicate a pause in the reading. Readers should not mistake these for ellipsis marks, which indicate an omission from the original text.

other you sleep, and there love goes on. Karintha had seen or
heard, perhaps she had felt her parents loving. One could but imitate one's parents, for to follow them was the way of God. She
played "home" with a small boy who was not afraid to do her bid-
ding. That started the whole thing. Old men could no longer ride
her hobby-horse upon their knees. But young men counted faster.

> Her skin is like dusk,
> O cant you see it,
> Her skin is like dusk,
> When the sun goes down.

Karintha is a woman. She who carries beauty, perfect as dusk
when the sun goes down. She has been married many times. Old
men remind her that a few years back they rode her hobby-horse
upon their knees. Karintha smiles, and indulges them when she is
in the mood for it. She has contempt for them. Karintha is a
woman. Young men run stills[5] to make her money. Young men go to
the big cities and run on the road.[6] Young men go away to college.
They all want to bring her money. These are the young men who
thought that all they had to do was to count time. But Karintha is
a woman, and she has had a child. A child fell out of her womb
onto a bed of pine-needles in the forest. Pine-needles are smooth
and sweet. They are elastic to the feet of rabbits. . . A sawmill was
nearby. Its pyramidal sawdust pile smouldered. It is a year before
one completely burns. Meanwhile, the smoke curls up and hangs in
odd wraiths about the trees, curls up, and spreads itself out over the
valley. . . Weeks after Karintha returned home the smoke was so
heavy you tasted it in water. Some one made a song:

> Smoke is on the hills. Rise up.
> Smoke is on the hills, O rise
> And take my soul to Jesus.

Karintha is a woman. Men do not know that the soul of her was a
growing thing ripened too soon. They will bring their money; they
will die not having found it out. . . Karintha at twenty, carrying
beauty, perfect as dusk when the sun goes down. Karintha. . .

> Her skin is like dusk on the eastern horizon,
> O cant you see it, O cant you see it,
> Her skin is like dusk on the eastern horizon
> . . . When the sun goes down.

Goes down. . .

---

5. Apparatus for distilling whiskey. The men using
stills were making and selling whiskey illegally.

6. Work for the railroad, as porters, stewards, or
members of the dining-car staff.

Reapers

Black reapers with the sound of steel on stones
Are sharpening scythes. I see them place the hones[1]
In their hip-pockets as a thing that's done,
And start their silent swinging, one by one.
Black horses drive a mower through the weeds,
And there, a field rat, startled, squealing bleeds.
His belly close to ground. I see the blade,
Blood-stained, continue cutting weeds and shade.

1. Instruments for sharpening blades.

November Cotton Flower [1]

Boll-weevil's coming, and the winter's cold,
Made cotton-stalks look rusty, seasons old,
And cotton, scarce as any southern snow,
Was vanishing; the branch, so pinched and slow,
Failed in its function as the autumn rake;
Drouth fighting soil had caused the soil to take
All water from the streams; dead birds were found
In wells a hundred feet below the ground—
Such was the season when the flower bloomed.
Old folks were startled, and it soon assumed
Significance. Superstition saw
Something it had never seen before:
Brown eyes that loved without a trace of fear,
Beauty so sudden for that time of year.

1. First published in *The Nomad* 2 (Summer 1923): 4.

Becky [1]

Becky was the white woman who had two Negro sons. She's dead; they've gone away. The pines whisper to Jesus. The Bible flaps its leaves with an aimless rustle on her mound.

Becky had one Negro son. Who gave it to her? Damn buck nigger, said the white folks' mouths. She wouldnt tell. Common, God-forsaken, insane white shameless wench, said the white folks' mouths. Her eyes were sunken, her neck stringy, her breasts fallen, till then. Taking their words, they filled her, like a bubble rising— then she broke. Mouth setting in a twist that held her eyes, harsh, vacant, staring. . . Who gave it to her? Low-down nigger with no self-respect, said the black folks' mouths. She wouldnt tell. Poor Catholic [2] poor-white crazy woman, said the black folks' mouths. White folks and black folks built her cabin, fed her and her growing baby, prayed secretly to God who'd put His cross upon her and cast her out.

When the first was born, the white folks said they'd have no more to do with her. And black folks, they too joined hands to cast her out. . . The pines whispered to Jesus. . The railroad boss said not to say he said it, but she could live, if she wanted to, on the narrow strip of land between the railroad and the road. John Stone, [3] who owned the lumber and the bricks, would have shot the man who told he gave the stuff to Lonnie Deacon, who stole out there at night and built the cabin. A single room held down to earth. . . O fly away to Jesus . . . by a leaning chimney. . .

Six trains each day rumbled past and shook the ground under her cabin. Fords, and horse- and mule-drawn buggies went back and forth along the road. No one ever saw her. Trainmen, and passengers who'd heard about her, threw out papers and food. Threw out little crumpled slips of paper scribbled with prayers, as they passed her eye-shaped piece of sandy ground. Ground islandized between the road and railroad track. Pushed up where a blue-sheen God [4] with listless eyes could look at it. Folks from the town took turns,

---

1. First published in *The Liberator* 5 (October 1922): 26.
2. Toomer suggests a variety of religious practices in the South. Imitating her parents (in their sexual relations), Karintha follows "the way of God"; that God seems to approve the behavior of nature rather than the laws of society. Becky is Catholic; Barlo and the narrator attend Ebenezer Church (probably Baptist); but the God of the story is a mechanized deity. "Fern" abounds with Jewish imagery.

3. A suggestion of the common locale of the stories in the first section of *Cane* is the occasional recurrence of names. John Stone is the father of Tom Stone ("Blood-Burning Moon"). A person named Barlo, possibly the same one as in this story, appears in "Esther." David Georgia is a character in "Blood-Burning Moon" as well as in "Becky." The Dixie Pike is named in "Carma" and "Fern."
4. The locomotive.

unknown, of course, to each other, in bringing corn and meat and sweet potatoes. Even sometimes snuff. . . O thank y Jesus. . . Old David Georgia, grinding cane and boiling syrup, never went her way without some sugar sap. No one ever saw her. The boy grew up and ran around. When he was five years old as folks reckoned it, Hugh Jourdon saw him carrying a baby. "Becky has another son," was what the whole town knew. But nothing was said, for the part of man that says things to the likes of that had told itself that if there was a Becky, that Becky now was dead.

The two boys grew. Sullen and cunning. . . O pines, whisper to Jesus; tell Him to come and press sweet Jesus-lips against their lips and eyes. . . It seemed as though with those two big fellows there, there could be no room for Becky. The part that prayed wondered if perhaps she'd really died, and they had buried her. No one dared ask. They'd beat and cut a man who meant nothing at all in mentioning that they lived along the road. White or colored? No one knew, and least of all themselves. They drifted around from job to job. We, who had cast out their mother because of them, could we take them in? They answered black and white folks by shooting up two men and leaving town. "Godam the white folks; godam the niggers," they shouted as they left town. Becky? Smoke curled up from her chimney; she must be there. Trains passing shook the ground. The ground shook the leaning chimney. Nobody noticed it. A creepy feeling came over all who saw that thin wraith of smoke and felt the trembling of the ground. Folks began to take her food again. They quit it soon because they had a fear. Becky if dead might be a hant,[5] and if alive—it took some nerve even to mention it. . . O pines, whisper to Jesus. . .

It was Sunday. Our congregation had been visiting at Pulverton, and were coming home. There was no wind. The autumn sun, the bell from Ebenezer Church, listless and heavy. Even the pines were stale, sticky, like the smell of food that makes you sick. Before we turned the bend of the road that would show us the Becky cabin, the horses stopped stock-still, pushed back their ears, and nervously whinnied. We urged, then whipped them on. Quarter of a mile away thin smoke curled up from the leaning chimney. . . O pines, whisper to Jesus. . . Goose-flesh came on my skin though there still was neither chill nor wind. Eyes left their sockets for the cabin. Ears burned and throbbed. Uncanny eclipse! fear closed my mind. We were just about to pass. . . Pines shout to Jesus! . . the ground trembled as a ghost train rumbled by. The chimney fell into the cabin. Its thud was like a hollow report, ages having passed since it

5. A "haunt," a ghost.

went off. Barlo and I were pulled out of our seats. Dragged to the door that had swung open. Through the dust we saw the bricks in a mound upon the floor. Becky, if she was there, lay under them. I thought I heard a groan. Barlo, mumbling something, threw his Bible on the pile. (No one has ever touched it.) Somehow we got away. My buggy was still on the road. The last thing that I remember was whipping old Dan like fury; I remember nothing after that—that is, until I reached town and folks crowded round to get the true word of it.

Becky was the white woman who had two Negro sons. She's dead; they've gone away. The pines whisper to Jesus. The Bible flaps its leaves with an aimless rustle on her mound.

Face [1]

Hair—
silver-gray,
like streams of stars,
Brows—
recurved canoes
quivered by the ripples blown by pain,
Her eyes—
mist of tears
condensing on the flesh below
And her channeled muscles
are cluster grapes of sorrow
purple in the evening sun
nearly ripe for worms.

---

1. First published as number one of three "Georgia Portraits," *Modern Review* 1 (January 1923): 81.

Cotton Song

Come, brother, come. Lets lift it;
Come now, hewit! roll away!
Shackles fall upon the Judgment Day
But lets not wait for it.

God's body's got a soul,
Bodies like to roll the soul,
Cant blame God if we dont roll,
Come, brother, roll, roll!

Cotton bales are the fleecy way
Weary sinner's bare feet trod,
Softly, softly to the throne of God,
"We aint agwine t wait until th Judgment Day!

Nassur; nassur,
Hump.
Eoho, eoho, roll away!
We aint agwine t wait until th Judgment Day!"

God's body's got a soul,
Bodies like to roll the soul,
Cant blame God if we dont roll,
Come, brother, roll, roll!

Carma [1]

Wind is in the cane. Come along.
Cane leaves swaying, rusty with talk,
Scratching choruses above the guinea's squawk,
Wind is in the cane. Come along.

Carma, in overalls, and strong as any man, stands behind the old
brown mule, driving the wagon home. It bumps, and groans, and
shakes as it crosses the railroad track. She, riding it easy. I leave
the men around the stove to follow her with my eyes down the red
dust road. Nigger woman driving a Georgia chariot down an old
dust road. Dixie Pike is what they call it. Maybe she feels my gaze,
perhaps she expects it. Anyway, she turns. The sun, which has
been slanting over her shoulder, shoots primitive rockets into her
mangrove-gloomed, yellow flower face. Hi! Yip! God has left the
Moses-people for the nigger. "Gedap." Using reins to slap the mule,
she disappears in a cloudy rumble at some indefinite point along the
road.
(The sun is hammered to a band of gold. Pine-needles, like
mazda, are brilliantly aglow. No rain has come to take the rustle
from the falling sweet-gum leaves. Over in the forest, across the
swamp, a sawmill blows its closing whistle. Smoke curls up.
Marvelous web spun by the spider sawdust pile. Curls up and
spreads itself pine-high above the branch, a single silver band along
the eastern valley. A black boy . . . you are the most sleepiest man
I ever seed, Sleeping Beauty . . . cradled on a gray mule, guided by
the hollow sound of cowbells, heads for them through a rusty
cotton field. From down the railroad track, the chug-chug of a gas
engine announces that the repair gang is coming home. A girl in
the yard of a whitewashed shack not much larger than the stack of
worn ties piled before it, sings. Her voice is loud. Echoes, like rain,
sweep the valley. Dusk takes the polish from the rails. Lights twin-
kle in scattered houses. From far away, a sad strong song. Pungent
and composite, the smell of farmyards is the fragrance of the
woman. She does not sing; her body is a song. She is in the forest,
dancing. Torches flare . . juju men,[2] greegree,[3] witch-doctors . .
torches go out. . . The Dixie Pike has grown from a goat path in
Africa.

Night.

Foxie, the bitch, slicks back her ears and barks at the rising moon.)

1. First published in *The Liberator* 5 (September
1922): 5. "Karma," from the Sanskrit word for "fate,"
is the force generated by a person's actions; it is
believed in Hinduism and Buddhism to perpetuate
the passage of the soul from one state to another
and to determine a person's destiny in his or her
next existence.
2. Conjurers, supposedly able to use powers of the
supernatural.
3. An African charm or amulet.

Wind is in the corn. Come along.
Corn leaves swaying, rusty with talk,
Scratching choruses above the guinea's squawk,
Wind is in the corn. Come along.

Carma's tale is the crudest melodrama. Her husband's in the gang.[4] And its her fault he got there. Working with a contractor, he was away most of the time. She had others. No one blames her for that. He returned one day and hung around the town where he picked up week-old boasts and rumors. . . Bane accused her. She denied. He couldnt see that she was becoming hysterical. He would have liked to take his fists and beat her. Who was strong as a man. Stronger. Words, like corkscrews, wormed to her strength. It fizzled out. Grabbing a gun, she rushed from the house and plunged across the road into a canebrake. . There, in quarter heaven shone the crescent moon. . . Bane was afraid to follow till he heard the gun go off. Then he wasted half an hour gathering the neighbor men. They met in the road where lamp-light showed tracks dissolving in the loose earth about the cane. The search began. Moths flickered the lamps. They put them out. Really, because she still might be live enough to shoot. Time and space have no meaning in a canefield. No more than the interminable stalks. . . Some one stumbled over her. A cry went up. From the road, one would have thought that they were cornering a rabbit or a skunk. . . It is difficult carrying dead weight through cane. They placed her on the sofa. A curious, nosey somebody looked for the wound. This fussing with her clothes aroused her. Her eyes were weak and pitiable for so strong a woman. Slowly, then like a flash, Bane came to know that the shot she fired, with averted head, was aimed to whistle like a dying hornet through the cane. Twice deceived, and one deception proved the other. His head went off. Slashed one of the men who'd helped, the man who'd stumbled over her. Now he's in the gang. Who was her husband. Should she not take others, this Carma, strong as a man, whose tale as I have told it is the crudest melodrama?

Wind is in the cane. Come along.
Cane leaves swaying, rusty with talk,
Scratching choruses above the guinea's squawk,
Wind is in the cane. Come along.

4. Chain gang: prisoners, chained at the feet, who repaired roads and performed other forms of labor.

Song of the Son [1]

Pour O pour that parting soul in song,
O pour it in the sawdust glow of night,
Into the velvet pine-smoke air to-night,
And let the valley carry it along.
And let the valley carry it along.

O land and soil, red soil and sweet-gum tree,
So scant of grass, so profligate of pines,
Now just before an epoch's sun declines
Thy son, in time, I have returned to thee,
Thy son, I have in time returned to thee.

In time, for though the sun is setting on
A song-lit race of slaves, it has not set;
Though late, O soil, it is not too late yet
To catch thy plaintive soul, leaving, soon gone,
Leaving, to catch thy plaintive soul soon gone.

O Negro slaves, dark purple ripened plums,
Squeezed, and bursting in the pine-wood air,
Passing, before they stripped the old tree bare
One plum was saved for me, one seed becomes

An everlasting song, a singing tree,
Caroling softly souls of slavery,
What they were, and what they are to me,
Caroling softly souls of slavery.

---

1. The poem expresses an important theme. After
Cane was published, Toomer stated his belief that,
in *Cane*, he was writing about a way of life that
was dying. The poem was first published in *The
Crisis* 23 (June 1922): 65.

Georgia Dusk[1]

The sky, lazily disdaining to pursue
    The setting sun, too indolent to hold
    A lengthened tournament for flashing gold,
Passively darkens for night's barbecue,

A feast of moon and men and barking hounds,
    An orgy for some genius of the South
    With blood-hot eyes and cane-lipped scented mouth,
Surprised in making folk-songs from soul sounds.

The sawmill blows its whistle, buzz-saws stop,
    And silence breaks the bud of knoll and hill,
    Soft settling pollen where plowed lands fulfill
Their early promise of a bumper crop.

Smoke from the pyramidal sawdust pile
    Curls up, blue ghosts of trees, tarrying low
    Where only chips and stumps are left to show
The solid proof of former domicile.

Meanwhile, the men, with vestiges of pomp,
    Race memories of king and caravan,
    High-priests, an ostrich, and a juju-man,
Go singing through the footpaths of the swamp.

Their voices rise . . the pine trees are guitars,
    Strumming, pine-needles fall like sheets of rain . .
    Their voices rise . . the chorus of the cane
Is caroling a vesper to the stars. .

O singers, resinous and soft your songs
    Above the sacred whisper of the pines,
    Give virgin lips to cornfield concubines,
Bring dreams of Christ to dusky cane-lipped throngs.

---

1. First published in *The Liberator* 5 (September 1922): 25.

Face actually, in sentence
flows into her eye (the word)   # Fern [1]

Face flowed into her eyes. Flowed in soft cream foam and plaintive ripples, in such a way that wherever your glance may momentarily have rested, it immediately thereafter wavered in the direction
of her eyes. The soft suggestion of down slightly darkened, like the
shadow of a bird's wing might, the creamy brown color of her upper
lip. Why, after noticing it, you sought her eyes, I cannot tell you.
Her nose was aquiline, Semitic. If you have heard a Jewish cantor
sing, if he has touched you and made your own sorrow seem trivial
when compared with his, you will know my feeling when I follow
the curves of her profile, like mobile rivers, to their common delta.
They were strange eyes. In this, that they sought nothing—that is,
nothing that was obvious and tangible and that one could see, and
they gave the impression that nothing was to be denied. When a
woman seeks, you will have observed, her eyes deny. Fern's eyes
desired nothing that you could give her; there was no reason why
they should withhold. Men saw her eyes and fooled themselves.
Fern's eyes said to them that she was easy. When she was young, a
few men took her, but got no joy from it. And then, once done,
they felt bound to her (quite unlike their hit and run with other
girls), felt as though it would take them a lifetime to fulfill an obli-
gation which they could find no name for. They became attached
to her, and hungered after finding the barest trace of what she
might desire. As she grew up, new men who came to town felt as
almost everyone did who ever saw her: that they would not be
denied. Men were everlastingly bringing her their bodies.
Something inside of her got tired of them, I guess, for I am certain
that for the life of her she could not tell why or how she began to
turn them off. A man in fever is no trifling thing to send away.
They began to leave her, baffled and ashamed, yet vowing to themselves that some day they would do some fine thing for her: send
her candy every week and not let her know whom it came from,
watch out for her wedding-day and give her a magnificent something with no name on it, buy a house and deed it to her, rescue
her from some unworthy fellow who had tricked her into marrying
him. As you know, men are apt to idolize or fear that which they
cannot understand, especially if it be a woman. She did not deny
them, yet the fact was that they were denied. A sort of superstition
crept into their consciousness of her being somehow above them.
Being above them meant that she was not to be approached by
anyone. She became a virgin. Now a virgin in a small southern

1. First published in *Little Review* 9 (Autumn 1922): 25–29.

town is by no means the usual thing, if you will believe me. That the sexes were made to mate is the practice of the South. Particularly, black folks were made to mate. And it is black folks whom I have been talking about thus far. What white men thought of Fern I can arrive at only by analogy. They let her alone.

Anyone, of course, could see her, could see her eyes. If you walked up the Dixie Pike most any time of day, you'd be most like to see her resting listless-like on the railing of her porch, back propped against a post, head tilted a little forward because there was a nail in the porch post just where her head came which for some reason or other she never took the trouble to pull out. Her eyes, if it were sunset, rested idly where the sun, molten and glorious, was pouring down between the fringe of pines. Or maybe they gazed at the gray cabin on the knoll from which an evening folk-song was coming. Perhaps they followed a cow that had been turned loose to roam and feed on cotton-stalks and corn leaves. Like as not they'd settle on some vague spot above the horizon, though hardly a trace of wistfulness would come to them. If it were dusk, then they'd wait for the search-light of the evening train which you could see miles up the track before it flared across the Dixie Pike, close to her home. Wherever they looked, you'd follow them and then waver back. Like her face, the whole countryside seemed to flow into her eyes. Flowed into them with the soft listless cadence of Georgia's South. A young Negro, once, was looking at her, spellbound, from the road. A white man passing in a buggy had to flick him with his whip if he was to get by without running him over. I first saw her on her porch. I was passing with a fellow whose crusty numbness (I was from the North and suspected of being prejudiced and stuck-up)[2] was melting as he found me warm. I asked him who she was. "That's Fern," was all that I could get from him. Some folks already thought that I was given to nosing around; I let it go at that, so far as questions were concerned. But at first sight of her I felt as if I heard a Jewish cantor sing. As if his singing rose above the unheard chorus of a folk-song. And I felt bound to her. I too had my dreams: something I would do for her. I have knocked about from town to town too much not to know the futility of mere change of place. Besides, picture if you can, this cream-colored solitary girl sitting at a tenement window looking down on the indifferent throngs of Harlem. Better that she listen to folk-songs at dusk in Georgia, you would say, and so would I. Or, suppose she came up North and married. Even a doctor or a lawyer, say, one who would be sure to get along—that is, make

---

2. Note the similarity between the Black people's concept of the anonymous narrator here and their concept of Lewis in "Kabnis."

money. You and I know, who have had experience in such things, that love is not a thing like prejudice which can be bettered by changes of town. Could men in Washington, Chicago, or New York, more than the men of Georgia, bring her something left vacant by the bestowal of their bodies? You and I who know men in these cities will have to say, they could not. See her out and out a prostitute along State Street in Chicago. See her move into a southern town where white men are more aggressive. See her become a white man's concubine. . . Something I must do for her. There was myself. What could I do for her? Talk, of course. Push back the fringe of pines upon new horizons. To what purpose? and what for? Her? Myself? Men in her case seem to lose their selfishness. I lost mine before I touched her. I ask you, friend (it makes no difference if you sit in the Pullman or the Jim Crow[3] as the train crosses her road), what thoughts would come to you—that is, after you'd finished with the thoughts that leap into men's minds at the sight of a pretty woman who will not deny them; what thoughts would come to you, had you seen her in a quick flash, keen and intuitively, as she sat there on her porch when your train thundered by? Would you have got off at the next station and come back for her to take her where? Would you have completely forgotten her as soon as you reached Macon, Atlanta, Augusta, Pasadena, Madison, Chicago, Boston, or New Orleans? Would you tell your wife or sweetheart about a girl you saw? Your thoughts can help me, and I would like to know. Something I would do for her. . .

One evening I walked up the Pike on purpose, and stopped to say hello. Some of her family were about, but they moved away to make room for me. Damn if I knew how to begin. Would you? Mr. and Miss So-and-So, people, the weather, the crops, the new preacher, the frolic, the church benefit, rabbit and possum hunting, the new soft drink they had at old Pap's store, the schedule of the trains, what kind of town Macon was, Negro's migration north, bollweevils, syrup, the Bible—to all these things she gave a yassur or nassur, without further comment. I began to wonder if perhaps my own emotional sensibility had played one of its tricks on me. "Lets take a walk," I at last ventured. The suggestion, coming after so long an isolation, was novel enough, I guess, to surprise. But it wasnt that. Something told me that men before me had said just that as a prelude to the offering of their bodies. I tried to tell her

3. "Pullman" was the sleeping-car section of railway trains. During the time when Afro-Americans were legally segregated from whites on public transportation in the South (especially in the states that had formed the Confederacy during the Civil War), they were not permitted to ride in the sleeping-car section. Therefore, the Pullman riders alluded to are white. "Jim Crow" as a noun or adjective refers to the system of segregation or to the segregated facilities. Here, it refers to the railway coach or coaches to which Blacks were assigned because of Southern segregation.

with my eyes. I think she understood. The thing from her that made my throat catch, vanished. Its passing left her visible in a way I'd thought, but never seen. We walked down the Pike with people on all the porches gaping at us. "Doesnt it make you mad?" She meant the row of petty gossiping people. She meant the world. Through a canebrake that was ripe for cutting, the branch was reached. Under a sweet-gum tree, and where reddish leaves had dammed the creek a little, we sat down. Dusk, suggesting the almost imperceptible procession of giant trees, settled with a purple haze about the cane. I felt strange, as I always do in Georgia, particularly at dusk. I felt that things unseen to men were tangibly immediate. It would not have surprised me had I had vision. People have them in Georgia more often than you would suppose. A black woman once saw the mother of Christ and drew her in charcoal on the courthouse wall. . .[4] When one is on the soil of one's ancestors, most anything can come to one. . . From force of habit, I suppose, I held Fern in my arms—that is, without at first noticing it. Then my mind came back to her. Her eyes, unusually weird and open, held me. Held God. He flowed in as I've seen the countryside flow in. Seen men. I must have done something— what, I dont know, in the confusion of my emotion. She sprang up. Rushed some distance from me. Fell to her knees, and began swaying, swaying. Her body was tortured with something it could not let out. Like boiling sap it flooded arms and fingers till she shook them as if they burned her. It found her throat, and spattered inarticulately in plaintive, convulsive sounds, mingled with calls to Christ Jesus. And then she sang, brokenly. A Jewish cantor singing with a broken voice. A child's voice, uncertain, or an old man's. Dusk hid her; I could hear only her song. It seemed to me as though she were pounding her head in anguish upon the ground. I rushed to her. She fainted in my arms.

There was talk about her fainting with me in the canefield. And I got one or two ugly looks from town men who'd set themselves up to protect her. In fact, there was talk of making me leave town. But they never did. They kept a watch-out for me, though. Shortly after, I came back North. From the train window I saw her as I crossed her road. Saw her on her porch, head tilted a little forward where the nail was, eyes vaguely focused on the sunset. Saw her face flow into them, the countryside and something that I call God, flowing into them. . . Nothing ever really happened. Nothing ever came to Fern, not even I. Something I would do for her. Some fine unnamed thing. . . And, friend, you? She is still living, I have reason to know. Her name, against the chance that you might happen down that way, is Fernie May Rosen.

---

4. See also in "Esther" (p. 22) this reference to a Black madonna drawn by a Black woman.

Nullo

A spray of pine-needles,
Dipped in western horizon gold,
Fell onto a path.
Dry moulds of cow-hoofs.
In the forest.
Rabbits knew not of their falling,
Nor did the forest catch aflame.

Evening Song

Full moon rising on the waters of my heart,
Lakes and moon and fires,
Cloine tires,
Holding her lips apart.

Promises of slumber leaving shore to charm the moon,
Miracle made vesper-keeps,
Cloine sleeps,
And I'll be sleeping soon.

Cloine, curled like the sleepy waters where the moon-waves start,
Radiant, resplendently she gleams,
Cloine dreams,
Lips pressed against my heart.

Esther[1]

1

Nine.

Esther's hair falls in soft curls about her high-cheek-boned chalk-white face. Esther's hair would be beautiful if there were more gloss to it. And if her face were not prematurely serious, one would call it pretty. Her cheeks are too flat and dead for a girl of nine. Esther looks like a little white child, starched, frilled, as she walks slowly from her home towards her father's grocery store. She is about to turn in Broad from Maple Street. White and black men loafing on the corner hold no interest for her. Then a strange thing happens. A clean-muscled, magnificent, black-skinned Negro, whom she had heard her father mention as King Barlo, suddenly drops to his knees on a spot called the Spittoon. White men, unaware of him, continue squirting tobacco juice in his direction. The saffron fluid splashes on his face. His smooth black face begins to glisten and to shine. Soon, people notice him, and gather round. His eyes are rapturous upon the heavens. Lips and nostrils quiver. Barlo is in a religious trance. Town folks know it. They are not startled. They are not afraid. They gather round. Some beg boxes from the grocery stores. From old McGregor's notion shop. A coffin-case is pressed into use. Folks line the curb-stones. Business men close shop. And Banker Warply parks his car close by. Silently, all await the prophet's voice. The sheriff, a great florid fellow whose leggings never meet around his bulging calves, swears in three deputies. "Wall, y cant never tell what a nigger like King Barlo might be up t." Soda bottles, five fingers full of shine, are passed to those who want them. A couple of stray dogs start a fight. Old Goodlow's cow comes flopping up the street. Barlo, still as an Indian fakir,[2] has not moved. The town bell strikes six. The sun slips in behind a heavy mass of horizon cloud. The crowd is hushed and expectant. Barlo's under jaw relaxes, and his lips begin to move.

"Jesus has been awhisperin strange words deep down, O way down deep, deep in my ears."

Hums of awe and of excitement.

"He called me to His side an said, 'Git down on your knees beside me, son, Ise gwine t whisper in your ears.' "

An old sister cries, "Ah, Lord."

1. First published in *Modern Review* 1 (January 1923): 50–54.   2. Magician.

" 'Ise agwine t whisper in your ears,' he said, an I replied, 'Thy will be done on earth as it is in heaven.' "

"Ah, Lord. Amen. Amen."

"An Lord Jesus whispered strange good words deep down, O way down deep, deep in my ears. An He said, 'Tell em till you feel your throat on fire.' I saw a vision. I saw a man arise, an he was big an black an powerful—"

Some one yells, "Preach it, preacher, preach it!"

"—but his head was caught up in th clouds. An while he was agazin at th heavens, heart filled up with th Lord, some little white-ant biddies came an tied his feet to chains. They led him t th coast, they led him t th sea, they led him across th ocean an they didnt set him free. The old coast didnt miss him, an th new coast wasnt free, he left the old-coast brothers, t give birth t you an me. O Lord, great God Almighty, t give birth t you an me."

Barlo pauses. Old gray mothers are in tears. Fragments of melodies are being hummed. White folks are touched and curiously awed. Off to themselves, white and black preachers confer as to how best to rid themselves of the vagrant, usurping fellow. Barlo looks as though he is struggling to continue. People are hushed. One can hear weevils work. Dusk is falling rapidly, and the customary store lights fail to throw their feeble glow across the gray dust and flagging of the Georgia town. Barlo rises to his full height. He is immense. To the people he assumes the outlines of his visioned African. In a mighty voice he bellows:

"Brothers an sisters, turn your faces t th sweet face of the Lord, an fill your hearts with glory. Open your eyes an see th dawnin of th mornin light. Open your ears—"

Years afterwards Esther was told that at that very moment a great, heavy, rumbling voice actually was heard. That hosts of angels and of demons paraded up and down the streets all night. That King Barlo rode out of town astride a pitch-black bull that had a glowing gold ring in its nose. And that old Limp Underwood, who hated niggers, woke up next morning to find that he held a black man in his arms. This much is certain: an inspired Negress, of wide reputation for being sanctified, drew a portrait of a black madonna on the courthouse wall. And King Barlo left town. He left his image indelibly upon the mind of Esther. He became the starting point of the only living patterns that her mind was to know.

2

Sixteen.[3]

Esther begins to dream. The low evening sun sets the windows
of McGregor's notion shop aflame. Esther makes believe that they
really are aflame. The town fire department rushes madly down the
road. It ruthlessly shoves black and white idlers to one side. It
whoops. It clangs. It rescues from the second-story window a dim-
pled infant which she claims for her own. How had she come by
it? She thinks of it immaculately. It is a sin to think of it immaculately. She must dream no more. She must repent her sin.
Another dream comes. There is no fire department. There are no
heroic men. The fire starts. The loafers on the corner form a circle,
chew their tobacco faster, and squirt juice just as fast as they can
chew. Gallons on top of gallons they squirt upon the flames. The
air reeks with the stench of scorched tobacco juice. Women, fat
chunky Negro women, lean scrawny white women, pull their skirts
up above their heads and display the most ludicrous underclothes.
The women scoot in all directions from the danger zone. She
alone is left to take the baby in her arms. But what a baby! Black,
singed, woolly, tobacco-juice baby—ugly as sin. Once held to her
breast, miraculous thing: its breath is sweet and its lips can nibble.
She loves it frantically. Her joy in it changes the town folks' jeers
to harmless jealousy, and she is left alone.

Twenty-two.

Esther's schooling is over. She works behind the counter of her
father's grocery store. "To keep the money in the family," so he
said. She is learning to make distinctions between the business and
the social worlds. "Good business comes from remembering that
the white folks dont divide the niggers, Esther. Be just as black as
any man who has a silver dollar." Esther listlessly forgets that she
is near white, and that her father is the richest colored man in
town. Black folk who drift in to buy lard and snuff and flour of
her, call her a sweet-natured, accommodating girl. She learns their
names. She forgets them. She thinks about men. "I dont appeal
to them. I wonder why." She recalls an affair she had with a little

3. Esther's two dreams reveal the impossibility of
her resolving her conflict. Because of her "proper"
rearing, she dreams first of conceiving a child without sexual intercourse; but she believes that it is
sinful to dream of such an immaculate conception
because her religion has taught her that there has
been only one Immaculate Conception. But her
training has also taught her to consider sex to be
sinful. Therefore, in her second dream, when she
imagines a child conceived as a result of a sexual
act, the images are of ugliness and the child is
"ugly as sin." Notice the manner in which Toomer,
in this second dream, uses Freudian imagery to
transform the setting and the characters of the incident that occurred when Esther was nine years
old.

fair boy while still in school. It had ended in her shame when he as much as told her that for sweetness he preferred a lollipop. She remembers the salesman from the North who wanted to take her to the movies that first night he was in town. She refused, of course. And he never came back, having found out who she was. She thinks of Barlo. Barlo's image gives her a slightly stale thrill. She spices it by telling herself his glories. Black. Magnetically so. Best cotton picker in the county, in the state, in the whole world for that matter. Best man with his fists, best man with dice, with a razor. Promoter of church benefits. Of colored fairs. Vagrant preacher. Lover of all the women for miles and miles around. Esther decides that she loves him. And with a vague sense of life slipping by, she resolves that she will tell him so, whatever people say, the next time he comes to town. After the making of this resolution which becomes a sort of wedding cake for her to tuck beneath her pillow and go to sleep upon, she sees nothing of Barlo for five years. Her hair thins. It looks like the dull silk on puny corn ears. Her face pales until it is the color of the gray dust that dances with dead cotton leaves.

3

Esther is twenty-seven.

Esther sells lard and snuff and flour to vague black faces that drift in her store to ask for them. Her eyes hardly see the people to whom she gives change. Her body is lean and beaten. She rests listlessly against the counter, too weary to sit down. From the street some one shouts, "King Barlo has come back to town." He passes her window, driving a large new car. Cut-out open.[4] He veers to the curb, and steps out. Barlo has made money on cotton during the war.[5] He is as rich as anyone. Esther suddenly is animate. She goes to her door. She sees him at a distance, the center of a group of credulous men. She hears the deep-bass rumble of his talk. The sun swings low. McGregor's windows are aflame again. Pale flame.[6] A sharply dressed white girl passes by. For a moment Esther wishes that she might be like her. Not white; she has no need for being that. But sharp, sporty, with get-up about her. Barlo is connected with that wish. She mustnt wish. Wishes only make you restless. Emptiness is a thing that grows by being moved. "I'll not think. Not wish. Just set my mind against it." Then the thought

4. A valve in the exhaust pipe of an internal combustion engine through which exhaust gases may escape without going through the muffler.
5. World War I (1914-18).
6. Notice the manner in which Toomer uses images of flame to contrast Esther's emotions at this stage of her life with the deeper emotions that she experienced at the age of sixteen. Notice also that Toomer again uses the windows of McGregor's shop in the setting to remind readers of the original setting in which Barlo appeared.

comes to her that those purposeless, easy-going men will possess him, if she doesnt. Purpose is not dead in her, now that she comes to think of it. That loose women will have their arms around him at Nat Bowle's place to-night. As if her veins are full of fired sun-bleached southern shanties, a swift heat sweeps them. Dead dreams, and a forgotten resolution are carried upward by the flames. Pale flames. "They shant have him. Oh, they shall not. Not if it kills me they shant have him." Jerky, aflutter, she closes the store and starts home. Folks lazing on store windowsills wonder what on earth can be the matter with Jim Crane's gal, as she passes them. "Come to remember, she always was a little off, a little crazy, I reckon." Esther seeks her own room, and locks the door. Her mind is a pink meshbag filled with baby toes.

Using the noise of the town clock striking twelve to cover the creaks of her departure, Esther slips into the quiet road. The town, her parents, most everyone is sound asleep. This fact is a stable thing that comforts her. After sundown a chill wind came up from the west. It is still blowing, but to her it is a steady, settled thing like the cold. She wants her mind to be like that. Solid, contained, and blank as a sheet of darkened ice. She will not permit herself to notice the peculiar phosphorescent glitter of the sweet-gum leaves. Their movement would excite her. Exciting too, the recession of the dull familiar homes she knows so well. She doesnt know them at all. She closes her eyes, and holds them tightly. Wont do. Her being aware that they are closed recalls her purpose. She does not want to think of it. She opens them. She turns now into the deserted business street. The corrugated iron canopies and mule- and horse-gnawed hitching posts bring her a strange composure. Ghosts of the commonplaces of her daily life take stride with her and become her companions. And the echoes of her heels upon the flagging are rhythmically monotonous and soothing. Crossing the street at the corner of McGregor's notion shop, she thinks that the windows are a dull flame. Only a fancy. She walks faster. Then runs. A turn into a side street brings her abruptly to Nat Bowle's place. The house is squat and dark. It is always dark. Barlo is within. Quietly she opens the outside door and steps in. She passes through a small room. Pauses before a flight of stairs down which people's voices, muffled, come. The air is heavy with fresh tobacco smoke. It makes her sick. She wants to turn back. She goes up the steps. As if she were mounting to some great height, her head spins. She is violently dizzy. Blackness rushes to her eyes. And then she finds that she is in a large room. Barlo is before her.

"Well, I'm sholy damned—skuse me, but what, what brought you here, lil milk-white gal?"

"You." Her voice sounds like a frightened child's that calls homeward from some point miles away.

"Me?"

"Yes, you Barlo."

"This aint th place fer y. This aint th place fer y."

"I know. I know. But I've come for you."

"For me for what?"

She manages to look deep and straight into his eyes. He is slow at understanding. Guffaws and giggles break out from all around the room. A coarse woman's voice remarks, "So. thats how th dictie niggers does it." Laughs. "Mus give em credit fo their gall."

Esther doesnt hear. Barlo does. His faculties are jogged. She sees a smile, ugly and repulsive to her, working upward through thick licker fumes. Barlo seems hideous. The thought comes suddenly, that conception with a drunken man must be a mighty sin. She draws away, frozen. Like a somnambulist she wheels around and walks stiffly to the stairs. Down them. Jeers and hoots pelter bluntly upon her back. She steps out. There is no air, no street, and the town has completely disappeared.

Conversion[1]

African Guardian of Souls,
Drunk with rum,
Feasting on a strange cassava,[2]
Yielding to new words and a weak palabra[3]
Of a white-faced sardonic god—
Grins, cries
Amen,
Shouts hosanna.

1. This poem was first published as number three of three "Georgia Portraits," *Modern Review* 1 (January 1923): 81. Earlier, Toomer had intended to use the first five lines of this poem as part of a longer, untitled poem in a short story, "Withered Skin of Berries." Not published in Toomer's lifetime, the story now appears in *The Wayward and the Seeking: A Collection of Writings by Jean Toomer*, pp. 138–65. The entire poem (p. 161) is as follows:

> Court-house tower,
> Bell-buoy of the Whites,
> Charting the white-man's channel,
> Bobs on the agitated crests of pines
> And sends its mellow monotone,

Satirically sweet,
To guide the drift of barges . .
Black barges . . .

> African Guardian of Souls,
> Drunk with rum,
> Feasting on a strange cassava,
> Yielding to new words and a weak palabra
> Of a white-faced sardonic God—

2. A tuberous root of the West Indies and tropical America and a staple vegetable; also the name for the starch or flour obtained from the plant's roots; bread and tapioca are made from it.
3. Talk.

Portrait in Georgia[1]

Hair—braided chestnut,
      coiled like a lyncher's rope,
Eyes—fagots,
Lips—old scars, or the first red blisters,
Breath—the last sweet scent of cane,
And her slim body, white as the ash
      of black flesh after flame.

1. First published as number two of three "Georgia Portraits," *Modern Review* 1 (January 1923): 81.

Blood-Burning Moon[1]

1

Up from the skeleton stone walls, up from the rotting floor boards and the solid hand-hewn beams of oak of the pre-war cotton factory, dusk came. Up from the dusk the full moon came. Glowing like a fired pine-knot, it illumined the great door and soft showered the Negro shanties aligned along the single street of factory town. The full moon in the great door was an omen. Negro women improvised songs against its spell.

Louisa sang as she came over the crest of the hill from the white folks' kitchen. Her skin was the color of oak leaves on young trees in fall. Her breasts, firm and up-pointed like ripe acorns. And her singing had the low murmur of winds in fig trees. Bob Stone, younger son of the people she worked for, loved her. By the way the world reckons things, he had won her. By measure of that warm glow which came into her mind at thought of him, he had won her. Tom Burwell, whom the whole town called Big Boy, also loved her. But working in the fields all day, and far away from her, gave him no chance to show it. Though often enough of evenings he had tried to. Somehow, he never got along. Strong as he was with hands upon the ax or plow, he found it difficult to hold her. Or so he thought. But the fact was that he held her to factory town more firmly than he thought for. His black balanced, and pulled against, the white of Stone, when she thought of them. And her mind was vaguely upon them as she came over the crest of the hill, coming from the white folks' kitchen. As she sang softly at the evil face of the full moon.

A strange stir was in her. Indolently, she tried to fix upon Bob or Tom as the cause of it. To meet Bob in the canebrake, as she was going to do an hour or so later, was nothing new. And Tom's proposal which she felt on its way to her could be indefinitely put off. Separately, there was no unusual significance to either one. But for some reason, they jumbled when her eyes gazed vacantly at the rising moon. And from the jumble came the stir that was strangely within her. Her lips trembled. The slow rhythm of her song grew agitant and restless. Rusty black and tan spotted hounds, lying in the dark corners of porches or prowling around back yards, put their noses in the air and caught its tremor. They began plaintively to

1. Superstition insists that a night when the moon has a reddish coloring will be a night of violence. Bernard Bell, in "Portrait of the Artist as High Priest of Soul," considers this image in *Cane* an allusion to the Book of Revelation 6.12: ". . . and the moon became as blood." The story was first published in *Prairie* (March–April 1923): 18.

yelp and howl. Chickens woke up and cackled. Intermittently, all over the countryside dogs barked and roosters crowed as if heralding a weird dawn or some ungodly awakening. The women sang lustily. Their songs were cotton-wads to stop their ears. Louisa came down into factory town and sank wearily upon the step before her home. The moon was rising towards a thick cloud-bank which soon would hide it.

> Red nigger moon. Sinner!
> Blood-burning moon. Sinner!
> Come out that fact'ry door.

2

Up from the deep dusk of a cleared spot on the edge of the forest a mellow glow arose and spread fan-wise into the low-hanging heavens. And all around the air was heavy with the scent of boiling cane. A large pile of cane-stalks lay like ribboned shadows upon the ground. A mule, harnessed to a pole, trudged lazily round and round the pivot of the grinder. Beneath a swaying oil lamp, a Negro alternately whipped out at the mule, and fed cane-stalks to the grinder. A fat boy waddled pails of fresh ground juice between the grinder and the boiling stove. Steam came from the copper boiling pan. The scent of cane came from the copper pan and drenched the forest and the hill that sloped to factory town, beneath its fragrance. It drenched the men in circle seated around the stove. Some of them chewed at the white pulp of stalks, but there was no need for them to, if all they wanted was to taste the cane. One tasted it in factory town. And from factory town one could see the soft haze thrown by the glowing stove upon the low-hanging heavens.

Old David Georgia stirred the thickening syrup with a long ladle, and ever so often drew it off. Old David Georgia tended his stove and told tales about the white folks, about moonshining and cotton picking, and about sweet nigger gals, to the men who sat there about his stove to listen to him. Tom Burwell chewed cane-stalk and laughed with the others till some one mentioned Louisa. Till some one said something about Louisa and Bob Stone, about the silk stockings she must have gotten from him. Blood ran up Tom's neck hotter than the glow that flooded from the stove. He sprang up. Glared at the men and said, "She's my gal." Will Manning laughed. Tom strode over to him. Yanked him up and knocked him to the ground. Several of Manning's friends got up to fight for him. Tom whipped out a long knife and would have cut them to shreds if they hadnt ducked into the woods. Tom had had enough. He nodded to Old David Georgia and swung down the path to factory town. Just then, the dogs started barking and the roosters began to crow. Tom felt funny. Away from the fight, away from the stove, chill got to him. He shivered. He shuddered when he saw the full moon rising towards the cloud-bank. He who didnt give a godam for the fears of old women. He forced his mind to fasten on Louisa. Bob Stone. Better not be. He turned into the street and saw Louisa sitting before her home. He went towards her, ambling, touched the brim of a marvelously shaped, spotted, felt hat, said he wanted to say something to her, and then found that he didnt know what he had to say, or if he did, that he couldnt say it. He shoved his big fists in his overalls, grinned, and started to move off.

"Youall want me, Tom?"

"Thats what us wants, sho, Louisa."

"Well, here I am—"

"An here I is, but that aint ahelpin none, all th same."

"You wanted to say something? . ."

"I did that, sho. But words is like th spots on dice: no matter how y fumbles em, there's times when they jes wont come. I dunno why. Seems like th love I feels fo yo done stole m tongue. I got it now. Whee! Louisa, honey, I oughtnt tell y, I feel I oughtnt cause yo is young an goes t church an I has had other gals, but Louisa I sho do love y. Lil gal, Ise watched y from them first days when youall sat right here befo yo door befo th well an sang sometimes in a way that like t broke m heart. Ise carried y with me into th fields, day after day, an after that, an I sho can plow when yo is there, an I can pick cotton. Yassur! Come near beatin Barlo yesterday. I sho did. Yassur! An next year if ole Stone'll trust me, I'll have a farm. My own. My bales will buy yo what y gets from white folks now. Silk stockings an purple dresses—course I dont believe what some folks been whisperin as t how y gets them things now. White folks always did do for niggers what they likes. An they jes cant help alikin yo, Louisa. Bob Stone likes y. Course he does. But not th way folks is awhisperin. Does he, hon?"

"I dont know what you mean, Tom."

"Course y dont. Ise already cut two niggers. Had t hon, t tell em so. Niggers always tryin t make somethin out a nothin. An then besides, white folks aint up t them tricks so much nowadays. Godam better not be. Leastawise not with yo. Cause I wouldnt stand f it. Nassur."

"What would you do, Tom?"

"Cut him jes like I cut a nigger."

"No, Tom—"

"I said I would an there aint no mo to it. But that aint th talk f now. Sing, honey Louisa, an while I'm listenin t y I'll be makin love."

Tom took her hand in his. Against the tough thickness of his own, hers felt soft and small. His huge body slipped down to the step beside her. The full moon sank upward into the deep purple of the cloud-bank. An old woman brought a lighted lamp and hung it on the common well whose bulky shadow squatted in the middle of the road, opposite Tom and Louisa. The old woman lifted the well-lid, took hold the chain, and began drawing up the heavy bucket. As she did so, she sang. Figures shifted, restlesslike, between lamp and window in the front rooms of the shanties. Shadows of the figures fought each other on the gray dust of the road. Figures raised the windows and joined the old woman in song. Louisa and Tom, the whole street, singing:

> Red nigger moon. Sinner!
> Blood-burning moon. Sinner!
> Come out that fact'ry door.

3

Bob Stone sauntered from his veranda out into the gloom of fir trees and magnolias. The clear white of his skin paled, and the flush of his cheeks turned purple. As if to balance this outer change, his mind became consciously a white man's. He passed the house with its huge open hearth which, in the days of slavery, was the plantation cookery. He saw Louisa bent over that hearth. He went in as a master should and took her. Direct, honest, bold. None of this sneaking that he had to go through now. The contrast was repulsive to him. His family had lost ground. Hell no, his family still owned the niggers, practically. Damned if they did, or he wouldnt have to duck around so. What would they think if they knew? His mother? His sister? He shouldnt mention them, shouldnt think of them in this connection. There in the dusk he blushed at doing so. Fellows about town were all right, but how about his friends up North? He could see them incredible, repulsed. They didnt know. The thought first made him laugh. Then, with their eyes still upon him, he began to feel embarrassed. He felt the need of explaining things to them. Explain hell. They wouldnt understand, and moreover, who ever heard of a Southerner getting on his knees to any Yankee, or anyone. No sir. He was going to see Louisa to-night, and love her. She was lovely—in her way. Nigger way. What way was that? Damned if he knew. Must know. He'd known her long enough to know. Was there something about niggers that you couldnt know? Listening to them at church didnt tell you anything. Looking at them didnt tell you anything. Talking to them didnt tell you anything—unless it was gossip, unless they wanted to talk. Of course, about farming, and licker, and craps—but those werent nigger. Nigger was something

more. How much more? Something to be afraid of, more? Hell
no. Who ever heard of being afraid of a nigger? Tom Burwell.
Cartwell had told him that Tom went with Louisa after she
reached home. No sir. No nigger had ever been with his girl. He'd
like to see one try. Some position for him to be in. Him, Bob
Stone, of the old Stone family, in a scrap with a nigger over a
nigger girl. In the good old days. . . Ha! Those were the days. His
family had lost ground. Not so much, though. Enough for him to
have to cut through old Lemon's canefield by way of the woods,
that he might meet her. She was worth it. Beautiful nigger gal.
Why nigger? Why not, just gal? No, it was because she was
nigger that he went to her. Sweet. . . The scent of boiling cane
came to him. Then he saw the rich glow of the stove. He heard
the voices of the men circled around it. He was about to skirt the
clearing when he heard his own name mentioned. He stopped.
Quivering. Leaning against a tree, he listened.

"Bad nigger. Yassur, he sho is one bad nigger when he gets
started."

"Tom Burwell's been on th gang three times fo cuttin men."

"What y think he's agwine t do t Bob Stone?"

"Dunno yet. He aint found out. When he does— Baby!"

"Aint no tellin."

"Young Stone aint no quitter an I ken tell y that. Blood of th
old uns in his veins."

"Thats right. He'll scrap, sho."

"Be gettin too hot f niggers round this away."

"Shut up, nigger. Y dont know what y talkin bout."

Bob Stone's ears burned as though he had been holding them
over the stove. Sizzling heat welled up within him. His feet felt as
if they rested on red-hot coals. They stung him to quick movement.
He circled the fringe of the glowing. Not a twig cracked beneath
his feet. He reached the path that led to factory town. Plunged
furiously down it. Halfway along, a blindness within him veered
him aside. He crashed into the bordering canebrake. Cane leaves
cut his face and lips. He tasted blood. He threw himself down and
dug his fingers in the ground. The earth was cool. Cane-roots took
the fever from his hands. After a long while, or so it seemed to
him, the thought came to him that it must be time to see Louisa.
He got to his feet and walked calmly to their meeting place. No
Louisa. Tom Burwell had her. Veins in his forehead bulged and
distended. Saliva moistened the dried blood on his lips. He bit
down on his lips. He tasted blood. Not his own blood; Tom Burwell's blood. Bob drove through the cane and out again upon the
road. A hound swung down the path before him towards factory
town. Bob couldnt see it. The dog loped aside to let him pass.

Bob's blind rushing made him stumble over it. He fell with a thud
that dazed him. The hound yelped. Answering yelps came from all
over the countryside. Chickens cackled. Roosters crowed, heralding
the bloodshot eyes of southern awakening. Singers in the town
were silenced. They shut their windows down. Palpitant between
the rooster crows, a chill hush settled upon the huddled forms of
Tom and Louisa. A figure rushed from the shadow and stood
before them. Tom popped to his feet.

"Whats y want?"

"I'm Bob Stone."

"Yassur—an I'm Tom Burwell. Whats y want?"

Bob lunged at him. Tom side-stepped, caught him by the
shoulder, and flung him to the ground. Straddled him.

"Let me up."

"Yassur—but watch yo doins,[2] Bob Stone."

A few dark figures, drawn by the sound of scuffle, stood about
them. Bob sprang to his feet.

"Fight like a man, Tom Burwell, an I'll lick y."

Again he lunged. Tom side-stepped and flung him to the ground.
Straddled him.

"Get off me, you godam nigger you."

"Yo sho has started somethin now. Get up."

Tom yanked him up and began hammering at him. Each blow
sounded as if it smashed into a precious, irreplaceable soft something. Beneath them, Bob staggered back. He reached in his
pocket and whipped out a knife.

"Thats my game, sho."

Blue flash, a steel blade slashed across Bob Stone's throat. He
had a sweetish sick feeling. Blood began to flow. Then he felt a
sharp twitch of pain. He let his knife drop. He slapped one hand
against his neck. He pressed the other on top of his head as if to
hold it down. He groaned. He turned, and staggered towards the
crest of the hill in the direction of white town. Negroes who had
seen the fight slunk into their homes and blew the lamps out.
Louisa, dazed, hysterical, refused to go indoors. She slipped, crumbled, her body loosely propped against the woodwork of the well.
Tom Burwell leaned against it. He seemed rooted there.

Bob reached Broad Street. White men rushed up to him. He
collapsed in their arms.

"Tom Burwell. . . ."

White men like ants upon a forage rushed about. Except for
the taut hum of their moving, all was silent. Shotguns, revolvers,
rope, kerosene, torches. Two high-powered cars with glaring search-

2. "Doings," actions.

lights. They came together. The taut hum rose to a low roar. Then nothing could be heard but the flop of their feet in the thick dust of the road. The moving body of their silence preceded them over the crest of the hill into factory town. It flattened the Negroes beneath it. It rolled to the wall of the factory, where it stopped. Tom knew that they were coming. He couldnt move. And then he saw the search-lights of the two cars glaring down on him. A quick shock went through him. He stiffened. He started to run. A yell went up from the mob. Tom wheeled about and faced them. They poured down on him. They swarmed. A large man with dead-white face and flabby cheeks came to him and almost jabbed a gun-barrel through his guts.

"Hands behind y, nigger."

Tom's wrists were bound. The big man shoved him to the well. Burn him over it, and when the woodwork caved in, his body would drop to the bottom. Two deaths for a godam nigger. Louisa was driven back. The mob pushed in. Its pressure, its momentum was too great. Drag him to the factory. Wood and stakes already there. Tom moved in the direction indicated. But they had to drag him. They reached the great door. Too many to get in there. The mob divided and flowed around the walls to either side. The big man shoved him through the door. The mob pressed in from the sides. Taut humming. No words. A stake was sunk into the ground. Rotting floor boards piled around it. Kerosene poured on the rotting floor boards. Tom bound to the stake. His breast was bare. Nails' scratches let little lines of blood trickle down and mat into the hair. His face, his eyes were set and stony. Except for irregular breathing, one would have thought him already dead. Torches were flung onto the pile. A great flare muffled in black smoke shot upward. The mob yelled. The mob was silent. Now Tom could be seen within the flames. Only his head, erect, lean, like a blackened stone. Stench of burning flesh soaked the air. Tom's eyes popped. His head settled downward. The mob yelled. Its yell echoed against the skeleton stone walls and sounded like a hundred yells. Like a hundred mobs yelling. Its yell thudded against the thick front wall and fell back. Ghost of a yell slipped through the flames and out the great door of the factory. It fluttered like a dying thing down the single street of factory town. Louisa, upon the step before her home, did not hear it, but her eyes opened slowly. They saw the full moon glowing in the great door. The full moon, an evil thing, an omen, soft showering the homes of folks she knew. Where were they, these people? She'd sing, and perhaps they'd come out and join her. Perhaps Tom Burwell would come. At any rate, the full moon in the great door was an omen which she must sing to:

Red nigger moon. Sinner!
Blood-burning moon. Sinner!
Come out that fact'ry door.

Seventh Street[1]

Money burns the pocket, pocket hurts,
Bootleggers in silken shirts,
Ballooned, zooming Cadillacs,
Whizzing, whizzing down the street-car tracks.

Seventh Street is a bastard of Prohibition and the War.[2] A crude-boned, soft-skinned wedge of nigger life breathing its loafer air, jazz songs and love, thrusting unconscious rhythms, black reddish blood into the white and whitewashed wood of Washington. Stale soggy wood of Washington. Wedges rust in soggy wood. . . Split it! In two! Again! Shred it! . . the sun. Wedges are brilliant in the sun; ribbons of wet wood dry and blow away. Black reddish blood. Pouring for crude-boned soft-skinned life, who set you flowing? Blood suckers of the War would spin in a frenzy of dizziness if they drank your blood. Prohibition would put a stop to it. Who set you flowing? White and whitewash disappear in blood. Who set you flowing? Flowing down the smooth asphalt of Seventh Street, in shanties, brick office buildings, theaters, drug stores, restaurants, and cabarets? Eddying on the corners? Swirling like a blood-red smoke up where the buzzards fly in heaven? God would not dare to suck black red blood. A Nigger God! He would duck his head in shame and call for the Judgment Day. Who set you flowing?

Money burns the pocket, pocket hurts,
Bootleggers in silken shirts,
Ballooned, zooming Cadillacs,
Whizzing, whizzing down the street-car tracks.

1. The stories and sketches in this section are set in Washington, D.C., except for "Bona and Paul," which is set in Chicago. Notice the emphasis on street images that contrast with the forest images of the earlier, Georgia section. "Seventh Street" was first published in *Broom* 4 (December 1922): 3.
2. World War I.

Rhobert

Rhobert wears a house, like a monstrous diver's helmet, on his head. His legs are banty-bowed and shaky because as a child he had rickets. He is way down. Rods of the house like antennæ of a dead thing, stuffed, prop up in the air. He is way down. He is sinking. His house is a dead thing that weights him down. He is sinking as a diver would sink in mud should the water be drawn off. Life is a murky, wiggling, microscopic water that compresses him. Compresses his helmet and would crush it the minute that he pulled his head out. He has to keep it in. Life is water that is being drawn off.

> Brother, life is water that is being drawn off.
> Brother, life is water that is being drawn off.

The dead house is stuffed. The stuffing is alive. It is sinful to draw one's head out of live stuffing in a dead house. The propped-up antennæ would cave in and the stuffing be strewn . . shredded life-pulp . . in the water. It is sinful to have one's own head crushed. Rhobert is an upright man whose legs are banty-bowed and shaky because as a child he had rickets. The earth is round. Heaven is a sphere that surrounds it. Sink where you will. God is a Red Cross man with a dredge and a respiration-pump who's waiting for you at the opposite periphery. God built the house. He blew His breath into its stuffing. It is good to die obeying Him who can do these things.

A futile something like the dead house wraps the live stuffing of the question: how long before the water will be drawn off? Rhobert does not care. Like most men who wear monstrous helmets, the pressure it exerts is enough to convince him of its practical infinity. And he cares not two straws as to whether or not he will ever see his wife and children again. Many a time he's seen them drown in his dreams and has kicked about joyously in the mud for days after. One thing about him goes straight to the heart. He has an Adam's-apple which strains sometimes as if he were painfully gulping great globules of air . . air floating shredded life-pulp. It is a sad thing to see a banty-bowed, shaky, ricket-legged man straining the raw insides of his throat against smooth air. Holding furtive thoughts about the glory of pulp-heads strewn in water. . He is way down. Down. Mud, coming to his banty knees, almost hides them. Soon people will be looking at him and calling him a strong man. No doubt he is for one who has had rickets. Lets give it to him. Lets call him great when the water shall have been all drawn off.

Lets build a monument and set it in the ooze where he goes down. A monument of hewn oak, carved in nigger-heads. Lets open our throats, brother, and sing "Deep River"[1] when he goes down.

> Brother, Rhobert is sinking.
> Lets open our throats, brother,
> Lets sing Deep River when he goes down.

1. Black-American spiritual.

Avey

For a long while she was nothing more to me than one of those skirted beings whom boys at a certain age disdain to play with. Just how I came to love her, timidly, and with secret blushes, I do not know. But that I did was brought home to me one night, the first night that Ned wore his long pants. Us fellers were seated on the curb before an apartment house where she had gone in. The young trees had not outgrown their boxes then. V Street[1] was lined with them. When our legs grew cramped and stiff from the cold of the stone, we'd stand around a box and whittle it. I like to think now that there was a hidden purpose in the way we hacked them with our knives. I like to feel that something deep in me responded to the trees, the young trees that whinnied like colts impatient to be let free... On the particular night I have in mind, we were waiting for the top-floor light to go out. We wanted to see Avey leave the flat. This night she stayed longer than usual and gave us a chance to complete the plans of how we were going to stone and beat that feller on the top floor out of town. Ned especially had it in for him. He was about to throw a brick up at the window when at last the room went dark. Some minutes passed. Then Avey, as unconcerned as if she had been paying an old-maid aunt a visit, came out. I dont remember what she had on, and all that sort of thing. But I do know that I turned hot as bare pavements in the summertime at Ned's boast: "Hell, bet I could get her too if you little niggers weren't always spying and crabbing everything." I didnt say a word to him. It wasnt my way then. I just stood there like the others, and something like a fuse burned up inside of me. She never noticed us, but swung along lazy and easy as anything. We sauntered to the corner and watched her till her door banged to. Ned repeated what he'd said. I didnt seem to care. Sitting around old Mush-Head's bread box, the discussion began. "Hang if I can see how she gets away with it," Doc started. Ned knew, of course. There was nothing he didnt know when it came to women. He dilated on the emotional needs of girls. Said they werent much different from men in that respect. And concluded with the solemn avowal: "It does em good." None of us liked Ned much. We all talked dirt; but it was the way he said it. And then too, a couple of the fellers had sisters and had caught Ned playing with them. But there was no disputing the superiority of his smutty wisdom. Bubs Sanborn, whose mother was friendly with Avey's, had overheard the old ladies talking. "Avey's mother's ont her," he said. We thought

1. Like Seventh, "V" Street was (and is) a street passing through a densely populated Afro-American neighborhood in Washington, D.C.

that only natural and began to guess at what would happen. Some one said she'd marry that feller on the top floor. Ned called that a lie because Avey was going to marry nobody but him. We had our doubts about that, but we did agree that she'd soon leave school and marry some one. The gang broke up, and I went home, picturing myself as married.

Nothing I did seemed able to change Avey's indifference to me. I played basket-ball, and when I'd make a long clean shot she'd clap with the others, louder than they, I thought. I'd meet her on the street, and there'd be no difference in the way she said hello. She never took the trouble to call me by my name. On the days for drill,[2] I'd let my voice down a tone and call for a complicated maneuver when I saw her coming. She'd smile appreciation, but it was an impersonal smile, never for me. It was on a summer excursion down to Riverview that she first seemed to take me into account. The day had been spent riding merry-go-rounds, scenic-railways, and shoot-the-chutes. We had been in swimming and we had danced. I was a crack swimmer then. She didnt know how. I held her up and showed her how to kick her legs and draw her arms. Of course she didnt learn in one day, but she thanked me for bothering with her. I was also somewhat of a dancer. And I had already noticed that love can start on a dance floor. We danced. But though I held her tightly in my arms, she was way away. That college feller who lived on the top floor was somewhere making money for the next year. I imagined that she was thinking, wishing for him. Ned was along. He treated her until his money gave out. She went with another feller. Ned got sore. One by one the boys' money gave out. She left them. And they got sore. Every one of them but me got sore. This is the reason, I guess, why I had her to myself on the top deck of the *Jane Mosely* that night as we puffed up the Potomac, coming home. The moon was brilliant. The air was sweet like clover. And every now and then, a salt tang, a stale drift of sea-weed. It was not my mind's fault if it went romancing. I should have taken her in my arms the minute we were stowed in that old lifeboat. I dallied, dreaming. She took me in hers. And I could feel by the touch of it that it wasnt a man-to-woman love. It made me restless. I felt chagrined. I didnt know what it was, but I did know that I couldnt handle it. She ran her fingers through my hair and kissed my forehead. I itched to break through her tenderness to passion. I wanted her to take me in her arms as I knew she had that college feller. I wanted her to love me passionately as she did him. I gave her one burning kiss. Then she laid me in her lap as if I were a child. Helpless. I got sore when she started to

---

2. Marching as part of the military training in high school.

hum a lullaby. She wouldnt let me go. I talked. I knew damned well that I could beat her at that. Her eyes were soft and misty, the curves of her lips were wistful, and her smile seemed indulgent of the irrelevance of my remarks. I gave up at last and let her love me, silently, in her own way. The moon was brilliant. The air was sweet like clover, and every now and then, a salt tang, a stale drift of sea-weed. . .

The next time I came close to her was the following summer at Harpers Ferry. We were sitting on a flat projecting rock they give the name of Lover's Leap. Some one is supposed to have jumped off it. The river is about six hundred feet beneath. A railroad track runs up the valley and curves out of sight where part of the mountain rock had to be blasted away to make room for it. The engines of this valley have a whistle, the echoes of which sound like iterated gasps and sobs. I always think of them as crude music from the soul of Avey. We sat there holding hands. Our palms were soft and warm against each other. Our fingers were not tight. She would not let them be. She would not let me twist them. I wanted to talk. To explain what I meant to her. Avey was as silent as those great trees whose tops we looked down upon. She has always been like that. At least, to me. I had the notion that if I really wanted to, I could do with her just what I pleased. Like one can strip a tree. I did kiss her. I even let my hands cup her breasts. When I was through, she'd seek my hand and hold it till my pulse cooled down. Evening after evening we sat there. I tried to get her to talk about that college feller. She never would. There was no set time to go home. None of my family had come down. And as for hers, she didnt give a hang about them. The general gossips could hardly say more than they had. The boarding-house porch was always deserted when we returned. No one saw us enter, so the time was set conveniently for scandal. This worried me a little, for I thought it might keep Avey from getting an appointment in the schools. She didnt care. She had finished normal school.[3] They could give her a job if they wanted to. As time went on, her indifference to things began to pique me; I was ambitious. I left the Ferry earlier than she did. I was going off to college. The more I thought of it, the more I resented, yes, hell, thats what it was, her downright laziness. Sloppy indolence. There was no excuse for a healthy girl taking life so easy.[4] Hell! she was no better than a cow. I was certain that she was a cow when I felt an udder in a Wiscon-

---

3. A teacher-training institution. Although a normal school was not considered the equivalent of a four-year college, during the 1920's completion of a normal-school degree program was considered sufficient qualification for teaching in elementary or secondary schools.

4. Contrast the narrator's reaction here with the narrator's more sanguine reaction to Fern's laziness.

sin stock-judging class. Among those energetic Swedes, or whatever they are, I decided to forget her. For two years I thought I did. When I'd come home for the summer she'd be away. And before she returned, I'd be gone. We never wrote; she was too damned lazy for that. But what a bluff I put up about forgetting her. The girls up that way, at least the ones I knew, havent got the stuff: they dont know how to love. Giving themselves completely was tame beside just the holding of Avey's hand. One day I received a note from her. The writing, I decided, was slovenly. She wrote on a torn bit of note-book paper. The envelope had a faint perfume that I remembered. A single line told me she had lost her school and was going away. I comforted myself with the reflection that shame held no pain for one so indolent as she. Nevertheless, I left Wisconsin that year for good. Washington had seemingly forgotten her. I hunted Ned. Between curses, I caught his opinion of her. She was no better than a whore. I saw her mother on the street. The same old pinch-beck, jerky-gaited creature that I'd always known.

Perhaps five years passed. The business of hunting a job or something or other had bruised my vanity so that I could recognize it. I felt old. Avey and my real relation to her, I thought I came to know. I wanted to see her. I had been told that she was in New York. As I had no money, I hiked and bummed my way there. I got work in a ship-yard and walked the streets at night, hoping to meet her. Failing in this, I saved enough to pay my fare back home. One evening in early June, just at the time when dusk is most lovely on the eastern horizon, I saw Avey, indolent as ever, leaning on the arm of a man, strolling under the recently lit arc-lights of U Street.[5] She had almost passed before she recognized me. She showed no surprise. The puff over her eyes had grown heavier. The eyes themselves were still sleepy-large, and beautiful. I had almost concluded—indifferent. "You look older," was what she said. I wanted to convince her that I was, so I asked her to walk with me. The man whom she was with, and whom she never took the trouble to introduce, at a nod from her, hailed a taxi, and drove away. That gave me a notion of what she had been used to. Her dress was of some fine, costly stuff. I suggested the park, and then added that the grass might stain her skirt. Let it get stained, she said, for where it came from there are others.

I have a spot in Soldier's Home[6] to which I always go when I want the simple beauty of another's soul. Robins spring about the lawn

<hr />

5. Like Seventh, "U" Street was (and is) a street passing through a densely populated Afro-American neighborhood in Washington, D.C.
6. A park.

all day. They leave their footprints in the grass. I imagine that the grass at night smells sweet and fresh because of them. The ground is high. Washington lies below. Its light spreads like a blush against the darkened sky. Against the soft dusk sky of Washington. And when the wind is from the South, soil of my homeland falls like a fertile shower upon the lean streets of the city. Upon my hill in Soldier's Home, I know the policeman who watches the place of nights. When I go there alone, I talk to him. I tell him I come there to find the truth that people bury in their hearts. I tell him that I do not come there with a girl to do the thing he's paid to watch out for. I look deep in his eyes when I say these things, and he believes me. He comes over to see who it is on the grass. I say hello to him. He greets me in the same way and goes off searching for other black splotches upon the lawn. Avey and I went there. A band in one of the buildings a fair distance off was playing a march. I wished they would stop. Their playing was like a tin spoon in one's mouth. I wanted the Howard[7] Glee Club to sing "Deep River,"[8] from the road. To sing "Deep River, Deep River," from the road. . . Other than the first comments, Avey had been silent. I started to hum a folk-tune. She slipped her hand in mine. Pillowed her head as best she could upon my arm. Kissed the hand that she was holding and listened, or so I thought, to what I had to say. I traced my development from the early days up to the present time, the phase in which I could understand her. I described her own nature and temperament. Told how they needed a larger life for their expression. How incapable Washington was of under-standing that need. How it could not meet it. I pointed out that in lieu of proper channels, her emotions had overflowed into paths that dissipated them. I talked, beautifully I thought, about an art that would be born, an art that would open the way for women the likes of her. I asked her to hope, and build up an inner life against the coming of that day. I recited some of my own things to her. I sang, with a strange quiver in my voice, a promise-song. And then I began to wonder why her hand had not once returned a single pres-sure. My old-time feeling about her laziness came back. I spoke sharply. My policeman friend passed by. I said hello to him. As he went away, I began to visualize certain possibilities. An immediate and urgent passion swept over me. Then I looked at Avey. Her heavy eyes were closed. Her breathing was as faint and regular as a child's in slumber. My passion died. I was afraid to move lest I dis-turb her. Hours and hours, I guess it was, she lay there. My body grew numb. I shivered. I coughed. I wanted to get up and whittle at the boxes of young trees. I withdrew my hand. I raised her head to waken her. She did not stir. I got up and walked around. I

7. Howard University.   8. Black-American spiritual.

found my policeman friend and talked to him. We both came up, and bent over her. He said it would be all right for her to stay there just so long as she got away before the workmen came at dawn. A blanket was borrowed from a neighbor house. I sat beside her through the night. I saw the dawn steal over Washington. The Capitol dome looked like a gray ghost ship drifting in from sea. Avey's face was pale, and her eyes were heavy. She did not have the gray crimson-splashed beauty of the dawn. I hated to wake her. Orphan-woman. . .

Beehive

Within this black hive to-night
There swarm a million bees;
Bees passing in and out the moon,
Bees escaping out the moon,
Bees returning through the moon,
Silver bees intently buzzing,
Silver honey dripping from the swarm of bees
Earth is a waxen cell of the world comb,
And I, a drone,
Lying on my back,
Lipping honey,
Getting drunk with silver honey,
Wish that I might fly out past the moon
And curl forever in some far-off farmyard flower.

Storm Ending[1]

Thunder blossoms gorgeously above our heads,
Great, hollow, bell-like flowers,
Rumbling in the wind,
Stretching clappers to strike our ears . .
Full-lipped flowers
Bitten by the sun
Bleeding rain
Dripping rain like golden honey—
And the sweet earth flying from the thunder.

1. First published in *Double Dealer* 4 (September 1922): 118.

Theater

Life of nigger alleys, of pool rooms and restaurants and near-beer saloons soaks into the walls of Howard Theater[1] and sets them throbbing jazz songs. Black-skinned, they dance and shout above the tick and trill of white-walled buildings. At night, they open doors to people who come in to stamp their feet and shout. At night, road-shows volley songs into the mass-heart of black people. Songs soak the walls and seep out to the nigger life of alleys and near-beer saloons, of the Poodle Dog and Black Bear cabarets. Afternoons, the house is dark, and the walls are sleeping singers until rehearsal begins. Or until John comes within them. Then they start throbbing to a subtle syncopation. And the space-dark air grows softly luminous.

John is the manager's brother. He is seated at the center of the theater, just before rehearsal. Light streaks down upon him from a window high above. One half his face is orange in it. One half his face is in shadow.[2] The soft glow of the house rushes to, and compacts about, the shaft of light. John's mind coincides with the shaft of light. Thoughts rush to, and compact about it. Life of the house and of the slowly awakening stage swirls to the body of John, and thrills it. John's body is separate from the thoughts that pack his mind.

Stage-lights, soft, as if they shine through clear pink fingers. Beneath them, hid by the shadow of a set, Dorris. Other chorus girls drift in. John feels them in the mass. And as if his own body were the mass-heart of a black audience listening to them singing, he wants to stamp his feet and shout. His mind, contained above desires of his body, singles the girls out, and tries to trace origins and plot destinies.

A pianist slips into the pit and improvises jazz. The walls awake. Arms of the girls, and their limbs, which . . jazz, jazz . . by lifting up their tight street skirts they set free, jab the air and clog the floor in rhythm to the music. (Lift your skirts, Baby, and talk t papa!) Crude, individualized, and yet . . monotonous. . .

John: Soon the director will herd you, my full-lipped, distant beauties, and tame you, and blunt your sharp thrusts in loosely suggestive movements, appropriate to Broadway. (O dance!) Soon the audience will paint your dusk faces white, and call you beauti-

1. A theater in the Afro-American section of Washington, D.C.; the audiences and the performers were also Afro-American.
2. As Toomer uses images of flame to suggest the varying degrees of intensity of Esther's passion, so here he uses light and shadow to suggest the in-

ternal conflict of John. Daylight shining through a theater window tints his face orange when he surrenders to his sensuality. His face is shadowed whenever he is using intellect (mind) to control and repress his sensuality.

ful.[3] (O dance!) Soon I... (O dance!) I'd like...

Girls laugh and shout. Sing discordant snatches of other jazz songs. Whirl with loose passion into the arms of passing show-men.

John: Too thick. Too easy. Too monotonous. Her whom I'd love I'd leave before she knew that I was with her. Her? Which? (O dance!) I'd like to...

Girls dance and sing. Men clap. The walls sing and press inward. They press the men and girls, they press John towards a center of physical ecstasy. Go to it, Baby! Fan yourself, and feed your papa! Put .. nobody lied .. and take .. when they said I cried over you. No lie! The glitter and color of stacked scenes, the gilt and brass and crimson of the house, converge towards a center of physical ecstasy. John's feet and torso and his blood press in. He wills thought to rid his mind of passion.

"All right, girls. Alaska. Miss Reynolds, please."

The director wants to get the rehearsal through with.

The girls line up. John sees the front row: dancing ponies. The rest are in shadow. The leading lady fits loosely in the front. Lacklife, monotonous. "One, two, three—" Music starts. The song is somewhere where it will not strain the leading lady's throat. The dance is somewhere where it will not strain the girls. Above the staleness, one dancer throws herself into it. Dorris. John sees her. Her hair, crisp-curled, is bobbed. Bushy, black hair bobbing about her lemon-colored face. Her lips are curiously full, and very red. Her limbs in silk purple stockings are lovely. John feels them. Desires her. Holds off.

John: Stage-door johnny;[4] chorus-girl. No, that would be all right. Dictie,[5] educated, stuck-up; show-girl. Yep. Her suspicion would be stronger than her passion. It wouldnt work. Keep her loveliness. Let her go.

Dorris sees John and knows that he is looking at her. Her own glowing is too rich a thing to let her feel the slimness of his diluted passion.

"Who's that?" she asks her dancing partner.

"Th manager's brother. Dictie. Nothin doin, hon."

Dorris tosses her head and dances for him until she feels she has him. Then, withdrawing disdainfully, she flirts with the director.

Dorris: Nothin doin? How come? Aint I as good as him?

---

3. During the 1920's, producers and directors of all-Black musical shows gave preference to Afro-American females who were light-skinned. Here, however, Toomer probably refers to a refusal by the predominantly white Broadway audience to accept Afro-American beauty. Instead, the audience will instinctively consider the Afro-American dancers to be dusky-skinned whites. Then the audience can judge them beautiful while still believing that only whites are beautiful.

4. Slang term referring to men who dated actresses, singers, and dancers and who, after performances, waited for them at the stage door.

5. Slang term referring to educated, middle-class Afro-Americans who behave as though they consider themselves socially superior to other Afro-Americans—similar to "stuck-up," "snobbish."

Couldnt I have got an education if I'd wanted one? Dont I know respectable folks, lots of em, in Philadelphia and New York and Chicago? Aint I had men as good as him? Better. Doctors an lawyers. Whats a manager's brother, anyhow?

Two steps back, and two steps front.

"Say, Mame, where do you get that stuff?"

"Whatshmean, Dorris?"

"If you two girls cant listen to what I'm telling you, I know where I can get some who can. Now listen."

Mame: Go to hell, you black bastard.

Dorris: Whats eatin at him, anyway?

"Now follow me in this, you girls. Its three counts to the right, three counts to the left, and then you shimmy—"[6]

John: —and then you shimmy. I'll bet she can. Some good cabaret, with rooms upstairs. And what in hell do you think you'd get from it? Youre going wrong. Here's right: get her to herself— (Christ, but how she'd bore you after the first five minutes)—not if you get her right she wouldnt. Touch her, I mean. To herself—in some room perhaps. Some cheap, dingy bedroom. Hell no. Cant be done. But the point is, brother John, it can be done. Get her to herself somewhere, anywhere. Go down in yourself—and she'd be calling you all sorts of asses while you were in the process of going down. Hold em, bud. Cant be done. Let her go. (Dance and I'll love you!) And keep her loveliness.

"All right now, Chicken Chaser.[7] Dorris and girls. Where's Dorris? I told you to stay on the stage, didnt I? Well? Now thats enough. All right. All right there, Professor?[8] All right. One, two, three—"

Dorris swings to the front. The line of girls, four deep, blurs within the shadow of suspended scenes. Dorris wants to dance. The director feels that and steps to one side. He smiles, and picks her for a leading lady, one of these days. Odd ends of stage-men emerge from the wings, and stare and clap. A crap game in the alley suddenly ends. Black faces crowd the rear stage doors. The girls, catching joy from Dorris, whip up within the footlights' glow. They forget set steps; they find their own. The director forgets to bawl them out. Dorris dances.[9]

John: Her head bobs to Broadway. Dance from yourself. Dance! O just a little more.

Dorris' eyes burn across the space of seats to him.

Dorris: I bet he can love. Hell, he cant love. He's too skinny.

6. A popular dance movement that emphasized an erotic vibration of the torso.
7. Another dance.
8. A nickname for a band leader or pianist. See also p. 88.

9. Toomer believed that individuals could express their emotions and their souls through dancing. Dorris, therefore, intends to use her dance to "tell" John who she is and how she feels.

His lips are too skinny. He wouldnt love me anyway, only for that. But I'd get a pair of silk stockings out of it. Red silk. I got purple. Cut it, kid. You cant win him to respect you that away. He wouldnt anyway. Maybe he would. Maybe he'd love. I've heard em say that men who look like him (what does he look like?) will marry if they love. O will you love me? And give me kids, and a home, and everything? (I'd like to make your nest, and honest, hon, I wouldnt run out on you.) You will if I make you. Just watch me.

Dorris dances. She forgets her tricks.[1] She dances.

Glorious songs are the muscles of her limbs.

And her singing is of canebrake loves and mangrove feastings.

The walls press in, singing. Flesh of a throbbing body, they press close to John and Dorris. They close them in. John's heart beats tensely against her dancing body. Walls press his mind within his heart. And then, the shaft of light goes out the window high above him. John's mind sweeps up to follow it. Mind pulls him upward into dream. Dorris dances. . .

John dreams:

> Dorris is dressed in a loose black gown splashed with lemon ribbons. Her feet taper long and slim from trim ankles. She waits for him just inside the stage door. John, collar and tie colorful and flaring, walks towards the stage door. There are no trees in the alley. But his feet feel as though they step on autumn leaves whose rustle has been pressed out of them by the passing of a million satin slippers. The air is sweet with roasting chestnuts, sweet with bonfires of old leaves. John's melancholy is a deep thing that seals all senses but his eyes, and makes him whole.
>
> Dorris knows that he is coming. Just at the right moment she steps from the door, as if there were no door. Her face is tinted like the autumn alley. Of old flowers, or of a southern canefield, her perfume. "Glorious Dorris." So his eyes speak. And their sadness is too deep for sweet untruth. She barely touches his arm. They glide off with footfalls softened on the leaves, the old leaves powdered by a million satin slippers.
>
> They are in a room. John knows nothing of it. Only, that the flesh and blood of Dorris are its walls. Singing walls. Lights, soft, as if they shine through clear pink fingers. Soft lights, and warm.
>
> John reaches for a manuscript of his, and reads. Dorris, who has no eyes, has eyes to understand him. He comes to a dancing scene. The scene is Dorris. She dances. Dorris dances. Glorious Dorris. Dorris whirls, whirls, dances. . .

Dorris dances.

The pianist crashes a bumper chord. The whole stage claps. Dorris, flushed, looks quick at John. His whole face is in shadow.

---

1. Her practiced or stylized dance routine.

She seeks for her dance in it. She finds it a dead thing in the shadow which is his dream. She rushes from the stage. Falls down the steps into her dressing-room. Pulls her hair. Her eyes, over a floor of tears, stare at the whitewashed ceiling. (Smell of dry paste, and paint, and soiled clothing.) Her pal comes in. Dorris flings herself into the old safe arms, and cries bitterly.

"I told you nothin doin," is what Mame says to comfort her.

Her Lips Are Copper Wire[1]

whisper of yellow globes
gleaming on lamp-posts that sway
like bootleg licker[2] drinkers in the fog

and let your breath be moist against me
like bright beads on yellow globes

telephone the power-house
that the main wires are insulate

(her words play softly up and down
dewy corridors of billboards)

then with your tongue remove the tape
and press your lips to mine
till they are incandescent

1. First published in S4N (May–August 1923).
2. Liquor illegally distilled, especially during Prohibition, a period during the 1920's and early 1930's when federal laws in the United States prohibited the manufacture, transportation, sale, and possession of alcoholic beverages. The term "bootleg liquor" now applies to liquor that manufacturers distill and distribute without paying the required state and federal taxes.

Calling Jesus[1]

Her soul is like a little thrust-tailed dog that follows her, whimpering. She is large enough, I know, to find a warm spot for it. But each night when she comes home and closes the big outside storm door, the little dog is left in the vestibule, filled with chills till morning. Some one . . . eoho[2] Jesus . . . soft as a cotton boll brushed against the milk-pod cheek of Christ, will steal in and cover it that it need not shiver, and carry it to her where she sleeps upon clean hay cut in her dreams.

When you meet her in the daytime on the streets, the little dog keeps coming. Nothing happens at first, and then, when she has forgotten the streets and alleys, and the large house where she goes to bed of nights, a soft thing like fur begins to rub your limbs, and you hear a low, scared voice, lonely, calling, and you know that a cool something nozzles moisture in your palms. Sensitive things like nostrils, quiver. Her breath comes sweet as honeysuckle whose pistils bear the life of coming song. And her eyes carry to where builders find no need for vestibules, for swinging on iron hinges, storm doors.

Her soul is like a little thrust-tailed dog, that follows her, whimpering. I've seen it tagging on behind her, up streets where chestnut trees flowered, where dusty asphalt had been freshly sprinkled with clean water. Up alleys where niggers sat on low door-steps before tumbled shanties and sang and loved. At night, when she comes home, the little dog is left in the vestibule, nosing the crack beneath the big storm door, filled with chills till morning. Some one . . . eoho Jesus . . . soft as the bare feet of Christ moving across bales of southern cotton, will steal in and cover it that it need not shiver, and carry it to her where she sleeps: cradled in dream-fluted cane.

1. Originally entitled "Nora" when first published   2. A call.
in *Double Dealer* 4 (September 1922): 132.

Box Seat[1]

1

Houses are shy girls whose eyes shine reticently upon the dusk body of the street. Upon the gleaming limbs and asphalt torso of a dreaming nigger. Shake your curled wool-blossoms, nigger. Open your liver lips to the lean, white spring. Stir the root-life of a withered people. Call them from their houses, and teach them to dream.

Dark swaying forms of Negroes are street songs that woo virginal houses.

Dan Moore walks southward on Thirteenth Street. The low limbs of budding chestnut trees recede above his head. Chestnut buds and blossoms are wool he walks upon. The eyes of houses faintly touch him as he passes them. Soft girl-eyes, they set him singing. Girl-eyes within him widen upward to promised faces. Floating away, they dally wistfully over the dusk body of the street. Come on, Dan Moore, come on. Dan sings. His voice is a little hoarse. It cracks. He strains to produce tones in keeping with the houses' loveliness. Cant be done. He whistles. His notes are shrill. They hurt him. Negroes open gates, and go indoors, perfectly. Dan thinks of the house he's going to. Of the girl. Lips, flesh-notes of a forgotten song, plead with him. . .

Dan turns into a side-street, opens an iron gate, bangs it to. Mounts the steps, and searches for the bell. Funny, he cant find it. He fumbles around. The thought comes to him that some one passing by might see him, and not understand. Might think that he is trying to sneak, to break in.

Dan:[2] Break in. Get an ax and smash in. Smash in their faces. I'll show em. Break into an engine-house, steal a thousand horse-power fire truck. Smash in with the truck. I'll show em. Grab an ax and brain em. Cut em up. Jack the Ripper.[3] Baboon from the zoo. And then the cops come. "No, I aint a baboon. I aint Jack the Ripper. I'm a poor man out of work. Take your hands off me, you bull-necked bears. Look into my eyes. I am Dan Moore. I was born in a canefield. The hands of Jesus touched me. I am come to a sick world to heal it. Only the other day, a dope fiend brushed against me— Dont laugh, you mighty, juicy, meat-hook men. Give

---

1. Expensive theater seats usually located along a side wall, box seats were considered the best seats in the theater. They were above stage level, and the closest were within arms' reach of the stage.
2. Throughout this story, a colcn following the name of Dan or Muriel indicates that the thoughts, not the spoken words, of the character will follow.
3. The name given by newspapers to an unidentified individual in nineteenth-century London, England, who killed and mutilated several prostitutes.

me your fingers and I will peel them as if they were ripe bananas."

Some one might think he is trying to break in. He'd better knock. His knuckles are raw bone against the thick glass door. He waits. No one comes. Perhaps they havent heard him. He raps again. This time, harder. He waits. No one comes. Some one is surely in. He fancies that he sees their shadows on the glass. Shadows of gorillas. Perhaps they saw him coming and dont want to let him in. He knocks. The tension of his arms makes the glass rattle. Hurried steps come towards him. The door opens.

"Please, you might break the glass—the bell—oh, Mr. Moore! I thought it must be some stranger. How do you do? Come in, wont you? Muriel? Yes. I'll call her. Take your things off, wont you? And have a seat in the parlor. Muriel will be right down. Muriel! Oh Muriel! Mr. Moore to see you. She'll be right down. You'll pardon me, wont you? So glad to see you."

Her eyes are weak. They are bluish and watery from reading newspapers. The blue is steel. It gimlets[4] Dan while her mouth flaps amiably to him.

Dan: Nothing for you to see, old mussel-head. Dare I show you? If I did, delirium would furnish you headlines for a month. Now look here. Thats enough. Go long, woman. Say some nasty thing and I'll kill you. Huh. Better damned sight not. Ta-ta, Mrs. Pribby.

Mrs. Pribby retreats to the rear of the house. She takes up a newspaper. There is a sharp click as she fits into her chair and draws it to the table. The click is metallic like the sound of a bolt being shot into place. Dan's eyes sting. Sinking into a soft couch, he closes them. The house contracts about him. It is a sharp-edged, massed, metallic house. Bolted. About Mrs. Pribby. Bolted to the endless rows of metal houses. Mrs. Pribby's house. The rows of houses belong to other Mrs. Pribbys. No wonder he couldn't sing to them.

Dan: What's Muriel doing here? God, what a place for her. Whats she doing? Putting her stockings on? In the bathroom. Come out of there, Dan Moore. People must have their privacy. Peeping-toms. I'll never peep. I'll listen. I like to listen.

Dan goes to the wall and places his ear against it. A passing street car and something vibrant from the earth sends a rumble to him. That rumble comes from the earth's deep core. It is the mutter of powerful underground races. Dan has a picture of all the people rushing to put their ears against walls, to listen to it. The next world-savior is coming up that way. Coming up. A continent sinks down. The new-world Christ will need consummate skill to walk upon the waters where huge bubbles burst. . . Thuds of

4. A gimlet is a small tool for piercing holes. Toomer uses the verb to suggest the piercing quality of the blue eyes.

Muriel coming down. Dan turns to the piano and glances through a stack of jazz music sheets. Ji-ji-bo, JI-JI-BO! . .

"Hello, Dan, stranger, what brought you here?"

Muriel comes in, shakes hands, and then clicks into a high-armed seat under the orange glow of a floor-lamp. Her face is fleshy. It would tend to coarseness but for the fresh fragrant something which is the life of it. Her hair like an Indian's. But more curly and bushed and vagrant. Her nostrils flare. The flushed ginger of her cheeks is touched orange by the shower of color from the lamp.

"Well, you havent told me, you havent answered my question, stranger. What brought you here?"

Dan feels the pressure of the house, of the rear room, of the rows of houses, shift to Muriel. He is light. He loves her. He is doubly heavy.

"Dont know, Muriel—wanted to see you—wanted to talk to you —to see you and tell you that I know what you've been through— what pain the last few months must have been—"

"Lets dont mention that."

"But why not, Muriel? I—"

"Please."

"But Muriel, life is full of things like that. One grows strong and beautiful in facing them. What else is life?"

"I dont know, Dan. And I dont believe I care. Whats the use? Lets talk about something else. I hear there's a good show at the Lincoln this week."

"Yes, so Harry was telling me. Going?"

"To-night."

Dan starts to rise.

"I didnt know. I dont want to keep you."

"Its all right. You dont have to go till Bernice comes. And she wont be here till eight. I'm all dressed. I'll let you know."

"Thanks."

Silence. The rustle of a newspaper being turned comes from the rear room.

Muriel: Shame about Dan. Something awfully good and fine about him. But he dont fit in. In where? Me? Dan, I could love you if I tried. I dont have to try. I do. O Dan, dont you know I do? Timid lover, brave talker that you are. Whats the good of all you know if you dont know that? I wont let myself. I? Mrs. Pribby who reads newspapers all night wont. What has she got to do with me? She *is* me, somehow. No she's not. Yes she is. She is the town, and the town wont let me love you, Dan. Dont you know? You could make it let me if you would. Why wont you? Youre selfish. I'm not strong enough to buck it. Youre too selfish to buck it, for me. I wish you'd go. You irritate me. Dan, please go.

"What are you doing now, Dan?"

"Same old thing, Muriel. Nothing, as the world would have it. Living, as I look at things. Living as much as I can without—"

"But you cant live without money, Dan. Why dont you get a good job and settle down?"

Dan: Same old line. Shoot it at me, sister. Hell of a note, this loving business. For ten minutes of it youve got to stand the torture of an intolerable heaviness and a hundred platitudes. Well, damit, shoot on.

"To what? my dear. Rustling newspapers?"

"You mustnt say that, Dan. It isnt right. Mrs. Pribby has been awfully good to me."

"Dare say she has. Whats that got to do with it?"

"Oh, Dan, youre so unconsiderate and selfish. All you think of is yourself."

"I think of you."

"Too much—I mean, you ought to work more and think less. Thats the best way to get along."

"Mussel-heads get along, Muriel. There is more to you than that—"

"Sometimes I think there is, Dan. But I dont know. I've tried. I've tried to do something with myself. Something real and beautiful, I mean. But whats the good of trying? I've tried to make people, every one I come in contact with, happy—"

Dan looks at her, directly. Her animalism, still unconquered by zoo-restrictions and keeper-taboos, stirs him. Passion tilts upward, bringing with it the elements of an old desire. Muriel's lips become the flesh-notes of a futile, plaintive longing. Dan's impulse to direct her is its fresh life.

"Happy, Muriel? No, not happy. Your aim is wrong. There is no such thing as happiness. Life bends joy and pain, beauty and ugliness, in such a way that no one may isolate them. No one should want to. Perfect joy, or perfect pain, with no contrasting element to define them, would mean a monotony of consciousness, would mean death. Not happy, Muriel. Say that you have tried to make them create. Say that you have used your own capacity for life to cradle them. To start them upward-flowing. Or if you cant say that you have, then say that you will. My talking to you will make you aware of your power to do so. Say that you will love, that you will give yourself in love—"

"To you, Dan?"

Dan's consciousness crudely swerves into his passions. They flare up in his eyes. They set up quivers in his abdomen. He is suddenly over-tense and nervous.

"Muriel—"

The newspaper rustles in the rear room.

"Muriel—"

Dan rises. His arms stretch towards her. His fingers and his palms, pink in the lamplight, are glowing irons. Muriel's chair is close and stiff about her. The house, the rows of houses locked about her chair. Dan's fingers and arms are fire to melt and bars to wrench and force and pry. Her arms hang loose. Her hands are hot and moist. Dan takes them. He slips to his knees before her.

"Dan, you mustnt."

"Muriel—"

"Dan, really you mustnt. No, Dan. No."

"Oh, come, Muriel. Must I—"

"Shhh. Dan, please get up. Please. Mrs. Pribby is right in the next room. She'll hear you. She may come in. Dont, Dan. She'll see you—"

"Well then, lets go out."

"I cant. Let go, Dan. Oh, wont you please let go."

Muriel tries to pull her hands away. Dan tightens his grip. He feels the strength of his fingers. His muscles are tight and strong. He stands up. Thrusts out his chest. Muriel shrinks from him. Dan becomes aware of his crude absurdity. His lips curl. His passion chills. He has an obstinate desire to possess her.

"Muriel, I love you. I want you, whatever the world of Pribby says. Damn your Pribby. Who is she to dictate my love? I've stood enough of her. Enough of you. Come here."

Muriel's mouth works in and out. Her eyes flash and waggle. She wrenches her hands loose and forces them against his breast to keep him off. Dan grabs her wrists. Wedges in between her arms. Her face is close to him. It is hot and blue and moist. Ugly.

"Come here now."

"Dont, Dan. Oh, dont. What are you killing?"

"Whats weak in both of us and a whole litter of Pribbys. For once in your life youre going to face whats real, by God—"

A sharp rap on the newspaper in the rear room cuts between them. The rap is like cool thick glass between them. Dan is hot on one side. Muriel, hot on the other. They straighten. Gaze fearfully at one another. Neither moves. A clock in the rear room, in the rear room, the rear room, strikes eight. Eight slow, cool sounds. Bernice. Muriel fastens on her image. She smooths her dress. She adjusts her skirt. She becomes prim and cool. Rising, she skirts Dan as if to keep the glass between them. Dan, gyrating nervously above the easy swing of his limbs, follows her to the parlor door. Muriel retreats before him till she reaches the landing of the steps that lead upstairs. She smiles at him. Dan sees his face in the hall mirror. He runs his fingers through his hair. Reaches for his hat and coat and puts them on. He moves towards Muriel. Muriel steps backward up one step. Dan's jaw shoots out. Muriel jerks her arm in warning of Mrs. Pribby. She gasps and turns and starts to run. Noise of a chair scraping as Mrs. Pribby rises from it, ratchets down the hall. Dan stops. He makes a wry face, wheels round, goes out, and slams the door.

2

People come in slowly . . . mutter, laughs, flutter, whishadwash,[5] "I've changed my work-clothes—" . . . and fill vacant seats of Lincoln Theater. Muriel, leading Bernice who is a cross between a washerwoman and a blue-blood lady, a washer-blue, a washer-lady, wanders down the right aisle to the lower front box. Muriel has on an orange dress. Its color would clash with the crimson box-draperies, its color would contradict the sweet rose smile her face is bathed in, should she take her coat off. She'll keep it on. Pale purple shadows rest on the planes of her cheeks. Deep purple comes from her thick-shocked hair. Orange of the dress goes well with these. Muriel presses her coat down from around her shoulders. Teachers are not supposed to have bobbed hair.[6] She'll keep her hat on. She takes the first chair, and indicates that Bernice is to take the one directly behind her. Seated thus, her eyes are level with, and near to, the face of an imaginary man upon the stage. To speak to Berny she must turn. When she does, the audience is square upon her.

People come in slowly . . . "—for my Sunday-go-to-meeting dress. O glory God! O shout Amen!" . . . and fill vacant seats of Lincoln Theater. Each one is a bolt that shoots into a slot, and is locked there. Suppose the Lord should ask, where was Moses when the light went out? Suppose Gabriel should blow his trumpet![7] The seats are slots. The seats are bolted houses. The mass grows denser. Its weight at first is impalpable upon the box. Then Muriel begins to feel it. She props her arm against the brass box-rail, to ward it off. Silly. These people are friends of hers: a parent of a child she teaches, an old school friend. She smiles at them. They return her courtesy, and she is free to chat with Berny. Berny's tongue, started, runs on, and on. O washer-blue! O washer-lady!

Muriel: Never see Dan again. He makes me feel queer. Starts things he doesnt finish. Upsets me. I am not upset. I am perfectly calm. I am going to enjoy the show. Good show. I've had some show! This damn tame thing. O Dan. Wont see Dan again. Not alone. Have Mrs. Pribby come in. She *was* in. Keep Dan out. If I

5. Toomer's attempt to suggest the sounds made by a theater audience during the time before the curtain rises.
6. A short hairstyle of the 1920's that was considered fashionable and daring for women who rebelled against the conservative custom of long hair.
7. The Christian concept that, at the end of the world, the angel Gabriel will blow a horn to announce Judgment Day.

love him, can I keep him out? Well then, I dont love him. Now he's out. Who is that coming in? Blind as a bat. Ding-bat. Looks like Dan. He mustnt see me. Silly. He cant reach me. He wont dare come in here. He'd put his head down like a goring bull and charge me. He'd trample them. He'd gore. He'd rape! Berny! He wont dare come in here.

"Berny, who was that who just came in? I havent my glasses."

"A friend of yours, a *good* friend so I hear. Mr. Daniel Moore, Lord."

"Oh. He's no friend of mine."

"No? I hear he is."

"Well, he isnt."

Dan is ushered down the aisle. He has to squeeze past the knees of seated people to reach his own seat. He treads on a man's corns. The man grumbles, and shoves him off. He shrivels close beside a portly Negress whose huge rolls of flesh meet about the bones of seat-arms. A soil-soaked fragrance comes from her. Through the cement floor her strong roots sink down. They spread under the asphalt streets. Dreaming, the streets roll over on their bellies, and suck their glossy health from them. Her strong roots sink down and spread under the river and disappear in blood-lines that waver south. Her roots shoot down. Dan's hands follow them. Roots throb. Dan's heart beats violently. He places his palms upon the earth to cool them. Earth throbs. Dan's heart beats violently. He sees all the people in the house rush to the walls to listen to the rumble. A new-world Christ is coming up. Dan comes up. He is startled. The eyes of the woman dont belong to her. They look at him unpleasantly. From either aisle, bolted masses press in. He doesnt fit. The mass grows agitant. For an instant, Dan's and Muriel's eyes meet. His weight there slides the weight on her. She braces an arm against the brass rail, and turns her head away.

Muriel: Damn fool; dear Dan, what did you want to follow me here for? Oh cant you ever do anything right? Must you always pain me, and make me hate you? I do hate you. I wish some one would come in with a horse-whip and lash you out. I wish some one would drag you up a back alley and brain you with the whip-butt.

Muriel glances at her wrist-watch.

"Quarter of nine. Berny, what time have you?"

"Eight-forty. Time to begin. Oh, look Muriel, that woman with the plume; doesnt she look good! They say she's going with, oh, whats his name. You know. Too much powder.[8] I can see it from here. Here's the orchestra now. O fine! Jim Clem at the piano!"

The men fill the pit. Instruments run the scale and tune. The

8. Face powder to make the skin seem lighter.

saxophone moans and throws a fit. Jim Clem, poised over the piano, is ready to begin. His head nods forward. Opening crash. The house snaps dark. The curtain recedes upward from the blush of the footlights. Jazz overture is over. The first act is on.

Dan: Old stuff. Muriel—bored. Must be. But she'll smile and she'll clap. Do what youre bid, you she-slave. Look at her. Sweet, tame woman in a brass box seat. Clap, smile, fawn, clap. Do what youre bid. Drag me in with you. Dirty me. Prop me in your brass box seat. I'm there, am I not? because of you. He-slave. Slave of a woman who is a slave. I'm a damned sight worse than you are. I sing your praises, Beauty! I exalt thee, O Muriel! A slave, thou art greater than all Freedom because I love thee.

Dan fidgets, and disturbs his neighbors. His neighbors glare at him. He glares back without seeing them. The man whose corns have been trod upon speaks to him.

"Keep quiet, cant you, mister. Other people have paid their money besides yourself to see the show."

The man's face is a blur about two sullen liquid things that are his eyes. The eyes dissolve in the surrounding vagueness. Dan suddenly feels that the man is an enemy whom he has long been looking for.

Dan bristles. Glares furiously at the man.

"All right. All right then. Look at the show. I'm not stopping you."

"Shhh," from some one in the rear.

Dan turns around.

"Its that man there who started everything. I didnt say a thing to him until he tried to start something. What have I got to do with whether he has paid his money or not? Thats the manager's business. Do I look like the manager?"

"Shhhh. Youre right. Shhhh."

"Dont tell me to shhh. Tell him. That man there. He started everything. If what he wanted was to start a fight, why didnt he say so?"

The man leans forward.

"Better be quiet, sonny. I aint said a thing about fight, yet."

"Its a good thing you havent."

"Shhhh."

Dan grips himself. Another act is on. Dwarfs, dressed like prizefighters, foreheads bulging like boxing gloves, are led upon the stage. They are going to fight for the heavyweight championship. Gruesome. Dan glances at Muriel. He imagines that she shudders. His mind curves back into himself, and picks up tail-ends of experiences. His eyes are open, mechanically. The dwarfs pound and bruise and bleed each other, on his eyeballs.

Dan: Ah, but she was some baby! And not vulgar either. Funny

how some women can do those things. Muriel dancing like that!
Hell. She rolled and wabbled. Her buttocks rocked. She pulled up
her dress and showed her pink drawers. Baby! And then she
caught my eyes. Dont know what my eyes had in them. Yes I do.
God, dont I though! Sometimes I think, Dan Moore, that your
eyes could burn clean . . . burn clean . . . BURN CLEAN! . .

The gong rings. The dwarfs set to. They spar grotesquely, play-
fully, until one lands a stiff blow. This makes the other sore. He
commences slugging. A real scrap is on. Time! The dwarfs go to
their corners and are sponged and fanned off. Gloves bulge from
their wrists. Their wrists are necks for the tight-faced gloves. The
fellow to the right lets his eyes roam over the audience. He sights
Muriel. He grins.

Dan: Those silly women arguing feminism. Here's what I
should have said to them. "It should be clear to you women, that
the proposition must be stated thus:

> Me, horizontally above her.
> Action: perfect strokes downward oblique.
> Hence, man dominates because of limitation.
> Or, so it shall be until women learn their stuff.

So framed, the proposition is a mental-filler, Dentist, I want gold
teeth. It should become cherished of the technical intellect. I
hereby offer it to posterity as one of the important machine-age
designs. P. S. It should be noted, that because it *is* an achievement
of this age, its growth and hence its causes, up to the point of
maturity, antedate machinery. Ery . . ."

The gong rings. No fooling this time. The dwarfs set to. They
clinch. The referee parts them. One swings a cruel upper-cut and
knocks the other down. A huge head hits the floor. Pop! The
house roars. The fighter, groggy, scrambles up. The referee whispers to the contenders not to fight so hard. They ignore him. They
charge. Their heads jab like boxing-gloves. They kick and spit and
bite. They pound each other furiously. Muriel pounds. The house
pounds. Cut lips. Bloody noses. The referee asks for the gong.
Time! The house roars. The dwarfs bow, are made to bow. The
house wants more. The dwarfs are led from the stage.

Dan: Strange I never really noticed him before. Been sitting
there for years. Born a slave. Slavery not so long ago. He'll die in
his chair. Swing low, sweet chariot.[9] Jesus will come and roll him
down the river Jordan. Oh, come along, Moses, you'll get lost;
stretch out your rod and come across. LET MY PEOPLE GO!
Old man. Knows everyone who passes the corners. Saw the first

---

9. In Dan's description of the slave who has lived
long enough to see the first automobiles, Toomer
alludes to Afro-American spirituals expressing hope
for freedom on earth and freedom in heaven: "Swing
Low, Sweet Chariot," "Roll, Jordan, Roll," "Let
My People Go."

horse-cars. The first Oldsmobile. And he was born in slavery. I did
see his eyes. Never miss eyes. But they were bloodshot and watery.
It hurt to look at them. It hurts to look in most people's eyes. He
saw Grant and Lincoln. He saw Walt—old man, did you see Walt
Whitman?[1] Did you see Walt Whitman! Strange force that drew
me to him. And I went up to see. The woman thought I saw
crazy. I told him to look into the heavens. He did, and smiled. I
asked him if he knew what that rumbling is that comes up from the
ground. Christ, what a stroke that was. And the jabbering idiots
crowding around. And the crossing-cop leaving his job to come over
and wheel him away . . .

The house applauds. The house wants more. The dwarfs are led
back. But no encore. Must give the house something. The attend-
ant comes out and announces that Mr. Barry, the champion, will
sing one of his own songs, "for your approval." Mr. Barry grins at
Muriel as he wabbles from the wing. He holds a fresh white rose,
and a small mirror. He wipes blood from his nose. He signals Jim
Clem. The orchestra starts. A sentimental love song, Mr. Barry
sings, first to one girl, and then another in the audience. He holds
the mirror in such a way that it flashes in the face of each one he
sings to. The light swings around.

Dan: I am going to reach up and grab the girders of this building and pull them down. The crash will be a signal. Hid by the
smoke and dust Dan Moore will arise. In his right hand will be a
dynamo. In his left, a god's face that will flash white light from
ebony. I'll grab a girder and swing it like a walking-stick.
Lightning will flash. I'll grab its black knob and swing it like a
crippled cane. Lightning . . . Some one's flashing . . . some one's
flashing . . . Who in hell is flashing that mirror? Take it off me,
godam you.

Dan's eyes are half blinded. He moves his head. The light follows. He hears the audience laugh. He hears the orchestra. A man
with a high-pitched, sentimental voice is singing. Dan sees the
dwarf. Along the mirror flash the song comes. Dan ducks his head.
The audience roars. The light swings around to Muriel. Dan looks.
Muriel is too close. Mr. Barry covers his mirror. He sings to her.
She shrinks away. Nausea. She clutches the brass box-rail. She
moves to face away. The audience is square upon her. Its eyes
smile. Its hands itch to clap. Muriel turns to the dwarf and
forces a smile at him. With a showy blare of orchestration, the
song comes to its close. Mr. Barry bows. He offers Muriel the
rose, first having kissed it. Blood of his battered lips is a vivid
stain upon its petals. Mr. Barry offers Muriel the rose. The
house applauds. Muriel flinches back. The dwarf steps forward,

1. A nineteenth-century American poet who voiced many ideas about democracy, brotherhood, and a
new American race with which Toomer agreed, Whitman served as a nurse during the Civil War.

diffident; threatening. Hate pops from his eyes and crackles like a brittle heat about the box. The thick hide of his face is drawn in tortured wrinkles. Above his eyes, the bulging, tight-skinned brow. Dan looks at it. It grows calm and massive. It grows profound. It is a thing of wisdom and tenderness, of suffering and beauty. Dan looks down. The eyes are calm and luminous. Words come from them . . . Arms of the audience reach out, grab Muriel, and hold her there. Claps are steel fingers that manacle her wrists and move them forward to acceptance. Berny leans forward and whispers:

"Its all right. Go on—take it."

Words form in the eyes of the dwarf:

> Do not shrink. Do not be afraid of me.
> *Jesus*
> See how my eyes look at you.
> *the Son of God*
> I too was made in His image.
> *was once—*
> I give you the rose.

Muriel, tight in her revulsion, sees black, and daintily reaches for the offering. As her hand touches it, Dan springs up in his seat and shouts:

"JESUS WAS ONCE A LEPER!"

Dan steps down.

He is as cool as a green stem that has just shed its flower.

Rows of gaping faces strain towards him. They are distant, beneath him, impalpable. Squeezing out, Dan again treads upon the corn-foot man. The man shoves him.

"Watch where youre going, mister. Crazy or no, you aint going to walk over me. Watch where youre going there."

Dan turns, and serenely tweaks the fellow's nose. The man jumps up. Dan is jammed against a seat-back. A slight swift anger flicks him. His fist hooks the other's jaw.

"Now you have started something. Aint no man living can hit me and get away with it. Come on on the outside."

The house, tumultuously stirring, grabs its wraps and follows the men.

The man leads Dan up a black alley. The alley-air is thick and moist with smells of garbage and wet trash. In the morning, singing niggers will drive by and ring their gongs. . . Heavy with the scent of rancid flowers and with the scent of fight. The crowd, pressing forward, is a hollow roar. Eyes of houses, soft girl-eyes, glow reticently upon the hubbub and blink out. The man stops. Takes off his hat and coat. Dan, having forgotten him, keeps going on.

Prayer

My body is opaque to the soul.
Driven of the spirit, long have I sought to temper it unto the spirit's
    longing,
But my mind, too, is opaque to the soul.
A closed lid is my soul's flesh-eye.
O Spirits of whom my soul is but a little finger,
Direct it to the lid of its flesh-eye.
I am weak with much giving.
I am weak with the desire to give more.
(How strong a thing is the little finger!)
So weak that I have confused the body with the soul,
And the body with its little finger.
(How frail is the little finger.)
My voice could not carry to you did you dwell in stars,
O Spirits of whom my soul is but a little finger . .

Harvest Song [1]

I am a reaper whose muscles set at sundown. All my oats are
    cradled.
But I am too chilled, and too fatigued to bind them. And I hunger.

I crack a grain between my teeth. I do not taste it.
I have been in the fields all day. My throat is dry. I hunger.

My eyes are caked with dust of oatfields at harvest-time.
I am a blind man who stares across the hills, seeking stack'd fields
    of other harvesters.

It would be good to see them . . crook'd, split, and iron-ring'd han-
    dles of the scythes. It would be good to see them, dust-
    caked and blind. I hunger.

(Dusk is a strange fear'd sheath their blades are dull'd in.)
My throat is dry. And should I call, a cracked grain like the
    oats . . . eoho—

I fear to call. What should they hear me, and offer me their grain,
    oats, or wheat, or corn? I have been in the fields all day. I
    fear I could not taste it. I fear knowledge of my hunger.

My ears are caked with dust of oatfields at harvest-time.
I am a deaf man who strains to hear the calls of other harvesters
    whose throats are also dry.

It would be good to hear their songs . . reapers of the sweet-stalk'd
    cane, cutters of the corn . . even though their throats
    cracked and the strangeness of their voices deafened me.

I hunger. My throat is dry. Now that the sun has set and I am
    chilled, I fear to call. (Eoho, my brothers!)

I am a reaper. (Eoho!) All my oats are cradled. But I am too
    fatigued to bind them. And I hunger. I crack a grain. It
    has no taste to it. My throat is dry. . .

O my brothers, I beat my palms, still soft, against the stubble of my
    harvesting. (You beat your soft palms, too.) My pain is
    sweet. Sweeter than the oats or wheat or corn. It will not
    bring me knowledge of my hunger.

---

1. First published in *Double Dealer* 4 (December 1922): 258.

Bona and Paul[1]

1

On the school gymnasium floor, young men and women are drilling. They are going to be teachers, and go out into the world . . thud, thud . . and give precision to the movements of sick people who all their lives have been drilling. One man is out of step. In step. The teacher glares at him. A girl in bloomers, seated on a mat in the corner because she has told the director that she is sick, sees that the footfalls of the men are rhythmical and syncopated. The dance of his blue-trousered limbs thrills her.

Bona: He is a candle that dances in a grove swung with pale balloons.

Columns of the drillers thud towards her. He is in the front row. He is in no row at all. Bona can look close at him. His red-brown face—

Bona: He is a harvest moon. He is an autumn leaf. He is a nigger. Bona! But dont all the dorm girls say so? And dont you, when you are sane, say so? Thats why I love— Oh, nonsense. You have never loved a man who didnt first love you. Besides—

Columns thud away from her. Come to a halt in line formation. Rigid. The period bell rings, and the teacher dismisses them.

A group collects around Paul. They are choosing sides for basket-ball. Girls against boys. Paul has his. He is limbering up beneath the basket. Bona runs to the girl captain and asks to be chosen. The girls fuss. The director comes to quiet them. He hears what Bona wants.

"But, Miss Hale, you were excused—"

"So I was, Mr. Boynton, but—"

"—you can play basket-ball, but you are too sick to drill."

"If you wish to put it that way."

She swings away from him to the girl captain.

"Helen, I want to play, and you must let me. This is the first time I've asked and I dont see why—"

"Thats just it, Bona. We have our team."

"Well, team or no team, I want to play and thats all there is to it."

She snatches the ball from Helen's hands, and charges down the floor.

1. This story, set in Chicago, is the only story of the second part not located in Washington, D.C. While attending schools in Chicago in 1916, Toomer was romantically involved with a young white woman. According to Toomer, the woman's guardian, whom he suspected of jealousy, tried to end the relationship by telling her that Toomer was Afro-American. Toomer, however, continued to correspond with her after he left Chicago. Although Toomer included autobiographical details, readers should remember that the story is fiction rather than autobiography.

72

Helen shrugs. One of the weaker girls says that she'll drop out. Helen accepts this. The team is formed. The whistle blows. The game starts. Bona, in center, is jumping against Paul. He plays with her. Out-jumps her, makes a quick pass, gets a quick return, and shoots a goal from the middle of the floor. Bona burns crimson. She fights, and tries to guard him. One of her team-mates advises her not to play so hard. Paul shoots his second goal.

Bona begins to feel a little dizzy and all in. She drives on. Almost hugs Paul to guard him. Near the basket, he attempts to shoot, and Bona lunges into his body and tries to beat his arms. His elbow, going up, gives her a sharp crack on the jaw. She whirls. He catches her. Her body stiffens. Then becomes strangely vibrant, and bursts to a swift life within her anger. He is about to give way before her hatred when a new passion flares at him and makes his stomach fall. Bona squeezes him. He suddenly feels stifled, and wonders why in hell the ring of silly gaping faces that's caked about him doesnt make way and give him air. He has a swift illusion that it is himself who has been struck. He looks at Bona. Whir. Whir. They seem to be human distortions spinning tensely in a fog. Spinning . . dizzy . . spinning. . . Bona jerks herself free, flushes a startling crimson, breaks through the bewildered teams, and rushes from the hall.

2

Paul is in his room of two windows.

Outside, the South-Side L track cuts them in two.[2]

Bona is one window. One window, Paul.

Hurtling Loop-jammed[3] L trains throw them in swift shadow.

Paul goes to his. Gray slanting roofs of houses are tinted lavender in the setting sun. Paul follows the sun, over the stock-yards where a fresh stench is just arising, across wheat lands that are still waving above their stubble, into the sun. Paul follows the sun to a pine-matted hillock in Georgia. He sees the slanting roofs of gray unpainted cabins tinted lavender. A Negress chants a lullaby beneath the mate-eyes of a southern planter. Her breasts are ample for the suckling of a song. She weans it, and sends it, curiously weaving, among lush melodies of cane and corn. Paul follows the sun into himself in Chicago.

He is at Bona's window.

With his own glow he looks through a dark pane.

Paul's room-mate comes in.

2. The elevated train that runs through the South Side of Chicago.
3. The Loop: a downtown area of Chicago that once was the center of the shopping district; so-called because the elevated train ("L") tracks make a loop around the area. "Loop-jammed," consequently, means "crowded with passengers coming from the Loop."

"Say, Paul, I've got a date for you. Come on. Shake a leg, will you?"

His blond hair is combed slick. His vest is snug about him.

He is like the electric light which he snaps on.

"Whatdoysay, Paul? Get a wiggle on. Come on. We havent got much time by the time we eat and dress and everything."

His bustling concentrates on the brushing of his hair.

Art: What in hell's getting into Paul of late, anyway? Christ, but he's getting moony. Its his blood. Dark blood: moony. Doesnt get anywhere unless you boost it. You've got to keep it going—

"Say, Paul!"

—or it'll go to sleep on you. Dark blood; nigger? Thats what those jealous she-hens say. Not Bona though, or she . . from the South . . wouldnt want me to fix a date for him and her. Hell of a thing, that Paul's dark: youve got to always be answering questions.

"Say, Paul, for Christ's sake leave that window, cant you?"

"Whats it, Art?"

"Hell, I've told you about fifty times. Got a date for you. Come on."

"With who?"

Art: He didnt use to ask; now he does. Getting up in the air. Getting funny.

"Heres your hat. Want a smoke? Paul! Here. I've got a match. Now come on and I'll tell you all about it on the way to supper."

Paul: He's going to Life this time. No doubt of that. Quit your kidding. Some day, dear Art, I'm going to kick the living slats out of you, and you wont know what I've done it for. And your slats will bring forth Life . . beautiful woman. . .

Pure Food Restaurant.

"Bring me some soup with a lot of crackers, understand? And then a roast-beef dinner. Same for you, eh, Paul? Now as I was saying, you've got a swell chance with her. And she's game. Best proof: she dont give a damn what the dorm girls say about you and her in the gym, or about the funny looks that Boynton gives her, or about what they say about, well, hell, you know, Paul. And say, Paul, she's a sweetheart. Tall, not puffy and pretty, more serious and deep—the kind you like these days. And they say she's got a car. And say, she's on fire. But you know all about that. She got Helen to fix it up with me. The four of us—remember the last party? Crimson Gardens![4] Boy!"

Paul's eyes take on a light that Art can settle in.

---

4. A nightclub.

3

Art has on his patent-leather pumps and fancy vest. A loose fall coat is swung across his arm. His face has been massaged, and over a close shave, powdered. It is a healthy pink the blue of evening tints a purple pallor. Art is happy and confident in the good looks that his mirror gave him. Bubbling over with a joy he must spend now if the night is to contain it all. His bubbles, too, are curiously tinted purple as Paul watches them. Paul, contrary to what he had thought he would be like, is cool like the dusk, and like the dusk, detached. His dark face is a floating shade in evening's shadow. He sees Art, curiously. Art is a purple fluid, carbon-charged, that effervesces beside him. He loves Art. But is it not queer, this pale purple facsimile of a red-blooded Norwegian friend of his? Perhaps for some reason, white skins are not supposed to live at night. Surely, enough nights would transform them fantastically, or kill them. And their red passion? Night paled that too, and made it moony. Moony. Thats what Art thought of him. Bona didnt, even in the daytime. Bona, would she be pale? Impossible. Not that red glow. But the conviction did not set his emotion flowing.

"Come right in, wont you? The young ladies will be right down. Oh, Mr. Carlstrom, do play something for us while you are waiting. We just love to listen to your music. You play so well."

Houses, and dorm sitting-rooms are places where white faces seclude themselves at night. There is a reason. . .

Art sat on the piano and simply tore it down. Jazz. The picture of Our Poets hung perilously.

Paul: I've got to get the kid to play that stuff for me in the daytime. Might be different. More himself. More nigger. Different? There is. Curious, though.

The girls come in. Art stops playing, and almost immediately takes up a petty quarrel, where he had last left it, with Helen.

Bona, black-hair curled staccato, sharply contrasting with Helen's puffy yellow, holds Paul's hand. She squeezes it. Her own emotion supplements the return pressure. And then, for no tangible reason, her spirits drop. Without them, she is nervous, and slightly afraid. She resents this. Paul's eyes are critical. She resents Paul. She flares at him. She flares to poise and security.

"Shall we be on our way?"

"Yes, Bona, certainly."

The Boulevard is sleek in asphalt, and, with arc-lights and limousines, aglow. Dry leaves scamper behind the whir of cars. The scent of exploded gasoline that mingles with them is faintly sweet. Mellow stone mansions overshadow clapboard homes which now resemble Negro shanties in some southern alley. Bona and Paul, and Art and Helen, move along an island-like, far-stretching strip of leaf-soft ground. Above them, worlds of shadow-planes and solids, silently moving. As if on one of these, Paul looks down on Bona. No doubt of it: her face is pale. She is talking. Her words have no feel to them. One sees them. They are pink petals that fall upon velvet cloth. Bona is soft, and pale, and beautiful.

"Paul, tell me something about yourself—or would you rather wait?"

"I'll tell you anything you'd like to know."

"Not what I want to know, Paul; what you want to tell me."

"You have the beauty of a gem fathoms under sea."

"I feel that, but I dont want to be. I want to be near you. Perhaps I will be if I tell you something. Paul, I love you."

The sea casts up its jewel into his hands, and burns them furiously. To tuck her arm under his and hold her hand will ease the burn.

"What can I say to you, brave dear woman—I cant talk love. Love is a dry grain in my mouth unless it is wet with kisses."

"You would dare? right here on the Boulevard? before Arthur and Helen?"

"Before myself? I dare."

"Here then."

Bona, in the slim shadow of a tree trunk, pulls Paul to her. Suddenly she stiffens. Stops.

"But you have not said you love me."

"I cant—yet—Bona."

"Ach, you never will. Youre cold. Cold."

Bona: Colored; cold. Wrong somewhere.

She hurries and catches up with Art and Helen.

4

Crimson Gardens. Hurrah! So one feels. People . . . University of Chicago students, members of the stock exchange, a large Negro in crimson uniform who guards the door . . had watched them enter. Had leaned towards each other over ash-smeared tablecloths and highballs and whispered: What is he, a Spaniard, an Indian, an Italian, a Mexican, a Hindu, or a Japanese? Art had at first fidgeted under their stares . . what are *you* looking at, you godam pack of owl-eyed hyenas? . . but soon settled into his fuss with Helen, and forgot them. A strange thing happened to Paul. Suddenly he knew that he was apart from the people around him. Apart from the pain which they had unconsciously caused. Suddenly he knew that people saw, not attractiveness in his dark skin, but difference. Their stares, giving him to himself, filled something long empty within him, and were like green blades sprouting in his consciousness. There was fullness, and strength and peace about it all. He saw himself, cloudy, but real. He saw the faces of the people at the tables round him. White lights, or as now, the pink lights of the Crimson Gardens gave a glow and immediacy to white faces. The pleasure of it, equal to that of love or dream, of seeing this. Art and Bona and Helen? He'd look. They were wonderfully flushed and beautiful. Not for himself; because they were. Distantly. Who were they, anyway? God, if he knew them. He'd come in with them. Of that he was sure. Come where? Into life? Yes. No. Into the Crimson Gardens. A part of life. A carbon bubble. Would it look purple if he went out into the night and looked at it? His sudden starting to rise almost upset the table.

"What in hell—pardon—whats the matter, Paul?"

"I forgot my cigarettes—"

"Youre smoking one."

"So I am. Pardon me."

The waiter straightens them out. Takes their order.

Art: What in hell's eating Paul? Moony aint the word for it. From bad to worse. And those godam people staring so. Paul's a queer fish. Doesnt seem to mind. . . He's my pal, let me tell you, you horn-rimmed owl-eyed hyena at that table, and a lot better than you whoever you are. . . Queer about him. I could stick up for him if he'd only come out, one way or the other, and tell a feller. Besides, a room-mate has a right to know. Thinks I wont understand. Said so. He's got a swell head when it comes to brains, all right. God, he's a good straight feller, though. Only, moony. Nut. Nuttish. Nuttery. Nutmeg. . . "What'd you say, Helen?"

"I was talking to Bona, thank you."

"Well, its nothing to get spiffy about."

"What? Oh, of course not. Please lets dont start some silly argument all over again."

"Well."

"Well."

"Now thats enough. Say, waiter, whats the matter with our order? Make it snappy, will you?"

Crimson Gardens. Hurrah! So one feels. The drinks come. Four highballs. Art passes cigarettes. A girl dressed like a bareback rider in flaming pink, makes her way through tables to the dance floor. All lights are dimmed till they seem a lush afterglow of crimson. Spotlights the girl. She sings. "Liza, Little Liza Jane."

Paul is rosy before his window.

He moves, slightly, towards Bona.

With his own glow, he seeks to penetrate a dark pane.

Paul: From the South. What does that mean, precisely, except that you'll love or hate a nigger? Thats a lot. What does it mean

except that in Chicago you'll have the courage to neither love or
hate. A priori.⁵ But it would seem that you have. Queer words,
arent these, for a man who wears blue pants on a gym floor in the
daytime. Well, never matter. You matter. I'd like to know you
whom I look at. Know, not love. Not that knowing is a greater
pleasure; but that I have just found the joy of it. You came just a
month too late. Even this afternoon I dreamed. To-night, along
the Boulevard, you found me cold. Paul Johnson, cold! Thats a
good one, eh, Art, you fine old stupid fellow, you! But I feel good!
The color and the music and the song. . . A Negress chants a lullaby beneath the mate-eyes of a southern planter. O song! . . And
those flushed faces. Eager brilliant eyes. Hard to imagine them as
unawakened. Your own. Oh, they're awake all right. "And you
know it too, dont you Bona?"

"What, Paul?"

"The truth of what I was thinking."

"I'd like to know I know—something of you."

"You will—before the evening's over. I promise it."

Crimson Gardens. Hurrah! So one feels. The bare-back rider
balances agilely on the applause which is the tail of her song.
Orchestral instruments warm up for jazz. The flute is a cat that
ripples its fur against the deep-purring saxophone. The drum
throws sticks. The cat jumps on the piano keyboard. Hi diddle, hi
diddle, the cat and the fiddle. Crimson Gardens . . hurrah! . .
jumps over the moon. Crimson Gardens! Helen . . O Eliza . . rab-
bit-eyes sparkling, plays up to, and tries to placate what she considers to be Paul's contempt. She always does that . . Little Liza Jane.
. . Once home, she burns with the thought of what she's done.
She says all manner of snidy things about him, and swears that
she'll never go out again when he is along. She tries to get Art to
break with him, saying, that if Paul, whom the whole dormitory
calls a nigger, is more to him than she is, well, she's through. She
does not break with Art. She goes out as often as she can with Art
and Paul. She explains this to herself by a piece of information
which a friend of hers had given her: men like him (Paul) can fas-
cinate. One is not responsible for fascination. Not one girl had
really loved Paul; he fascinated them. Bona didnt; only thought she
did. Time would tell. And of course, *she* didn't. Liza. . . She plays
up to, and tries to placate, Paul.

"Paul is so deep these days, and I'm so glad he's found some one
to interest him."

"I dont believe I do."

The thought escapes from Bona just a moment before her anger
at having said it.

5. In advance of the fact. A priori conclusions are judgments based on preconceived theories rather than
on actual study and analysis.

Bona: You little puffy cat, I do. I do!

Dont I, Paul? her eyes ask.

Her answer is a crash of jazz from the palm-hidden orchestra. Crimson Gardens is a body whose blood flows to a clot upon the dance floor. Art and Helen clot. Soon, Bona and Paul. Paul finds her a little stiff, and his mind, wandering to Helen (silly little kid who wants every highball spoon her hands touch, for a souvenir), supple, perfect little dancer, wishes for the next dance when he and Art will exchange.

Bona knows that she must win him to herself.

"Since when have men like you grown cold?"

"The first philosopher."

"I thought you were a poet—or a gym director."

"Hence, your failure to make love."

Bona's eyes flare. Water. Grow red about the rims. She would like to tear away from him and dash across the clotted floor.

"What do you mean?"

"Mental concepts rule you. If they were flush with mine—good. I dont believe they are."

"How do you know, Mr. Philosopher?"

"Mostly a priori."

"You talk well for a gym director." [6]

"And you—"

"I hate you. Ou!"

She presses away. Paul, conscious of the convention in it, pulls her to him. Her body close. Her head still strains away. He nearly crushes her. She tries to pinch him. Then sees people staring, and lets her arms fall. Their eyes meet. Both, contemptuous. The dance takes blood from their minds and packs it, tingling, in the torsos of their swaying bodies.[7] Passionate blood leaps back into their eyes. They are a dizzy blood clot on a gyrating floor. They know that the pink-faced people have no part in what they feel. Their instinct leads them away from Art and Helen, and towards the big uniformed black man who opens and closes the gilded exit door. The cloak-room girl is tolerant of their impatience over such trivial things as wraps. And slightly superior. As the black man swings the door for them, his eyes are knowing. Too many couples have passed out, flushed and fidgety, for him not to know. The chill air is a shock to Paul. A strange thing happens. He sees the Gardens purple, as if he were way off. And a spot is in the purple. The spot comes furiously towards him. Face of the black man. It leers. It smiles sweetly like a child's. Paul leaves Bona and darts back so quickly that he doesnt give the door-man a chance to open.

6. When he first attended school in Chicago, Toomer was studying physical education.
7. Toomer often conceived dance to be more than a rhythmic movement of a couple. See p. 54, n. 9.

He swings in. Stops. Before the huge bulk of the Negro.

"Youre wrong."

"Yassur."

"Brother, youre wrong.

"I came back to tell you, to shake your hand, and tell you that you are wrong. That something beautiful is going to happen. That the Gardens are purple like a bed of roses would be at dusk. That I came into the Gardens, into life in the Gardens with one whom I did not know. That I danced with her, and did not know her. That I felt passion, contempt and passion for her whom I did not know. That I thought of her. That my thoughts were matches thrown into a dark window. And all the while the Gardens were purple like a bed of roses would be at dusk. I came back to tell you, brother, that white faces are petals of roses. That dark faces are petals of dusk. That I am going out and gather petals. That I am going out and know her whom I brought here with me to these Gardens which are purple like a bed of roses would be at dusk."

Paul and the black man shook hands.

When he reached the spot where they had been standing, Bona was gone.

to Waldo Frank.[1]

1. American author (1889–1967); wrote *Our America*, *Holiday*, and other works of fiction and nonfiction. A friend and admirer. Frank introduced Toomer's work and wrote a foreword for *Cane* (see p. 138).

Kabnis [1]

1

Ralph Kabnis, propped in his bed, tries to read. To read himself to sleep. An oil lamp[2] on a chair near his elbow burns unsteadily. The cabin room is spaced fantastically about it. Whitewashed hearth and chimney, black with sooty saw-teeth. Ceiling, patterned by the fringed globe of the lamp. The walls, unpainted, are seasoned a rosin yellow. And cracks between the boards are black. These cracks are the lips the night winds use for whispering. Night winds in Georgia are vagrant poets, whispering. Kabnis, against his will, lets his book slip down, and listens to them. The warm whiteness of his bed, the lamp-light, do not protect him from the weird chill of their song:

> White-man's land.
> Niggers,[3] sing.
> Burn, bear black children
> Till poor rivers bring
> Rest, and sweet glory
> In Camp Ground.[4]

Kabnis' thin hair is streaked on the pillow. His hand strokes the slim silk of his mustache. His thumb, pressed under his chin, seems to be trying to give squareness and projection to it. Brown eyes stare from a lemon face. Moisture gathers beneath his arm-pits. He slides down beneath the cover, seeking release.

Kabnis: Near me. Now. Whoever you are, my warm glowing sweetheart, do not think that the face that rests beside you is the real Kabnis. Ralph Kabnis is a dream. And dreams are faces with large eyes and weak chins and broad brows that get smashed by the fists of square faces. The body of the world is bull-necked. A dream is a soft face that fits uncertainly upon it. . . God, if I could develop that in words. Give what I know a bull-neck and a heaving body, all would go well with me, wouldnt it, sweetheart? If I could feel that I came to the South to face it. If I, the dream (not what

---

1. At one time, Toomer prepared this work as a drama, with the hope that it would be produced on stage. Apparently it was once considered for production in a small playhouse, but there is no evidence that it was staged. The famous American director-producer Kenneth Macgowan rejected it because, he stated, it lacked a strong plot. Selections from the version of "Kabnis" that appears in *Cane* were first published in two parts in *Broom* 5 (August and September 1923): 12–16, 83–94. In August, *Broom* published section 1 of "Kabnis" under that title (pp. 12–16). In September, it pub-

lished section 5 (pp. 83–94) under the same title.
2. Although the story is set in the twentieth century, Kabnis's cabin lacks electricity.
3. A derogatory, usually offensive epithet; here it seems to suggest the subservient position of Afro-Americans in "White-man's land."
4. This is probably an original poem created in imitation of the spirituals. "Camp Ground," a place where soldiers camp to rest during a march, here symbolizes a resting place for Blacks— probably in Heaven.

is weak and afraid in me) could become the face of the South.
How my lips would sing for it, my songs being the lips of its soul.
Soul. Soul hell. There aint no such thing. What in hell was that?

A rat had run across the thin boards of the ceiling. Kabnis
thrusts his head out from the covers. Through the cracks, a pow-
dery faded red dust sprays down on him. Dust of slavefields, dried,
scattered. . . No use to read. Christ, if he only could drink himself
to sleep. Something as sure as fate was going to happen. He
couldnt stand this thing much longer. A hen, perched on a shelf in
the adjoining room begins to tread. Her nails scrape the soft wood.
Her feathers ruffle.

"Get out of that, you egg-laying bitch."

Kabnis hurls a slipper against the wall. The hen flies from her
perch and cackles as if a skunk were after her.

"Now cut out that racket or I'll wring your neck for you."

Answering cackles arise in the chicken yard.

"Why in Christ's hell cant you leave me alone? Damn it, I wish
your cackle would choke you. Choke every mother's son of them in
this God-forsaken hole. Go away. By God I'll wring your neck for
you if you dont. Hell of a mess I've got in: even the poultry is hostile. Go way. Go way. By God, I'll . . ."

Kabnis jumps from his bed. His eyes are wild. He makes for the
door. Bursts through it. The hen, driving blindly at the window-
pane, screams. Then flies and flops around trying to elude him.
Kabnis catches her.

"Got you now, you she-bitch."

With his fingers about her neck, he thrusts open the outside door
and steps out into the serene loveliness of Georgian autumn moonlight. Some distance off, down in the valley, a band of pine-smoke,
silvered gauze, drifts steadily. The half-moon is a white child that
sleeps upon the tree-tops of the forest. White winds croon its
sleep-song:

> rock a-by baby . .[5]
> Black mother sways, holding a white child on her bosom.
> when the bough bends . .
> Her breath hums through pine-cones.
> cradle will fall . .
> Teat moon-children at your breasts,
> down will come baby . .
> Black mother.

Kabnis whirls the chicken by its neck, and throws the head away.
Picks up the hopping body, warm, sticky, and hides it in a clump
of bushes. He wipes blood from his hands onto the coarse scant
grass.

5. Toomer alternates the familiar lines of a lullaby for children with lines of poetry describing the forest
at night as a Black mother nursing a white moon-child.

Kabnis: Thats done. Old Chromo in the big house there will wonder whats become of her pet hen. Well, it'll teach her a lesson: not to make a hen-coop of my quarters. Quarters. Hell of a fine quarters, I've got. Five years ago; look at me now. Earth's child. The earth my mother. God is a profligate red-nosed man about town.[6] Bastardy; me. A bastard son has got a right to curse his maker. God. . .

Kabnis is about to shake his fists heavenward. He looks up, and the night's beauty strikes him dumb. He falls to his knees. Sharp stones cut through his thin pajamas. The shock sends a shiver over him. He quivers. Tears mist his eyes. He writhes.

"God Almighty, dear God, dear Jesus, do not torture me with beauty. Take it away. Give me an ugly world. Ha, ugly. Stinking like unwashed niggers. Dear Jesus, do not chain me to myself and set these hills and valleys, heaving with folk-songs, so close to me that I cannot reach them. There is a radiant beauty in the night that touches and . . . tortures me. Ugh. Hell. Get up, you damn fool. Look around. Whats beautiful there? Hog pens and chicken yards. Dirty red mud. Stinking outhouse. Whats beauty anyway but ugliness if it hurts you? God, he doesnt exist, but nevertheless He is ugly. Hence, what comes from Him is ugly. Lynchers and business men, and that cockroach Hanby, especially. How come that he gets to be principal of a school? Of the school I'm driven to teach in? God's handiwork, doubtless. God and Hanby, they belong together. Two godam moral-spouters. Oh, no, I wont let that emotion come up in me. Stay down. Stay down, I tell you. O Jesus, Thou art beautiful. . . Come, Ralph, pull yourself together. Curses and adoration dont come from what is sane. This loneliness, dumbness, awful, intangible oppression is enough to drive a man insane. Miles from nowhere. A speck on a Georgia hillside. Jesus, can you imagine it—an atom of dust in agony on a hillside? Thats a spectacle for you. Come, Ralph, old man, pull yourself together."

Kabnis has stiffened. He is conscious now of the night wind, and of how it chills him. He rises. He totters as a man would who for the first time uses artificial limbs. As a completely artificial man would. The large frame house, squatting on brick pillars, where the principal of the school, his wife, and the boarding girls sleep, seems a curious shadow of his mind. He tries, but cannot convince himself of its reality. His gaze drifts down into the vale, across the swamp, up over the solid dusk bank of pines, and rests, bewildered-like, on the court-house tower. It is dull silver in the moonlight. White child that sleeps upon the top of pines. Kabnis' mind clears. He sees himself yanked beneath that tower. He sees white

6. A red nose is said to be the result of excessive consumption of alcoholic beverages. A "man about town" is a playboy.

minds, with indolent assumption, juggle justice and a nigger. . .
Somewhere, far off in the straight line of his sight, is Augusta.
Christ, how cut off from everything he is. And hours, hours north,
why not say a lifetime north? Washington sleeps. Its still, peaceful
streets, how desirable they are. Its people whom he had always half-
way despised. New York? Impossible. It was a fiction. He had
dreamed it. An impotent nostalgia grips him. It becomes intolerable. He forces himself to narrow to a cabin silhouetted on a knoll
about a mile away. Peace. Negroes within it are content. They
farm. They sing. They love. They sleep. Kabnis wonders if perhaps they can feel him. If perhaps he gives them bad dreams.
Things are so immediate in Georgia.

Thinking that now he can go to sleep, he re-enters his room. He
builds a fire in the open hearth. The room dances to the tongues of
flames, and sings to the crackling and spurting of the logs. Wind
comes up between the floor boards, through the black cracks of the
walls.

Kabnis: Cant sleep. Light a cigarette. If that old bastard comes
over here and smells smoke, I'm done for. Hell of a note, cant even
smoke. The stillness of it: where they burn and hang men, you
cant smoke. Cant take a swig of licker.[7] What do they think this is,
anyway, some sort of temperance school? How did I ever land in
such a hole? Ugh. One might just as well be in his grave. Still as a
grave. Jesus, how still everything is. Does the world know how still
it is? People make noise. They are afraid of silence. Of what lives,
and God, of what dies in silence. There must be many dead things
moving in silence. They come here to touch me. I swear I feel
their fingers. . . Come, Ralph, pull yourself together. What in hell
was that? Only the rustle of leaves, I guess. You know, Ralph, old
man, it wouldnt surprise me at all to see a ghost. People dont think
there are such things. They rationalize their fear, and call their
cowardice science. Fine bunch, they are. Damit, that was a noise.
And not the wind either. A chicken maybe. Hell, chickens dont
wander around this time of night. What in hell is it?

A scraping sound, like a piece of wood dragging over the ground,
is coming near.

"Ha, ha. The ghosts down this way havent got any chains to
rattle, so they drag trees along with them. Thats a good one. But
no joke, something is outside this house, as sure as hell. Whatever
it is, it can get a good look at me and I cant see it. Jesus Christ!"

Kabnis pours water on the flames and blows his lamp out. He
picks up a poker and stealthily approaches the outside door. Swings
it open, and lurches into the night. A calf, carrying a yoke of wood,
bolts away from him and scampers down the road.

7. "Liquor."

"Well, I'm damned. This godam place is sure getting the best of me. Come, Ralph, old man, pull yourself together. Nights cant last forever. Thank God for that. Its Sunday already. First time in my life I've ever wanted Sunday to come. Hell of a day. And down here there's no such thing as ducking church. Well, I'll see Halsey and Layman, and get a good square meal. Thats something. And Halsey's a damn good feller. Cant talk to him, though. Who in Christ's world can I talk to? A hen. God. Myself. . . I'm going bats, no doubt of that. Come now, Ralph, go in and make yourself go to sleep. Come now . . in the door . . thats right. Put the poker down. There. All right. Slip under the sheets. Close your eyes. Think nothing . . a long time . . nothing, nothing. Dont even think nothing. Blank. Not even blank. Count. No, mustnt count. Nothing . . blank . . nothing . . blank . . space without stars in it. No, nothing . . nothing . .

Kabnis sleeps. The winds, like soft-voiced vagrant poets sing:

> White-man's land.
> Niggers, sing.
> Burn, bear black children
> Till poor rivers bring
> Rest, and sweet glory
> In Camp Ground.

2

The parlor of Fred Halsey's home. There is a seediness about it. It seems as though the fittings have given a frugal service to at least seven generations of middle-class shop-owners. An open grate burns cheerily in contrast to the gray cold changed autumn weather. An old-fashioned mantelpiece supports a family clock (not running), a figure or two in imitation bronze, and two small group pictures. Directly above it, in a heavy oak frame, the portrait of a bearded man. Black hair, thick and curly, intensifies the pallor of the high forehead. The eyes are daring. The nose, sharp and regular. The poise suggests a tendency to adventure checked by the necessities of absolute command. The portrait is that of an English gentleman who has retained much of his culture, in that money has enabled him to escape being drawn through a land-grubbing pioneer life. His nature and features, modified by marriage and circumstances, have been transmitted to his great-grandson, Fred. To the left of this picture, spaced on the wall, is a smaller portrait of the great-grandmother. That here there is a Negro strain, no one would doubt. But it is difficult to say in precisely what feature it lies. On close inspection, her mouth is seen to be wistfully twisted. The expression of her face seems to shift before one's gaze—now ugly, repulsive; now sad, and somehow beautiful in its pain. A tin wood-box rests on the floor below. To the right of the great-grandfather's portrait hangs a family group: the father, mother, two brothers, and one sister of Fred. It includes himself some thirty years ago when his face was an olive white, and his hair luxuriant and dark and wavy. The father is a rich brown. The mother, practically white. Of the children, the girl, quite young, is like Fred; the two brothers, darker. The walls of the room are plastered and painted green. An old upright piano is tucked into the corner near the window. The window looks out on a forlorn, box-like, whitewashed frame church. Negroes are gathering, on foot, driving questionable gray and brown mules, and in an occasional Ford, for afternoon service. Beyond, Georgia hills roll off into the distance, their dreary aspect heightened by the gray spots of unpainted one- and two-room shanties. Clumps of pine trees here and there are the dark points the whole landscape is approaching. The church bell tolls. Above its squat tower, a great spiral of buzzards reaches far into the heavens. An ironic comment upon the path that leads into the Christian land. . . Three rocking chairs are grouped around the grate. Sunday papers scattered on the floor indicate a recent usage. Halsey, a well-built, stocky fellow, hair cropped close, enters the room. His Sunday clothes smell of wood and glue, for it is his habit to potter around his wagon-shop even on the Lord's day. He is followed by Professor Layman, tall, heavy, loose-jointed Georgia Negro, by turns teacher and preacher, who has traveled in almost every nook and corner of the state and hence knows more than would be good for anyone other than a silent man. Kabnis, trying to force through a gathering heaviness, trails in behind them. They slip into chairs before the fire.

Layman: Sholy[8] fine, Mr. Halsey, sholy fine. This town's right good at feedin folks, better'n most towns in th state, even for preachers, but I ken[9] say this beats um all. Yassur. Now aint that right, Professor[1] Kabnis?

Kabnis: Yes sir, this beats them all, all right—best I've had, and thats a fact, though my comparison doesnt carry far, y'know.

Layman: Hows that, Professor?

Kabnis: Well, this is my first time out—

Layman: For a fact. Aint seed you round so much. Whats th trouble? Dont like our folks down this away?

Halsey: Aint that, Layman. He aint like most northern niggers that way. Aint a thing stuck-up about him. He likes us, you an me, maybe all—its that red[2] mud over yonder—gets stuck in it an

8. "Surely."
9. "Can."
1. Well into the twentieth century, "professor" was used as a term of respect by Southern Blacks for any male teacher on any grade level; sometimes also used to refer to preachers (see p. 90), pianists (see p. 54), or other educated or talented individuals.
2. The typical color of mud in parts of Georgia.

cant get out. (Laughs.) An then he loves th fire so, warm as its been. Coldest Yankee I've ever seen. But I'm goin t get him out now in a jiffy, eh, Kabnis?

Kabnis: Sure, I should say so, sure. Dont think its because I dont like folks down this way. Just the opposite, in fact. Theres more hospitality and everything. Its diff—that is, theres lots of northern exaggeration about the South. Its not half the terror they picture it. Things are not half bad, as one could easily figure out for himself without ever crossing the Mason and Dixie[3] line: all these people wouldnt stay down here, especially the rich, the ones that could easily leave, if conditions were so mighty bad. And then too, sometime back, my family were southerners y'know. From Georgia, in fact—

Layman: Nothin t feel proud about, Professor. Neither your folks nor mine.

Halsey (in a mock religious tone): Amen t that, brother Layman. Amen (turning to Kabnis, half playful, yet somehow dead in earnest). An Mr. Kabnis, kindly remember youre in th land of cotton—hell of a land. Th white folks get th boll; th niggers get th stalk. An dont you dare touch th boll, or even look at it. They'll swing y sho. (Laughs.)

Kabnis: But they wouldnt touch a gentleman—fellows, men like us three here—

Layman: Nigger's a nigger down this away, Professor. An only two dividins: good an bad. An even they aint permanent categories. They sometimes mixes um up when it comes t lynchin. I've seen um do it.

Halsey: Dont let th fear int y, though, Kabnis. This county's a good un. Aint been a stringin up I can remember. (Laughs.)

Layman: This is a good town an a good county. But theres some that makes up fer it.

Kabnis: Things are better now though since that stir about those peonage cases,[4] arent they?

Layman: Ever hear tell of a single shot killin moren one rabbit, Professor?

Kabnis: No, of course not, that is, but then—

Halsey: Now I know you werent born yesterday, sprung up so rapid like you aint heard of th brick thrown in th hornets' nest. (Laughs.)

Kabnis: Hardly, hardly, I know—

Halsey: Course y do. (To Layman) See, northern niggers aint as dumb as they make out t be.

3. Named for two surveyors, the imaginary Mason-Dixon line divides the North from the South. Toomer may have carelessly used "Dixie" rather than "Dixon" because "Dixie" is a name for the South.

4. In some Southern states, prisoners—especially Black prisoners—were leased to work, without pay, for white landowners.

Kabnis (overlooking the remark) : Just stirs them up to sting.

Halsey: T perfection. An put just like a professor should put it.

Kabnis: Thats what actually did happen?

Layman: Well, if it aint sos only because th stingers already movin jes as fast as they ken go. An been goin ever since I ken remember, an then some mo.[5] Though I dont usually make mention of it.

Halsey: Damn sight better not. Say, Layman, you come from where theyre always swarmin, dont y?

Layman: Yassur. I do that, sho. Dont want t mention it, but its a fact. I've seed th time when there werent no use t even stretch out flat upon th ground. Seen um shoot an cut a man t pieces who had died th night befo. Yassur. An they didnt stop when they found out he was dead—jes went on ahackin at him anyway.

Kabnis: What did you do? What did you say to them, Professor?

Layman: Thems th things you neither does a thing or talks about if y want t stay around this away, Professor.

Halsey: Listen t what he's tellin y, Kabnis. May come in handy some day.

Kabnis: Cant something be done? But of course not. This preacher-ridden race. Pray and shout. Theyre in the preacher's hands. Thats what it is. And the preacher's hands are in the white man's pockets.

Halsey: Present company always excepted.

Kabnis: The Professor knows I wasnt referring to him.

Layman: Preacher's a preacher anywheres you turn. No use exceptin.

Kabnis: Well, of course, if you look at it that way. I didnt mean— But cant something be done?

Layman: Sho. Yassur. An done first rate an well. Jes like Sam Raymon done it.

Kabnis: Hows that? What did he do?

Layman: Th white folks (reckon I oughtnt tell it) had jes knocked two others like you kill a cow—brained um with an ax, when they caught Sam Raymon by a stream. They was about t do fer him when he up an says, "White folks, I gotter die, I knows that. But wont y let me die in my own way?" Some was fer gettin after him, but th boss held um back an says, "Jes so longs th nigger dies—" An Sam fell down ont his knees an prayed, "O Lord, Ise comin to y," and he up an jumps int th stream.

Singing from the church becomes audible. Above it, rising and falling in a plaintive moan, a woman's voice swells to shouting. **Kabnis hears it. His face gives way to an expression of mingled fear, contempt, and pity. Layman takes no notice of it. Halsey**

5. "More."

grins at Kabnis. He feels like having a little sport with him.

Halsey: Lets go t church, eh, Kabnis?

Kabnis (seeking control): All right—no sir, not by a damn sight. Once a days enough for me. Christ, but that stuff gets to me. Meaning no reflection on you, Professor.

Halsey: Course not. Say, Kabnis, noticed y this morning. What'd y get up for an go out?

Kabnis: Couldnt stand the shouting, and thats a fact. We dont have that sort of thing up North. We do, but, that is, some one should see to it that they are stopped or put out when they get so bad the preacher has to stop his sermon for them.

Halsey: Is that th way youall sit on sisters up North?

Kabnis: In the church I used to go to no one ever shouted—

Halsey: Lungs weak?

Kabnis: Hardly, that is—

Halsey: Yankees are right up t th minute in tellin folk how t turn a trick. They always were good at talkin.

Kabnis: Well, anyway, they should be stopped.

Layman: Thats right. Thats true. An its th worst ones in th community that comes int th church t shout. I've sort a made a study of it. You take a man what drinks, th biggest licker-head around will come int th church an yell th loudest. An th sister whats done wrong, an is always doin wrong, will sit down in th Amen corner[6] an swing her arms an shout her head off. Seems as if they cant control themselves out in th world; they cant control themselves in church. Now dont that sound logical, Professor?

Halsey: Reckon its as good as any. But I heard that queer cuss over yonder—y know him, dont y, Kabnis? Well, y ought t. He had a run-in with your boss th other day—same as you'll have if you dont walk th chalk-line. An th quicker th better. I hate that Hanby. Ornery bastard. I'll mash his mouth in one of these days. Well, as I was sayin, that feller, Lewis's[7] name, I heard him sayin somethin about a stream whats dammed has got t cut loose somewheres. An that sounds good. I know th feelin myself. He strikes me as knowin a bucketful bout most things, that feller does. Seems like he doesnt want t talk, an does, sometimes, like Layman here. Damn queer feller, him.

Layman: Cant make heads or tails of him, an I've seen lots o queer possums in my day. Everybody's wonderin about him. White folks too. He'll have t leave here soon, thats sho. Always askin questions. An I aint seed his lips move once. Pokin round an notin somethin. Noted what I said th other day, an that werent fer notin down.

<hr/>

6. A front area of the church, generally occupied by older female members of the congregation; so-called because of their practice of shouting "amen" as approval and exhortation of the preacher.

7. Lewis resembles the self-portrait Toomer sometimes created in his fiction and drama.

Kabnis: What was that?

Layman: Oh, a lynchin that took place bout a year ago. Th worst I know of round these parts.

Halsey: Bill Burnam?

Layman: Na. Mame Lamkins.

Halsey grunts, but says nothing.

The preacher's voice rolls from the church in an insistent chanting monotone. At regular intervals it rises to a crescendo note. The sister begins to shout. Her voice, high-pitched and hysterical, is almost perfectly attuned to the nervous key of Kabnis. Halsey notices his distress, and is amused by it. Layman's face is expressionless. Kabnis wants to hear the story of Mame Lamkins. He does not want to hear it. It can be no worse than the shouting.

Kabnis (his chair rocking faster): What about Mame Lamkins?

Halsey: Tell him, Layman.

The preacher momentarily stops. The choir, together with the entire congregation, sings an old spiritual. The music seems to quiet the shouter. Her heavy breathing has the sound of evening winds that blow through pinecones. Layman's voice is uniformly low and soothing. A canebrake, murmuring the tale to its neighbor-road would be more passionate.

Layman: White folks know that niggers talk, an they dont mind jes so long as nothing comes of it, so here goes. She was in th family-way, Mame Lamkins was. They killed her in th street, an some white man seein th risin in her stomach as she lay there soppy in her blood like any cow, took an ripped her belly open, an th kid fell out. It was living; but a nigger baby aint supposed t live. So he jabbed his knife in it an stuck it t a tree. An then they all went away.[8]

Kabnis: Christ no! What had she done?

Layman: Tried t hide her husband when they was after him.

A shriek pierces the room. The bronze pieces on the mantel hum. The sister cries frantically: "Jesus, Jesus, I've found Jesus. O Lord, glory t God, one mo sinner is acomin home." At the height of this, a stone, wrapped round with paper, crashes through the window. Kabnis springs to his feet, terror-stricken. Layman is worried. Halsey picks up the stone. Takes off the wrapper, smooths it out, and reads: "You northern nigger, its time fer y t leave. Git along now." Kabnis knows that the command is meant for him. Fear squeezes him. Caves him in. As a violent external pressure would. Fear flows inside him. It fills him up. He bloats. He saves himself from bursting by dashing wildly from the room. Halsey and Layman stare stupidly at each other. The stone, the crumpled

8. This is an account of an actual lynching, described by Walter White of the National Association for the Advancement of Colored People and by others.

paper are things, huge things that weight them. Their thoughts are vaguely concerned with the texture of the stone, with the color of the paper. Then they remember the words, and begin to shift them about in sentences. Layman even construes them grammatically. Suddenly the sense of them comes back to Halsey. He grips Layman by the arm and they both follow after Kabnis.

A false dusk has come early. The countryside is ashen, chill. Cabins and roads and canebrakes whisper. The church choir, dipping into a long silence, sings:

> My Lord, what a mourning,
> My Lord, what a mourning,
> My Lord, what a mourning,
> When the stars begin to fall.

Softly luminous over the hills and valleys, the faint spray of a scattered star. . .

3

A splotchy figure drives forward along the cane- and corn-stalk hemmed-in road. A scarecrow replica of Kabnis, awkwardly animate. Fantastically plastered with red Georgia mud. It skirts the big house whose windows shine like mellow lanterns in the dusk. Its shoulder jogs against a sweet-gum tree. The figure caroms off against the cabin door, and lunges in. It slams the door as if to prevent some one entering after it.

"God Almighty, theyre here. After me. On me. All along the road I saw their eyes flaring from the cane. Hounds. Shouts. What in God's name did I run here for? A mud-hole trap. I stumbled on a rope. O God, a rope. Their clammy hands were like the love of death playing up and down my spine. Trying to trip my legs. To trip my spine. Up and down my spine. My spine. . . My legs. . . Why in hell didnt they catch me?"

Kabnis wheels around, half defiant, half numbed with a more immediate fear.

"Wanted to trap me here. Get out o there. I see you."

He grabs a broom from beside the chimney and violently pokes it under the bed. The broom strikes a tin wash-tub. The noise bewilders. He recovers.

"Not there. In the closet."

He throws the broom aside and grips the poker. Starts towards the closet door, towards somewhere in the perfect blackness behind the chimney.

"I'll brain you."

He stops short. The barks of hounds, evidently in pursuit, reach him. A voice, liquid in distance, yells, "Hi! Hi!"

"O God, theyre after me. Holy Father, Mother of Christ—hell, this aint no time for prayer—"

Voices, just outside the door:

"Reckon he's here."

"Dont see no light though."

The door is flung open.

Kabnis: Get back or I'll kill you.

He braces himself, brandishing the poker.

Halsey (coming in): Aint as bad as all that. Put that thing down.

Layman: Its only us, Professor. Nobody else after y.

Kabnis: Halsey. Layman. Close that door. Dont light that light. For godsake get away from there.

Halsey: Nobody's after y, Kabnis, I'm tellin y. Put that thing down an get yourself together.

Kabnis: I tell you they are. I saw them. I heard the hounds.

Halsey: These aint th days of hounds an Uncle Tom's Cabin,[9] feller. White folks aint in fer all them theatrics these days. Theys more direct than that. If what they wanted was t get y, theyd have just marched right in an took y where y sat. Somebodys down by th branch chasin rabbits an atreein possums.

A shot is heard.

Halsey: Got him, I reckon. Saw Tom goin out with his gun. Tom's pretty lucky most times.

He goes to the bureau and lights the lamp. The circular fringe is patterned on the ceiling. The moving shadows of the men are huge against the bare wall boards. Halsey walks up to Kabnis, takes the poker from his grip, and without more ado pushes him into a chair before the dark hearth.

Halsey: Youre a mess. Here, Layman. Get some trash an start a fire.

Layman fumbles around, finds some newspapers and old bags, puts them in the hearth, arranges the wood, and kindles the fire. Halsey sets a black iron kettle where it soon will be boiling. Then takes from his hip-pocket a bottle of corn licker which he passes to Kabnis.

Halsey: Here. This'll straighten y out a bit.

Kabnis nervously draws the cork and gulps the licker down.

Kabnis: Ha. Good stuff. Thanks. Thank y, Halsey.

Halsey: Good stuff! Youre damn right. Hanby there dont think so. Wonder he doesnt come over t find out whos burnin his oil.

9. In the South—and probably in other sections of the country—bloodhounds have been used to track escaping prisoners and slaves. Harriet Beecher Stowe wrote the novel *Uncle Tom's Cabin* (1852) to show the horrors of slavery and to persuade read-ers to abolish it. One of the most dramatic incidents in the novel, and in the many stage adaptations of it, occurs when bloodhounds pursue a fleeing slave mother and her infant child who are trying to cross the frozen Ohio River to find freedom.

Miserly bastard, him. Th boys what made this stuff—are y listenin t me, Kabnis? th boys what made this stuff have got th art down like I heard you say youd like t be with words. Eh? Have some, Layman?

Layman: Dont think I care for none, thank y jes th same, Mr. Halsey.

Halsey: Care hell. Course y care. Everybody cares around these parts. Preachers an school teachers an everybody. Here. Here, take it. Dont try that line on me.

Layman limbers up a little, but he cannot quite forget that he is on school ground.

Layman: Thats right. Thats true, sho. Shinin[1] is th only business what pays in these hard times.

He takes a nip, and passes the bottle to Kabnis. Kabnis is in the middle of a long swig when a rap sounds on the door. He almost spills the bottle, but manages to pass it to Halsey just as the door swings open and Hanby enters. He is a well-dressed, smooth, rich, black-skinned Negro who thinks there is no one quite so suave and polished as himself. To members of his own race, he affects the manners of a wealthy white planter. Or, when he is up North, he lets it be known that his ideas are those of the best New England tradition. To white men he bows, without ever completely humbling himself. Tradesmen in the town tolerate him because he spends his money with them. He delivers his words with a full consciousness of his moral superiority.

Hanby: Hum. Erer, Professor Kabnis, to come straight to the point: the progress of the Negro race is jeopardized whenever the personal habits and examples set by its guides and mentors fall below the acknowledged and hard-won standard of its average member. This institution, of which I am the humble president,[2] was founded, and has been maintained at a cost of great labor and untold sacrifice. Its purpose is to teach our youth to live better, cleaner, more noble lives. To prove to the world that the Negro race can be just like any other race. It hopes to attain this aim partly by the salutary examples set by its instructors. I cannot hinder the progress of a race simply to indulge a single member. I have thought the matter out beforehand, I can assure you. Therefore, if I find your resignation on my desk by to-morrow morning, Mr. Kabnis, I shall not feel obliged to call in the sheriff. Otherwise. . ."

Kabnis: A fellow can take a drink in his own room if he wants to, in the privacy of his own room.

Hanby: His room, but not the institution's room, Mr. Kabnis.

1. "Moonshining": the practice of making and selling liquor illegally (without paying tax to the government).
2. Principal.

Kabnis: This is my room while I'm in it.

Hanby: Mr. Clayborn (the sheriff) can inform you as to that.

Kabnis: Oh, well, what do I care—glad to get out of this mud-hole.

Hanby: I should think so from your looks.

Kabnis: You neednt get sarcastic about it.

Hanby: No, that is true. And I neednt wait for your resignation either, Mr. Kabnis.

Kabnis: Oh, you'll get that all right. Dont worry.

Hanby: And I should like to have the room thoroughly aired and cleaned and ready for your successor by to-morrow noon, Professor.

Kabnis (trying to rise): You can have your godam room right away. I dont want it.

Hanby: But I wont have your cursing.

Halsey pushes Kabnis back into his chair.

Halsey: Sit down, Kabnis, till I wash y.

Hanby (to Halsey): I would rather not have drinking men on the premises, Mr. Halsey. You will oblige me—

Halsey: I'll oblige you by stayin right on this spot, this spot, get me? till I get damned ready t leave.

He approaches Hanby. Hanby retreats, but manages to hold his dignity.

Halsey: Let me get you told right now, Mr. Samuel Hanby. Now listen t me. I aint no slick an span[3] slave youve hired, an dont y think it for a minute. Youve bullied enough about this town. An besides, wheres that bill youve been owin me? Listen t me. If I dont get it paid in by tmorrer noon, Mr. Hanby (he mockingly assumes Hanby's tone and manner), I shall feel obliged t call th sheriff. An that sheriff'll be myself who'll catch y in th road an pull y out your buggy an rightly attend t y. You heard me. Now leave him alone. I'm takin him home with me. I got it fixed. Before you came in. He's goin t work with me. Shapin shafts and buildin wagons'll make a man of him what nobody, y get me? what nobody can take advantage of. Thats all. . .

Halsey burrs off into vague and incoherent comment.

Pause. Disagreeable.

Layman's eyes are glazed on the spurting fire.

Kabnis wants to rise and put both Halsey and Hanby in their places. He vaguely knows that he must do this, else the power of direction will completely slip from him to those outside. The conviction is just strong enough to torture him. To bring a feverish, quick-passing flare into his eyes. To mutter words soggy in hot saliva. To jerk his arms upward in futile protest. Halsey, noticing his gestures, thinks it is water that he desires. He brings a glass to

---

3. Possibly "spic and span," i.e., spotlessly clean.

him. Kabnis slings it to the floor. Heat of the conviction dies. His arms crumple. His upper lip, his mustache, quiver. Rap! rap, on the door. The sounds slap Kabnis. They bring a hectic color to his cheeks. Like huge cold finger tips they touch his skin and gooseflesh it. Hanby strikes a commanding pose. He moves toward Layman. Layman's face is innocently immobile.

Halsey: Whos there?

Voice: Lewis.

Halsey: Come in, Lewis. Come on in.

Lewis enters. He is the queer fellow who has been referred to. A tall wiry copper-colored man, thirty perhaps. His mouth and eyes suggest purpose guided by an adequate intelligence. He is what a stronger Kabnis might have been, and in an odd faint way resembles him. As he steps towards the others, he seems to be issuing sharply from a vivid dream. Lewis shakes hands with Halsey.[4] Nods perfunctorily to Hanby, who has stiffened to meet him. Smiles rapidly at Layman, and settles with real interest on Kabnis.

Lewis: Kabnis passed me on the road. Had a piece of business of my own, and couldnt get here any sooner. Thought I might be able to help in some way or other.

Halsey: A good baths bout all he needs now. An somethin t put his mind t rest.

Lewis: I think I can give him that. That note was meant for me. Some Negroes have grown uncomfortable at my being here—

Kabnis: You mean, Mr. Lewis, some colored folks threw it? Christ Almighty!

Halsey: Thats what he means. An just as I told y. White folks more direct than that.

Kabnis: What are they after you for?

Lewis: Its a long story, Kabnis. Too long for now. And it might involve present company. (He laughs pleasantly and gestures vaguely in the direction of Hanby.) Tell you about it later on perhaps.

Kabnis: Youre not going?

Lewis: Not till my month's up.

Halsey: Hows that?

Lewis: I'm on a sort of contract with myself. (Is about to leave.) Well, glad its nothing serious—

Halsey: Come round t th shop sometime why dont y, Lewis? I've asked y enough. I'd like t have a talk with y. I aint as dumb as I look. Kabnis an me'll be in most any time. Not much work these days. Wish t hell there was. This burg[5] gets to me when there aint. (In answer to Lewis' question.) He's goin t work with

4. Here and later Toomer uses Lewis as a touchstone—that is, the reader is expected to accept Lewis's response to each character as the correct assessment of that individual's merit.

5. Town.

me. Ya. Night air this side th branch aint good fer him. (Looks at Hanby. Laughs.)

Lewis: I see. . .

His eyes turn to Kabnis. In the instant of their shifting, a vision of the life they are to meet. Kabnis, a promise of a soil-soaked beauty; uprooted, thinning out. Suspended a few feet above the soil whose touch would resurrect him.[6] Arm's length removed from him[7] whose will to help. . . There is a swift intuitive interchange of consciousness. Kabnis has a sudden need to rush into the arms of this man. His eyes call, "Brother." And then a savage, cynical twist-about within him mocks his impulse and strengthens him to repulse Lewis. His lips curl cruelly. His eyes laugh. They are glittering needles, stitching. With a throbbing ache they draw Lewis to. Lewis brusquely wheels on Hanby.

Lewis: I'd like to see you, sir, a moment, if you dont mind.

Hanby's tight collar and vest effectively preserve him.

Hanby: Yes, erer, Mr. Lewis. Right away.

Lewis: See you later, Halsey.

Halsey: So long—thanks—sho hope so, Lewis.

As he opens the door and Hanby passes out, a woman, miles down the valley, begins to sing. Her song is a spark that travels swiftly to the near-by cabins. Like purple tallow flames, songs jet up. They spread a ruddy haze over the heavens. The haze swings low. Now the whole countryside is a soft chorus. Lord. O Lord. . . Lewis closes the door behind him. A flame jets out. . .

The kettle is boiling. Halsey notices it. He pulls the wash-tub from beneath the bed. He arranges for the bath before the fire.

Halsey: Told y them theatrics didnt fit a white man. Th niggers, just like I told y. An after him. Aint surprisin though. He aint bowed t none of them. Nassur. T nairy a one of them nairy an inch nairy a time. An only mixed when he was good an ready—

Kabnis: That song, Halsey, do you hear it?

Halsey: Thats a man. Hear me, Kabnis? A man—

Kabnis: Jesus, do you hear it.

Halsey: Hear it? Hear what? Course I hear it. Listen t what I'm tellin y. A man, get me? They'll get him yet if he dont watch out.

Kabnis is jolted into his fear.

Kabnis: Get him? What do you mean? How? Not lynch him?

Halsey: Na. Take a shotgun an shoot his eyes clear out. Well, anyway, it wasnt fer you, just like I told y. You'll stay over at th house an work with me, eh, boy? Good t get away from his nobs,

---

6. Toomer alludes to the classical myth of a giant who regained full strength every time he came in contact with the earth. To defeat him, Hercules must lift him from the ground. Here, of course, Toomer suggests that, although Kabnis has come to the South, he cannot gain strength by rooting himself in the culture of that region.

7. Lewis.

eh? Damn big stiff though, him. An youre not th first an I can tell y. (Laughs.)

He bustles and fusses about Kabnis as if he were a child. Kabnis submits, wearily. He has no will to resist him.

Layman (his voice is like a deep hollow echo): Thats right. Thats true, sho. Everybody's been expectin that th bust up was comin. Surprised um all y held on as long as y did. Teachin in th South aint th thing fer y. Nassur. You ought t be way back up North where sometimes I wish I was. But I've hung on down this away so long—

Halsey: An there'll never be no leavin time fer y.

4

A month has passed.

Halsey's work-shop. It is an old building just off the main street of Sempter.[8] The walls to within a few feet of the ground are of an age-worn cement mixture. On the outside they are considerably crumbled and peppered with what looks like musket-shot. Inside, the plaster has fallen away in great chunks, leaving the laths, grayed and cobwebbed, exposed. A sort of loft above the shop proper serves as a break-water for the rain and sunshine which otherwise would have free entry to the main floor. The shop is filled with old wheels and parts of wheels, broken shafts, and wooden litter. A double door, midway the street wall. To the left of this, a work-bench that holds a vise and a variety of wood-work tools. A window with as many panes broken as whole, throws light on the bench. Opposite, in the rear wall, a second window looks out upon the back yard. In the left wall, a rickety smoke-blackened chimney, and hearth with fire blazing. Smooth-worn chairs grouped about the hearth suggest the village meeting-place. Several large wooden blocks, chipped and cut and sawed on their upper surfaces are in the middle of the floor. They are the supports used in almost any sort of wagon-work. Their idleness means that Halsey has no worth-while job on foot. To the right of the central door is a junk heap, and directly behind this, stairs that lead down into the cellar. The cellar is known as "The Hole." Besides being the home of a very old man, it is used by Halsey on those occasions when he spices up the life of the small town.

Halsey, wonderfully himself in his work overalls, stands in the doorway and gazes up the street, expectantly. Then his eyes grow listless. He slouches against the smooth-rubbed frame. He lights a cigarette. Shifts his position. Braces an arm against the door. Kabnis passes the window and stoops to get in under Halsey's arm. He is awkward and ludicrous, like a schoolboy in his big brother's

8. The name Toomer gives to the town. Sparta was the actual town he visited.

new overalls. He skirts the large blocks on the floor, and drops into
a chair before the fire. Halsey saunters towards him.

Kabnis: Time f lunch.

Halsey: Ya.

He stands by the hearth, rocking backward and forward. He
stretches his hands out to the fire. He washes them in the warm
glow of the flames. They never get cold, but he warms them.

Kabnis: Saw Lewis up th street. Said he'd be down.

Halsey's eyes brighten. He looks at Kabnis. Turns away. Says
nothing. Kabnis fidgets. Twists his thin blue cloth-covered[9] limbs.
Pulls closer to the fire till the heat stings his shins. Pushes back.
Pokes the burned logs. Puts on several fresh ones. Fidgets. The
town bell strikes twelve.

Kabnis: Fix it up f tnight?

Halsey: Leave it t me.

Kabnis: Get Lewis in?

Halsey: Tryin t.

The air is heavy with the smell of pine and resin. Green logs
spurt and sizzle. Sap trickles from an old pine-knot into the flames.
Layman enters. He carries a lunch-pail. Kabnis, for the moment,
thinks that he is a day laborer.

Layman: Evenin, gen'lemun.

Both: Whats say, Layman.

Layman squares a chair to the fire and droops into it. Several
town fellows, silent unfathomable men for the most part, saunter
in. Overalls. Thick tan shoes. Felt hats marvelously shaped and
twisted. One asks Halsey for a cigarette. He gets it. The blacksmith, a tremendous black man, comes in from the forge. Not even
a nod from him. He picks up an axle and goes out. Lewis enters.
The town men look curiously at him. Suspicion and an open liking
contest for possession of their faces. They are uncomfortable. One
by one they drift into the street.

Layman: Heard y was leavin, Mr. Lewis.

Kabnis: Months up, eh? Hell of a month I've got.

Halsey: Sorry y goin, Lewis. Just gettin acquainted like.

Lewis: Sorry myself, Halsey, in a way—

Layman: Gettin t like our town, Mr. Lewis?

Lewis: I'm afraid its on a different basis, Professor.

Halsey: An I've yet t hear about that basis. Been waitin long
enough, God knows. Seems t me like youd take pity on a feller if
nothin more.

Kabnis: Somethin that old black cockroach over yonder doesnt
like, whatever it is.

Layman: Thats right. Thats right, sho.

Halsey: A feller dropped in here tother day an said he knew

9. Overalls.

what you was about. Said you had queer opinions. Well, I could
have told him you was a queer one, myself. But not th way he was
driftin. Didnt mean anything by it, but just let drop he thought
you was a little wrong up here—crazy, y'know. (Laughs.)

Kabnis: Y mean old Blodson? Hell, he's bats himself.

Lewis: I remember him. We had a talk. But what he found
queer, I think, was not my opinions, but my lack of them. In half
an hour he had settled everything: boll weevils, God, the World
War. Weevils and wars are the pests that God sends against the
sinful. People are too weak to correct themselves: the Redeemer is
coming back. Get ready, ye sinners, for the advent of Our Lord.
Interesting, eh, Kabnis? but not exactly what we want.

Halsey: Y could have come t me. I've sho been after y enough.
Most every time I've seen y.

Kabnis (sarcastically): Hows it y never came t us professors?

Lewis: I did—to one.

Kabnis: Y mean t say y got somethin from that celluloid-collar-
eraser-cleaned old codger over in th mud hole?

Halsey: Rough on th old boy, aint he? (Laughs.)

Lewis: Something, yes. Layman here could have given me quite
a deal, but the incentive to his keeping quiet is so much greater
than anything I could have offered him to open up, that I crossed
him off my mind. And you—

Kabnis: What about me?

Halsey: Tell him, Lewis, for godsake tell him. I've told him.
But its somethin else he wants so bad I've heard him downstairs
mumblin with th old man.

Lewis: The old man?

Kabnis: What about me? Come on now, you know so much.

Halsey: Tell him, Lewis. Tell it t him.

Lewis: Life has already told him more than he is capable of
knowing. It has given him in excess of what he can receive. I have
been offered. Stuff in his stomach curdled, and he vomited me.

Kabnis' face twitches. His body writhes.

Kabnis: You know a lot, you do. How about Halsey?

Lewis: Yes. . . Halsey? Fits here. Belongs here. An artist in
your way, arent you, Halsey?

Halsey: Reckon I am, Lewis. Give me th work and fair pay an I
aint askin nothin better. Went over-seas an saw France; an I come
back. Been up North; an I come back. Went t school; but there
aint no books whats got th feel t them of them there tools. Nassur.
An I'm atellin y.

A shriveled, bony white man passes the window and enters the
shop. He carries a broken hatchet-handle and the severed head. He
speaks with a flat, drawn voice to Halsey, who comes forward to
meet him.

Mr. Ramsay: Can y fix this fer me, Halsey?

Halsey (looking it over): Reckon so, Mr. Ramsay. Here, Kabnis. A little practice fer y.

Halsey directs Kabnis, showing him how to place the handle in the vise, and cut it down. The knife hangs. Kabnis thinks that it must be dull. He jerks it hard. The tool goes deep and shaves too much off. Mr. Ramsay smiles brokenly at him.

Mr. Ramsay (to Halsey): Still breakin in the new hand, eh, Halsey? Seems like a likely enough faller once he gets th hang of it.

He gives a tight laugh at his own good humor. Kabnis burns red. The back of his neck stings him beneath his collar. He feels stifled. Through Ramsay, the whole white South weighs down upon him. The pressure is terrific. He sweats under the arms. Chill beads run down his body. His brows concentrate upon the handle as though his own life was staked upon the perfect shaving of it. He begins to out and out botch the job. Halsey smiles.

Halsey: He'll make a good un some of these days, Mr. Ramsay.

Mr. Ramsay: Y ought t know. Yer daddy was a good un before y. Runs in th family, seems like t me.

Halsey: Thats right, Mr. Ramsay.

Kabnis is hopeless. Halsey takes the handle from him. With a few deft strokes he shaves it. Fits it. Gives it to Ramsay.

Mr. Ramsay: How much on this?

Halsey: No charge, Mr. Ramsay.

Mr. Ramsay (going out): All right, Halsey. Come down an take it out in trade. Shoe-strings or something.

Halsey: Yassur, Mr. Ramsay.

Halsey rejoins Lewis and Layman. Kabnis, hangdog-fashion, follows him.

Halsey: They like y if y work fer them.

Layman: Thats right, Mr. Halsey. Thats right, sho.

The group is about to resume its talk when Hanby enters. He is all energy, bustle, and business. He goes direct to Kabnis.

Hanby: An axle is out in the buggy which I would like to have shaped into a crow-bar. You will see that it is fixed for me.

Without waiting for an answer, and knowing that Kabnis will follow, he passes out. Kabnis, scowling, silent, trudges after him.

Hanby (from the outside): Have that ready for me by three o'clock, young man. I shall call for it.

Kabnis (under his breath as he comes in): Th hell you say, you old black swamp-gut.

He slings the axle on the floor.

Halsey: Wheeee!

Layman, lunch finished long ago, rises, heavily. He shakes hands with Lewis.

Layman: Might not see y again befo y leave, Mr. Lewis. I enjoys t hear y talk. Y might have been a preacher. Maybe a bishop some day. Sho do hope t see y back this away again sometime, Mr. Lewis.

Lewis: Thanks, Professor. Hope I'll see you.

Layman waves a long arm loosely to the others, and leaves. Kabnis goes to the door. His eyes, sullen, gaze up the street.

Kabnis: Carrie K.'s comin with th lunch. Bout time.

She passes the window. Her red girl's-cap, catching the sun, flashes vividly. With a stiff, awkward little movement she crosses the doorsill and gives Kabnis one of the two baskets which she is carrying. There is a slight stoop to her shoulders. The curves of her body blend with this to a soft rounded charm. Her gestures are stiffly variant. Black bangs curl over the forehead of her oval-olive face. Her expression is dazed, but on provocation it can melt into a wistful smile. Adolescent. She is easily the sister of Fred Halsey.

Carrie K.: Mother says excuse her, brother Fred an Ralph, fer bein late.

Kabnis: Everythings all right an O.K., Carrie Kate. O.K. an all right.

The two men settle on their lunch. Carrie, with hardly a glance in the direction of the hearth, as is her habit, is about to take the second basket down to the old man, when Lewis rises. In doing so he draws her unwitting attention. Their meeting is a swift sun-burst. Lewis impulsively moves towards her. His mind flashes images of her life in the southern town. He sees the nascent woman, her flesh already stiffening to cartilage, drying to bone. Her spirit-bloom, even now touched sullen, bitter. Her rich beauty fading. . . He wants to— He stretches forth his hands to hers. He takes them. They feel like warm cheeks against his palms. The sun-burst from her eyes floods up and haloes him. Christ-eyes, his eyes look to her. Fearlessly she loves into them. And then something happens. Her face blanches. Awkwardly she draws away. The sin-bogies of respectable southern colored folks clamor at her: "Look out! Be a *good* girl. A *good* girl. Look out!" She gropes for her basket that has fallen to the floor. Finds it, and marches with a rigid gravity to her task of feeding the old man. Like the glowing white ash of burned paper, Lewis' eyelids, wavering, settle down. He stirs in the direction of the rear window. From the back yard, mules tethered to odd trees and posts blink dumbly at him. They too seem burdened with an impotent pain. Kabnis and Halsey are still busy with their lunch. They havent noticed him. After a while he turns to them.

Lewis: Your sister, Halsey, whats to become of her? What are you going to do for her?

Halsey: Who? What? What am I goin t do? . .

Lewis: What I mean is, what does she do down there?

Halsey: Oh. Feeds th old man. Had lunch, Lewis?

Lewis: Thanks, yes. You have never felt her, have you, Halsey? Well, no, I guess not. I dont suppose you can. Nor can she. . . Old man? Halsey, some one lives down there? I've never heard of him. Tell me—

Kabnis takes time from his meal to answer with some emphasis:

Kabnis: Theres lots of things you aint heard of.

Lewis: Dare say. I'd like to see him.

Kabnis: You'll get all th chance you want tnight.

Halsey: Fixin a little somethin up fer tnight, Lewis. Th three of us an some girls. Come round bout ten-thirty.

Lewis: Glad to. But what under the sun does he do down there?

Halsey: Ask Kabnis. He blows off t him every chance he gets.

. Kabnis gives a grunting laugh. His mouth twists. Carrie returns from the cellar. Avoiding Lewis, she speaks to her brother.

Carrie K.: Brother Fred, father hasnt eaten now goin on th second week, but mumbles an talks funny, or tries t talk when I put his hands ont th food. He frightens me, an I dunno what t do. An oh, I came near fergettin, brother, but Mr. Marmon—he was eatin lunch when I saw him—told me t tell y that th lumber wagon busted down an he wanted y t fix it fer him. Said he reckoned he could get it t y after he ate.

Halsey chucks a half-eaten sandwich in the fire. Gets up. Arranges his blocks. Goes to the door and looks anxiously up the street. The wind whirls a small spiral in the gray dust road.

Halsey: Why didnt y tell me sooner, little sister?

Carrie K.: I fergot t, an just remembered it now, brother.

Her soft rolled words are fresh pain to Lewis. He wants to take her North with him What for?[1] He wonders what Kabnis could do for her. What she could do for him. Mother him. Carrie gathers the lunch things, silently, and in her pinched manner, curtsies, and departs. Kabnis lights his after-lunch cigarette. Lewis, who has sensed a change, becomes aware that he is not included in it. He starts to ask again about the old man. Decides not to. Rises to go.

Lewis: Think I'll run along, Halsey.

Halsey: Sure. Glad t see y any time.

Kabnis: Dont forget tnight.

Lewis: Dont worry. I wont. So long.

Kabnis: So long. We'll be expectin y.

Lewis passes Halsey at the door. Halsey's cheeks form a vacant smile. His eyes are wide awake, watching for the wagon to turn from Broad Street into his road.

Halsey: So long.

His words reach Lewis halfway to the corner.

1. Compare Lewis's attitude toward Carrie K. with the narrator's attitude toward Fern.

5

Night, soft belly of a pregnant Negress, throbs evenly against the torso of the South. Night throbs a womb-song to the South. Cane- and cotton-fields, pine forests, cypress swamps, sawmills, and facto- ries are fecund at her touch. Night's womb-song sets them singing. Night winds are the breathing of the unborn child whose calm throbbing in the belly of a Negress sets them somnolently singing. Hear their song.

> White-man's land.
> Niggers, sing.
> Burn, bear black children
> Till poor rivers bring
> Rest, and sweet glory
> In Camp Ground.

Sempter's streets are vacant and still. White paint on the wealth- ier houses has the chill blue glitter of distant stars. Negro cabins are a purple blur. Broad Street is deserted. Winds stir beneath the corrugated iron canopies and dangle odd bits of rope tied to horse- and mule-gnawed hitching-posts. One store window has a light in it. Chesterfield cigarette and Chero-Cola cardboard advertisements are stacked in it. From a side door two men come out. Pause, for a last word and then say good night. Soon they melt in shadows thicker than they. Way off down the street four figures sway beneath iron awnings which form a sort of corridor that imperfectly echoes and jumbles what they say. A fifth form joins them. They turn into the road that leads to Halsey's workshop. The old build- ing is phosphorescent above deep shade. The figures pass through the double door. Night winds whisper in the eaves. Sing weirdly in the ceiling cracks. Stir curls of shavings on the floor. Halsey lights a candle. A good-sized lumber wagon, wheels off, rests upon the blocks. Kabnis makes a face at it. An unearthly hush is upon the place. No one seems to want to talk. To move, lest the scraping of their feet . .

Halsey: Come on down this way, folks.

He leads the way. Stella follows. And close after her, Cora, Lewis, and Kabnis. They descend into the Hole. It seems huge, limitless in the candle light. The walls are of stone, wonderfully fitted. They have no openings save a small iron-barred window toward the top of each. They are dry and warm. The ground slopes away to the rear of the building and thus leaves the south wall exposed to the sun. The blacksmith's shop is plumb against the right wall. The floor is clay. Shavings have at odd times been matted into it. In the right-hand corner, under the stairs, two good-sized pine mattresses, resting on cardboard, are on either side of a wooden table. On this are several half-burned candles and an oil lamp. Behind the table, an irregular piece of mirror hangs on the wall. A loose something that looks to be a gaudy ball costume dangles from a near-by hook. To the front, a second table holds a lamp and several whiskey glasses. Six rickety chairs are near this table. Two old wagon wheels rest on the floor. To the left, sitting in a high-backed chair which stands upon a low platform, the old man. He is like a bust in black walnut. Gray-bearded. Gray-haired. Prophetic. Immobile. Lewis' eyes are sunk in him. The others, unconcerned, are about to pass on to the front table when Lewis grips Halsey and so turns him that the candle flame shines obliquely on the old man's features.

Lewis: And he rules over—
Kabnis: Th smoke an fire of th forge.
Lewis: Black Vulcan?[2] I wouldnt say so. That forehead. Great woolly beard. Those eyes. A mute John the Baptist of a new religion—or a tongue-tied shadow of an old.
Kabnis: His tongue is tied all right, an I can vouch f that.
Lewis: Has he never talked to you?
Halsey: Kabnis wont give him a chance.
He laughs. The girls laugh. Kabnis winces.
Lewis: What do you call him?
Halsey: Father.[3]
Lewis: Good. Father what?
Kabnis: Father of hell.
Halsey: Father's th only name we have fer him. Come on. Lets sit down an get t th pleasure of the evenin.
Lewis: Father John[4] it is from now on. . .
Slave boy whom some Christian mistress taught to read the Bible. Black man who saw Jesus in the ricefields, and began preaching to his people. Moses- and Christ-words used for songs. Dead blind father of a muted folk who feel their way upward to a life that crushes or absorbs them. (Speak, Father!) Suppose your eyes could see, old man. (The years hold hands. O Sing!) Suppose your lips. . .
Halsey, does he never talk?
Halsey: Na. But sometimes. Only seldom. Mumbles. Sis says he talks—
Kabnis: I've heard him talk.
Halsey: First I've ever heard of it. You dont give him a chance. Sis says she's made out several words, mostly one—an like as not cause it was "sin."

2. In Roman mythology, the blacksmith god; also the god of the hearth.
3. Not the biological father of Halsey and Carrie K.; see the portrait of their father, p. 88.
4. Probably an allusion to John the Baptist, with particular reference to John's ability to foretell the coming of the Savior.

Cora laughs in a loose sort of way. She is a tall, thin, mulatto woman. Her eyes are deep-set behind a pointed nose. Her hair is coarse and bushy. Seeing that Stella also is restless, she takes her arm and the two women move towards the table. They slip into chairs. Halsey follows and lights the lamp. He lays out a pack of cards. Stella sorts them as if telling fortunes. She is a beautifully proportioned, large-eyed, brown-skin girl. Except for the twisted line of her mouth when she smiles or laughs, there is about her no suggestion of the life she's been through. Kabnis, with great mock-solemnity, goes to the corner, takes down the robe, and dons it. He is a curious spectacle, acting a part, yet very real. He joins the others at the table. They are used to him. Lewis is surprised. He laughs. Kabnis shrinks and then glares at him with a furtive hatred. Halsey, bringing out a bottle of corn licker, pours drinks.

Halsey: Come on, Lewis. Come on, you fellers. Heres lookin at y.

Then, as if suddenly recalling something, he jerks away from the table and starts towards the steps.

Kabnis: Where y goin, Halsey?

Halsey: Where? Where y think? That oak beam in th wagon—

Kabnis: Come ere. Come ere. Sit down. What in hell's wrong with you fellers? You with your wagon. Lewis with his Father John. This aint th time fer foolin with wagons. Daytime's bad enough f that. Ere, sit down. Ere, Lewis, you too sit down. Have a drink. Thats right. Drink corn licker, love th girls, an listen t th old man mumblin sin.

There seems to be no good-time spirit to the party. Something in the air is too tense and deep for that. Lewis, seated now so that his eyes rest upon the old man, merges with his source and lets the pain and beauty of the South meet him there. White faces, pain-pollen, settle downward through a cane-sweet mist and touch the ovaries of yellow flowers. Cotton-bolls bloom, droop. Black roots twist in a parched red soil beneath a blazing sky. Magnolias, fragrant, a trifle futile, lovely, far off. . . His eyelids close. A force begins to heave and rise. . . Stella is serious, reminiscent.

Stella: Usall is brought up t hate sin worse than death—

Kabnis: An then before you have y eyes half open, youre made t love it if y want t live.

Stella: Us never—

Kabnis: Oh, I know your story: that old prim bastard over yonder,[5] an then old Calvert's office—

Stella: It wasnt them—

Kabnis: I know. They put y out of church, an then I guess th preacher came around an asked f some. But thats your body. Now me—

5. Probably Hanby.

Halsey (passing him the bottle): All right, kid, we believe y. Here, take another. Wheres Clover, Stel?

Stella: You know how Jim is when he's just out th swamp. Done up in shine[6] an wouldnt let her come. Said he'd bust her head open if she went out.

Kabnis: Dont see why he doesnt stay over with Laura, where he belongs.

Stella: Ask him, an I reckon he'll tell y. More than you want.

Halsey: Th nigger hates th sight of a black woman worse than death. Sorry t mix y up this way, Lewis. But y see how tis.

Lewis' skin is tight and glowing over the fine bones of his face. His lips tremble. His nostrils quiver. The others notice this and smile knowingly at each other. Drinks and smokes are passed around. They pay no neverminds to him. A real party is being worked up. Then Lewis opens his eyes and looks at them. Their smiles disperse in hot-cold tremors. Kabnis chokes his laugh. It sputters, gurgles. His eyes flicker and turn away. He tries to pass the thing off by taking a long drink which he makes considerable fuss over. He is drawn back to Lewis. Seeing Lewis' gaze still upon him, he scowls.

Kabnis: Whatsha lookin at me for? Y want t know who I am? Well, I'm Ralph Kabnis—lot of good its goin t do y. Well? Whatsha keep lookin for? I'm Ralph Kabnis. Aint that enough f y? Want th whole family history? Its none of your godam business, anyway. Keep off me. Do y hear? Keep off me. Look at Cora. Aint she pretty enough t look at? Look at Halsey, or Stella. Clover ought t be here an you could look at her. An love her. Thats what you need. I know—

Lewis: Ralph Kabnis gets satisfied that way?

Kabnis: Satisfied? Say, quit your kiddin. Here, look at that old man there. See him? He's satisfied. Do I look like him? When I'm dead I dont expect t be satisfied. Is that enough f y, with your godam nosin, or do you want more? Well, y wont get it, understand?

Lewis: The old man as symbol, flesh, and spirit of the past, what do you think he would say if he could see you? You look at him, Kabnis.

Kabnis: Just like any done-up preacher is what he looks t me. Jam some false teeth in his mouth and crank him, an youd have God Almighty spit in torrents all around th floor. Oh, hell, an he reminds me of that black cockroach over yonder. An besides, he aint my past. My ancestors were Southern blue-bloods—

Lewis: And black.

Kabnis: Aint much difference between blue an black.

Lewis: Enough to draw a denial from you. Cant hold them, can

6. Intoxicated, drunk.

you? Master; slave. Soil; and the overarching heavens. Dusk; dawn. They fight and bastardize you. The sun tint of your cheeks, flame of the great season's multi-colored leaves, tarnished, burned. Split, shredded: easily burned. No use . . .

His gaze shifts to Stella. Stella's face draws back, her breasts come towards him.

Stella: I aint got nothin f y, mister. Taint no use t look at me.

Halsey: Youre a queer feller, Lewis, I swear y are. Told y so, didnt I, girls? Just take him easy though, an he'll be ridin just th same as any Georgia mule, eh, Lewis? (Laughs.)

Stella: I'm goin t tell y somethin, mister. It aint t you, t th Mister Lewis what noses about. Its t somethin different, I dunno what. That old man there—maybe its him—is like m father used t look. He used t sing. An when he could sing no mo, they'd allus come f him an carry him t church an there he'd sit, befo th pulpit, aswayin an aleadin every song. A white man took m mother an it broke th old man's heart. He died; an then I didnt care what become of me, an I dont now. I dont care now. Dont get it in y head I'm some sentimental Susie askin for yo sop.[7] Nassur. But theres somethin t yo th others aint got. Boars an kids an fools— thats all I've known. Boars when their fever's up. When their fever's up they come t me. Halsey asks me over when he's off th job. Kabnis—it ud be a sin t play with him. He takes it out in talk.

Halsey knows that he has trifled with her. At odd things he has been inwardly penitent before her tasking him. But now he wants to hurt her. He turns to Lewis.

Halsey: Lewis, I got a little licker in me, an thats true. True's what I said. True. But th stuff just seems t wake me up an make my mind a man of me. Listen. You know a lot, queer as hell as y are, an I want t ask y some questions. Theyre too high fer them, Stella an Cora an Kabnis, so we'll just excuse em. A chat between ourselves. (Turns to the others.) You-all cant listen in on this. Twont interest y. So just leave th table t this gen'lemun an myself. Go long now.

Kabnis gets up, pompous in his robe, grotesquely so, and makes as if to go through a grand march with Stella. She shoves him off, roughly, and in a mood swings her body to the steps. Kabnis grabs Cora and parades around, passing the old man, to whom he bows in mock-curtsy. He sweeps by the table, snatches the licker bottle, and then he and Cora sprawl on the mattresses. She meets his weak approaches after the manner she thinks Stella would use.

Halsey contemptuously watches them until he is sure that they are settled.

Halsey: This aint th sort o thing f me, Lewis, when I got work

7. Food produced by sopping bread in gravy; here, the meaning seems to be "charity" or "pity."

upstairs. Nassur. You an me has got things t do. Wastin time on common low-down women—say, Lewis, look at her now—Stella—aint she a picture? Common wench—na she aint, Lewis. You know she aint. I'm only tryin t fool y. I used t love that girl. Yassur. An sometimes when th moon is thick an I hear dogs up th valley barkin an some old woman fetches out her song, an th winds seem like th Lord made them fer t fetch an carry th smell o pine an cane, an there aint no big job on foot, I sometimes get t thinkin that I still do. But I want t talk t y, Lewis, queer as y are. Y know, Lewis, I went t school once. Ya. In Augusta. But it wasnt a regular school. Na. It was a pussy Sunday-school masqueradin under a regular name. Some goody-goody teachers from th North had come down t teach th niggers. If you was nearly white, they liked y. If you was black, they didnt. But it wasnt that—I was all right, y see. I couldnt stand em messin an pawin over m business like I was a child. So I cussed em out an left. Kabnis there ought t have cussed out th old duck over yonder an left. He'd a been a better man tday. But as I was sayin, I couldnt stand their ways. So I left an came here an worked with my father. An been here ever since. He died. I set in f myself. An its always been; give me a good job an sure pay an I aint far from being satisfied, so far as satisfaction goes. Prejudice is everywheres about this country. An a nigger aint in much standin anywheres. But when it comes t pottin round an doin nothin, with nothin bigger'n an ax-handle t hold a feller down, like it was a while back befo I got this job—that beam ought t be—but tmorrow mornin early's time enough f that. As I was sayin, I gets t thinkin. Play dumb naturally t white folks. I gets t thinkin. I used to subscribe t th *Literary Digest*[8] an that helped along a bit. But there werent nothing I could sink m teeth int. Theres lots I want t ask y, Lewis. Been askin y t come around. Couldnt get y. Cant get in much tnight. (He glances at the others. His mind fastens on Kabnis.) Say, tell me this, whats on your mind t say on that feller there? Kabnis' name. One queer bird ought t know another, seems like t me.

Licker has released conflicts in Kabnis and set them flowing. He pricks his ears, intuitively feels that the talk is about him, leaves Cora, and approaches the table. His eyes are watery, heavy with passion. He stoops. He is a ridiculous pathetic figure in his showy robe.

Kabnis: Talkin bout me. I know. I'm th topic of conversation everywhere theres talk about this town. Girls an fellers. White folks as well. An if its me youre talkin bout, guess I got a right t listen in. Whats sayin? Whats sayin bout his royal guts, the Duke? Whats sayin, eh?

8. A literary magazine published from 1890 to 1938.

Halsey (to Lewis): We'll take it up another time.

Kabnis: No nother time bout it. Now. I'm here now an talkin's just begun. I was born an bred in a family of orators, thats what I was.

Halsey: Preachers.

Kabnis: Na. Preachers hell. I didnt say wind-busters. Y misapprehended me. Y understand what that means, dont y? All right then, y misapprehended me. I didnt say preachers. I said orators. O R A T O R S. Born one an I'll die one. You understand me, Lewis. (He turns to Halsey and begins shaking his finger in his face.) An as f you, youre all right f choppin things from blocks of wood. I was good at that th day I ducked th cradle. An since then, I've been shapin words after a design that branded here. Know whats here? M soul. Ever heard o that? Th hell y have. Been shapin words t fit m soul. Never told y that before, did I? Thought I couldnt talk. I'll tell y. I've been shapin words; ah, but sometimes theyre beautiful an golden an have a taste that makes them fine t roll over with y tongue. Your tongue aint fit f nothin but t roll an lick hog-meat.

Stella and Cora come up to the table.

Halsey: Give him a shove there, will y, Stel?

Stella jams Kabnis in a chair. Kabnis springs up.

Kabnis: Cant keep a good man down. Those words I was tellin y about, they wont fit int th mold thats branded on m soul. Rhyme, y see? Poet, too. Bad rhyme. Bad poet. Somethin else youve learned tnight. Lewis dont know it all, an I'm atellin y. Ugh. Th form thats burned int my soul is some twisted awful thing that crept in from a dream, a godam nightmare, an wont stay still unless I feed it. An it lives on words. Not beautiful words. God Almighty no. Misshapen, split-gut, tortured, twisted words. Layman was feedin it back there that day you thought I ran out fearin things. White folks feed it cause their looks are words. Niggers, black niggers[9] feed it cause theyre evil an their looks are words. Yallar niggers[1] feed it. This whole damn bloated purple country feeds it cause its goin down t hell in a holy avalanche of words. I want t feed th soul—I know what that is; th preachers dont—but I've got t feed it. I wish t God some lynchin white man ud stick his knife through it an pin it to a tree.[2] An pin it to a tree. You hear me? Thats a wish f y, you little snot-nosed pups who've been makin fun of me, an fakin that I'm weak. Me, Ralph Kabnis weak. Ha.

Halsey: Thats right, old man. There, there. Here, so much exer-

9. Dark-skinned Afro-Americans. See also p. 83, n. 3.
1. Afro-Americans of lighter skin color ("yellow-ish").
2. See p. 92, n. 8.

tion merits a fittin reward. Help him t be seated, Cora.

Halsey gives him a swig of shine. Cora glides up, seats him, and then plumps herself down on his lap, squeezing his head into her breasts. Kabnis mutters. Tries to break loose. Curses. Cora almost stifles him. He goes limp and gives up. Cora toys with him. Ruffles his hair. Braids it. Parts it in the middle. Stella smiles contemptuously. And then a sudden anger sweeps her. She would like to lash Cora from the place. She'd like to take Kabnis to some distant pine grove and nurse and mother him. Her eyes flash. A quick tensioning throws her breasts and neck into a poised strain. She starts towards them. Halsey grabs her arm and pulls her to him. She struggles. Halsey pins her arms and kisses her. She settles, spurting like a pine-knot afire.

Lewis finds himself completely cut out. The glowing within him subsides. It is followed by a dead chill. Kabnis, Carrie, Stella, Halsey, Cora, the old man, the cellar, and the work-shop, the southern town descend upon him. Their pain is too intense. He cannot stand it. He bolts from the table. Leaps up the stairs. Plunges through the work-shop and out into the night.

6

The cellar swims in a pale phosphorescence. The table, the chairs, the figure of the old man are amœba-like shadows which move about and float in it. In the corner under the steps, close to the floor, a solid blackness. A sound comes from it. A forcible yawn. Part of the blackness detaches itself so that it may be seen against the grayness of the wall. It moves forward and then seems to be clothing itself in odd dangling bits of shadow. The voice of Halsey, vibrant and deepened, calls.

Halsey: Kabnis. Cora. Stella.

He gets no response. He wants to get them up, to get on the job. He is intolerant of their sleepiness.

Halsey: Kabnis! Stella! Cora!

Gutturals, jerky and impeded, tell that he is shaking them.

Halsey: Come now, up with you.

Kabnis (sleepily and still more or less intoxicated): Whats th big idea? What in hell—

Halsey: Work. But never you mind about that. Up with you.

Cora: Oooooo! Look here, mister, I aint used t bein thrown int th street befo day.

Stella: Any bunk whats worked is worth in wages moren this. But come on. Taint no use t arger.[3]

Kabnis: I'll arger. Its preposterous—

3. "Argue."

The girls interrupt him with none too pleasant laughs.

Kabnis: Thats what I said. Know what it means, dont y? All right, then. I said its preposterous t root an artist out o bed at this ungodly hour, when there aint no use t it. You can start your damned old work. Nobody's stoppin y. But what we got t get up for? Fraid somebody'll see th girls leavin? Some sport, you are. I hand it t y.

Halsey: Up you get, all th same.

Kabnis: Oh, th hell you say.

Halsey: Well, son, seeing that I'm th kindhearted father, I'll give y chance t open your eyes. But up y get when I come down.

He mounts the steps to the work-shop and starts a fire in the hearth. In the yard he finds some chunks of coal which he brings in and throws on the fire. He puts a kettle on to boil. The wagon draws him. He lifts an oak-beam, fingers it, and becomes abstracted. Then comes to himself and places the beam upon the work-bench. He looks over some newly cut wooden spokes. He goes to the fire and pokes it. The coals are red-hot. With a pair of long prongs he picks them up and places them in a thick iron bucket. This he carries downstairs. Outside, darkness has given way to the impalpable grayness of dawn. This early morning light, seeping through the four barred cellar windows, is the color of the stony walls. It seems to be an emanation from them. Halsey's coals throw out a rich warm glow. He sets them on the floor, a safe distance from the beds.

Halsey: No foolin now. Come. Up with you.

Other than a soft rustling, there is no sound as the girls slip into their clothes. Kabnis still lies in bed.

Stella (to Halsey): Reckon y could spare us a light?

Halsey strikes a match, lights a cigarette, and then bends over and touches flame to the two candles on the table between the beds. Kabnis asks for a cigarette. Halsey hands him his and takes a fresh one for himself. The girls, before the mirror, are doing up their hair. It is bushy hair that has gone through some straightening process. Character, however, has not all been ironed out. As they kneel there, heavy-eyed and dusky, and throwing grotesque moving shadows on the wall, they are two princesses in Africa going through the early-morning ablutions of their pagan prayers. Finished, they come forward to stretch their hands and warm them over the glowing coals. Red dusk of a Georgia sunset, their heavy, coal-lit faces. . . Kabnis suddenly recalls something.

Kabnis: Th old man talked last night.

Stella: And so did you.

Halsey: In your dreams.

Kabnis: I tell y, he did. I know what I'm talkin about. I'll tell y what he said. Wait now, lemme see.

Halsey: Look out, brother, th old man'll be getting int you by way o dreams. Come, Stel, ready? Cora? Coffee an eggs f both of you.

Halsey goes upstairs.

Stella: Gettin generous, aint he?

She blows the candles out. Says nothing to Kabnis. Then she and Cora follow after Halsey. Kabnis, left to himself, tries to rise. He has slept in his robe. His robe trips him. Finally, he manages to stand up. He starts across the floor. Half-way to the old man, he falls and lies quite still. Perhaps an hour passes. Light of a new sun is about to filter through the windows. Kabnis slowly rises to support upon his elbows. He looks hard, and internally gathers himself together. The side face of Father John is in the direct line of his eyes. He scowls at him. No one is around. Words gush from Kabnis.

Kabnis: You sit there like a black hound spiked to an ivory pedestal. An all night long I heard you murmurin that devilish word. They thought I didnt hear y, but I did. Mumblin, feedin that ornery thing thats livin on my insides. Father John. Father of Satan, more likely. What does it mean t you? Youre dead already. Death. What does it mean t you? To you who died way back there in th 'sixties. What are y throwin it in my throat for? Whats it goin t get y? A good smashin in th mouth, thats what. My fist'll sink int y black mush face clear t y gúts—if y got any. Dont believe y have. Never seen signs of none. Death. Death. Sin an Death. All night long y mumbled death. (He forgets the old man as his mind begins to play with the word and its associations.) Death . . . these clammy floors . . . just like th place they used t stow away th worn-out, no-count niggers in th days of slavery . . . that was long ago; not so long ago . . . no windows (he rises higher on his elbows to verify this assertion. He looks around, and, seeing no one but the old man, calls.) Halsey! Halsey! Gone an left me. Just like a nigger.[4] I thought he was a nigger all th time. Now I know it. Ditch y when it comes right down t it. Damn him anyway. Godam him. (He looks and re-sees the old man.) Eh, you? T hell with you too. What do I care whether you can see or hear? You know what hell is cause youve been there. Its a feelin an its ragin in my soul in a way that'll pop out of me an run you through, an scorch y, an burn an rip your soul. Your soul. Ha. Nigger soul. A gin soul that gets drunk on a preacher's words. An screams. An shouts. God Almighty, how I hate that shoutin. Where's th beauty in that? Gives a buzzard a windpipe an I'll bet a dollar t a dime th buzzard ud beat y to it. Aint surprisin th white folks hate y so. When you had eyes, did you ever see th beauty of th world?

---

4. See p. 83, n. 3.

Tell me that. Th hell y did. Now dont tell me. I know y didnt. You couldnt have. Oh, I'm drunk an just as good as dead, but no eyes that have seen beauty ever lose their sight. You aint got no sight. If you had, drunk as I am, I hope Christ will kill me if I couldnt see it. Your eyes are dull and watery, like fish eyes. Fish eyes are dead eyes. Youre an old man, a dead fish man, an black at that. Theyve put y here t die, damn fool y are not t know it. Do y know how many feet youre under ground? I'll tell y. Twenty. An do y think you'll ever see th light of day again, even if you wasnt blind? Do y think youre out of slavery? Huh? Youre where they used t throw th worked-out, no-count slaves. On a damp clammy floor of a dark scum-hole. An they called that an infirmary. Th sons-a . . . . Why I can already see you toppled off that stool an stretched out on th floor beside me—not beside me, damn you, by yourself, with th flies buzzin an lickin God knows what they'd find on a dirty, black, foul-breathed mouth like yours . . .

Some one is coming down the stairs. Carrie, bringing food for the old man. She is lovely in her fresh energy of the morning, in the calm untested confidence and nascent maternity which rise from the purpose of her present mission. She walks to within a few paces of Kabnis.

Carrie K.: Brother says come up now, brother Ralph.

Kabnis: Brother doesnt know what he's talkin bout.

Carrie K.: Yes he does, Ralph. He needs you on th wagon.

Kabnis: He wants me on th wagon, eh? Does he think some wooden thing can lift me up? Ask him that.

Carrie K.: He told me t help y.

Kabnis: An how would you help me, child, dear sweet little sister?

She moves forward as if to aid him.

Carrie K.: I'm not a child, as I've more than once told you, brother Ralph, an as I'll show you now.

Kabnis: Wait, Carrie. No, thats right. Youre not a child. But twont do t lift me bodily. You dont understand. But its th soul of me that needs th risin.

Carrie K.: Youre a bad brother an just wont listen t me when I'm tellin y t go t church.

Kabnis doesnt hear her. He breaks down and talks to himself.

Kabnis: Great God Almighty, a soul like mine cant pin itself onto a wagon wheel an satisfy itself in spinnin round. Iron prongs an hickory sticks, an God knows what all . . . all right for Halsey . . . use him. Me? I get my life down in this scum-hole. Th old man an me—

Carrie K.: Has he been talkin?

Kabnis: Huh? Who? Him? No. Dont need to. I talk. An when I really talk, it pays th best of them t listen. Th old man is

a good listener. He's deaf; but he's a good listener. An I can talk t
him. Tell him anything.

Carrie K.: He's deaf an blind, but I reckon he hears, an sees too,
from th things I've heard.

Kabnis: No. Cant. Cant I tell you. How's he do it?

Carrie K.: Dunno, except I've heard that th souls of old folks
have a way of seein things.

Kabnis: An I've heard them call that superstition.

The old man begins to shake his head slowly. Carrie and Kabnis
watch him, anxiously. He mumbles. With a grave motion his head
nods up and down. And then, on one of the down-swings—

Father John (remarkably clear and with great conviction): Sin.

He repeats this word several times, always on the downward nod-
ding. Surprised, indignant, Kabnis forgets that Carrie is with him.

Kabnis: Sin! Shut up. What do you know about sin, you old
black bastard. Shut up, an stop that swayin an noddin your head.

Father John: Sin.

Kabnis tries to get up.

Kabnis: Didnt I tell y t shut up?

Carrie steps forward to help him. Kabnis is violently shocked at
her touch. He springs back.

Kabnis: Carrie! What . . how . . Baby, you shouldnt be down
here. Ralph says things. Doesnt mean to. But Carrie, he doesnt
know what he's talkin about. Couldnt know. It was only a preacher's sin they knew in those old days, an that wasnt sin at all. Mind
me, th only sin is whats done against th soul. Th whole world is a
conspiracy t sin, especially in America, an against me. I'm th victim
of their sin. I'm what sin is. Does he look like me? Have you ever
heard him say th things youve heard me say? He couldnt if he had
th Holy Ghost t help him. Dont look shocked, little sweetheart,
you hurt me.

Father John: Sin.

Kabnis: Aw, shut up, old man.

Carrie K.: Leave him be. He wants t say somethin. (She turns
to the old man.) What is it, Father?

Kabnis: Whatsha talkin t that old deaf man for? Come away
from him.

Carrie K.: What is it, Father?

The old man's lips begin to work. Words are formed incoherently. Finally, he manages to articulate—

Father John: Th sin whats fixed . . . (Hesitates.)

Carrie K. (restraining a comment from Kabnis): Go on, Father.

Father John: . . . upon th white folks—

Kabnis: Suppose youre talkin about that bastard race thats
roamin round th country. It looks like sin, if thats what y mean.
Give us somethin new an up t date.

Father John:—f tellin Jesus—lies. O th sin th white folks 'mitted when they made th Bible lie.

Boom. Boom. BOOM! Thuds on the floor above. The old man sinks back into his stony silence. Carrie is wet-eyed. Kabnis, contemptuous.

Kabnis: So thats your sin. All these years t tell us that th white folks made th Bible lie. Well, I'll be damned. Lewis ought t have been here. You old black fakir—

Carrie K.: Brother Ralph, is that your best Amen?

She turns him to her and takes his hot cheeks in her firm cool hands. Her palms draw the fever out. With its passing, Kabnis crumples. He sinks to his knees before her, ashamed, exhausted. His eyes squeeze tight. Carrie presses his face tenderly against her. The suffocation of her fresh starched dress feels good to him. Carrie is about to lift her hands in prayer, when Halsey, at the head of the stairs, calls down.

Halsey: Well, well. Whats up? Aint you ever comin? Come on. Whats up down there? Take you all mornin t sleep off a pint? Youre weakenin, man, youre weakenin. Th axle an th beam's all ready waitin f y. Come on.

Kabnis rises and is going doggedly towards the steps. Carrie notices his robe. She catches up to him, points to it, and helps him take it off. He hangs it, with an exaggerated ceremony, on its nail in the corner. He looks down on the tousled beds. His lips curl bitterly. Turning, he stumbles over the bucket of dead coals. He savagely jerks it from the floor. And then, seeing Carrie's eyes upon him, he swings the pail carelessly and with eyes downcast and swollen, trudges upstairs to the work-shop. Carrie's gaze follows him till he is gone. Then she goes to the old man and slips to her knees before him. Her lips murmur, "Jesus, come."

Light streaks through the iron-barred cellar window. Within its soft circle, the figures of Carrie and Father John.

Outside, the sun arises from its cradle in the tree-tops of the forest. Shadows of pines are dreams the sun shakes from its eyes. The sun arises. Gold-glowing child, it steps into the sky and sends a birth-song slanting down gray dust streets and sleepy windows of the southern town.

THE END

Backgrounds

DARWIN T. TURNER

Introduction [to the 1975 Edition of *Cane*]†

The publication of *Cane* (1923) brought wider attention to a new presence in American literature—twenty-eight-year-old Jean Toomer, who, in less than eighteen months, had attracted an enthusiastic following among a select circle of prominent editors, critics, and authors. In the foreword to *Cane*, Waldo Frank, a well-known novelist and social critic, declared:

> A poet has arisen among our American youth who has known how to turn the essences of materials of his Southland into the essences and materials of literature. . . . The fashioning of beauty is ever foremost in his inspiration. . . . He has made songs and lovely stories of his land. . . . [*Cane*] is a harbinger of a literary force of whose incalculable future I believe no reader of this book will be in doubt.

Earlier Lola Ridge, editor of *Broom*, had predicted that Toomer would be the most widely discussed author of his generation, which is remembered now for such individuals as Sherwood Anderson, Ernest Hemingway, F. Scott Fitzgerald, and William Faulkner. John McClure, editor of *Double Dealer*, had favorably compared Toomer's lyricism with Sherwood Anderson's. Anderson himself had acclaimed Toomer as the only Negro "to have consciously the artist's impulse." A reading of *Cane* added literary critics Robert Littell and Allen Tate, among others, to the list of Toomer's admirers.

Afro-American literary critics endorsed Toomer as fervently as others had. In 1925 William Stanley Braithwaite, widely known for his anthologies of magazine verse, concluded an essay on the history of Afro-American writers:

> In Jean Toomer, the author of *Cane*, we come upon the very first artist of the race, who with all an artist's passion and sympathy for life, its hurts, its sympathies, its desires, its joys, its defeats and strange yearnings, can write about the Negro without the surrender or the compromise of the author's vision. . . . *Cane* is a book of gold and bronze, of dusk and flame, of ecstasy and pain, and Jean Toomer is a bright morning star of a new day of the race in literature.

Braithwaite knew that Toomer was not the first Afro-American to earn a significant literary reputation. As early as the eighteenth century, Phillis Wheatley, an African slave in Boston, elicited praise for *Poems on Various Subjects, Religious and Moral* (1773). William Wells Brown, a

† The "Introduction" by Darwin T. Turner to CANE by Jean Toomer is reprinted by permission of Liveright Publishing Corporation. Copyright 1923 by Boni & Liveright. Copyright renewed 1951 by Jean Toomer. "Introduction" Copyright © 1975 by Darwin T. Turner.

fugitive slave, wrote a novel, *Clotel* (1853), which reputedly rivaled Harriet Beecher Stowe's *Uncle Tom's Cabin* (1852) in popularity among Union soldiers during the Civil War. Frances E. W. Harper's poetry sold widely during the Civil War era; and Charles W. Chesnutt, before becoming a novelist, published short stories in *The Atlantic*, one of the more exclusive, highly priced periodicals of the late nineteenth century. Paul Laurence Dunbar was one of America's most popular poets at the beginning of the twentieth century. There had been others—poets, novelists, essayists. Yet Jean Toomer's star sparkled high above these, a signal light for the writers of the Harlem Renaissance, as the North Star had been for their ancestors a century earlier.

Predicting a destined greatness, Waldo Frank described Toomer's future as "incalculable," a choice of words that proved ironically prophetic. Like a nova, Toomer's literary career exploded into brilliance with *Cane*, then faded from the view of all but the few who continuously scanned the literary galaxy. Although he published a few essays, poems, and stories during more than thirty years of subsequent effort, he never again sold a book to a commercial publisher. Time, however, has restored his reputation, and *Cane* is more widely read than it was while Toomer lived. Printed initially in a small quantity and reprinted only once during Toomer's life, *Cane*, now in the third edition of the past eight years, is the most frequently studied, the most respected of all the books of the Harlem Renaissance; and Jean Toomer is ranked among the finest artists in the history of Afro-American literature.

This recent recognition, however, carries an irony. After *Cane*, Toomer resisted identification with any race except the new one—the American race—that he envisioned coming to birth on the North American continent. A mixture of several races and nationalities, an individual who could be identified as an Indian or a dark-skinned European, Toomer argued that a Black label or a white label restricted one's access to both groups and limited one's growth. As evidence he bitterly cited publishers' rejections of his writings after *Cane*. Identifying him as Negro, he argued, they expected and desired nothing except a duplicate of his earlier work. Today, however, Toomer's reputation stands at a zenith primarily because he was "discovered" by numbers of scholars and students during the 1960s, when interest in Black consciousness impelled many Americans to search for Black literary treasures even more avidly than the generation of the twenties had sought young Afro-American writers to sponsor.

Unfortunately, the very fact that *Cane* was revived during that storm of Black consciousness has prompted a misunderstanding of the author and, to a slighter degree, has blurred a vision of the various themes—in addition to Black life—that permeate the work. Poetically ambiguous, *Cane* may appear to be a jungle through which original trails can be hacked by readers seeking their own myths and symbols. In a major sense, however, it is a landscape conceived and designed by a man who struggled for greatness but believed that he had experienced only failure; a man who wished to guide, to teach, to lead; a man whose thoughts did not end with racial issues, but swirled through naturalism, socialism, atheism, Christianity, Eastern teachings, occultism, history, psychology; and, above all, a man whose actual perceptions of women and of Black life in the South seem paradoxically different from those sometimes inferred from sentimental readings of *Cane.* Thus, to see *Cane* clearly, one needs first to look at its author.

Much of what is known about Toomer's family background and early life must be taken from his unpublished autobiographies, which I have used for this introduction. Frequently, his recollections conflict with the facts or with the memories of others in the Pinchback family. In such instances, however, fantasy may prove more important than truth; for Toomer's distortions reflect his own assessment of the significant influences on his life.

Nathan Eugene (later, Jean) Toomer was born December 26, 1894, only one day after the date which Christians celebrate as the anniversary of the birth of Jesus, the Messiah—a coincidence that may have intensified in significance for Toomer years afterwards when he undertook a comparable mission of reform in his varied roles as teacher, counselor, and spiritual leader. Named "Nathan" after a father whom he scarcely can have known, Toomer glamorized his sire as a handsome, elegant man who, the son of a wealthy plantation owner in Georgia, "had the air of a southern aristocrat of the old stamp." Jean Toomer's romanticism also colors his narrative of his father's courtship: the elder Toomer dazzled Nina Pinchback, temporarily wrested her from the control of her tyrannical and possessive father, but was driven off before the birth of his first child. This heroic portrait of Toomer's father is sullied by the Pinchbacks' suspicions that Nathan Toomer was merely a slave woman's impoverished son who married Nina Pinchback with the hope that she could finance his extravagances but deserted her as soon as he discovered that her father, Pinckney B. S. Pinchback, tightly controlled the family fortunes.

Regardless of the accuracy, Toomer's conceptualization of his father suggests reasons not only for his choice of agriculture as a major in college and his adult desire for farmland, but even for his ability in *Cane* to observe Black life in the South with that detachment and objectivity which impressed Waldo Frank, Braithwaite, and other early reviewers of *Cane.* If Toomer identified emotionally with the plantation-owner class, perhaps he subconsciously established distance between himself and the Black peasants. Furthermore, his loss of his father may have motivated his attraction to various father figures in his life.

In his early years in the Pinchback home, where his mother had been forced to return, Toomer—now called Eugene Pinchback—developed attitudes which seem to have influenced his adult behavior. Living in an affluent neighborhood where, as far as he remembered, no one worried about racial identity, Toomer enjoyed the companionship of children his age, frolicked in their pranks and sports, and assumed the role of a Napoleonic leader until a prolonged illness separated him from his companions while he was in the fourth grade. When he discovered that new leaders had replaced him during his absence, Toomer reacted in a manner foreshadowing his subsequent actions whenever he suspected or anticipated failure: withdrawing from the group, he became a detached observer.

Not an ideal retreat for a youth isolated from his peers, the Pinchback household was ruled by the almost legendary P. B. S., who, since 1868— the year of his daughter Nina's birth—had figured prominently and controversially in politics. A crusader for rights for Blacks, the only Negro known to have served as acting governor of Louisiana, twice denied a seat in the United States Senate because of allegedly fraudulent elections, Pinchback in 1890 had moved his family from their mansion in New Orleans to Washington, D.C., where despite ebbing fortunes he continued to command public respect, as Toomer recalled admiringly and perhaps enviously. Although Pinchback's concern for Blacks aligned him with "radicals" in politics, at home, Toomer asserted, he was a conservative who demanded strictness, order, and religious observance of the conventions and moralities. As evidence of Pinchback's dictatorial practices, Toomer recounted Pinchback's effort to curtail his son Bismarck's habit of reading late at night:

> Grandfather did not object to the reading, at least not openly, though I suppose he felt both anger and regret seeing a son of his at the prime of life spending so much time in bed. But, with his mania for petty economy, he did loudly and strongly object to Bismarck burning gas after ten o'clock. Perhaps his inner disappointment found vent in this curious small way. At any rate, he stormed against the large gas bill. If he passed Bis's room after ten o'clock and saw a light coming from it he would rap sharply, open the door, raise the very devil, and demand that the light be turned out. So Bis had to devise a means of outwitting the old gentleman.

But the same man who fretted about minor expenditures enjoyed luxury and, loving his children, permitted them—especially Nina—to cultivate a similar taste.

In this atmosphere, undoubtedly often uncomfortable for a mischievous, stubborn child who blamed his grandfather for his father's disappearance, Toomer derived comfort from his mother and his grandmother, but turned for inspiration and guidance to his Uncle Bismarck, whom he perhaps identified subconsciously as a substitute father. During frequent visits to Bismarck's room in the evenings, he acquired a vision of the nature of "the good life":

> This position—my uncle in bed surrounded by the materials of a literary man—was impressed upon me as one of the desirable positions

in life. It is no wonder that later on I responded positively to pictures of Robert Louis Stevenson and other writers spending most of their lives in bed. Nor is it surprising that in time I inclined to a career which would let me live this way if I wanted to.

Artistic, meditative Bismarck did more than provide a physical model; he stimulated Toomer's interests in science, reading (as a pleasure in itself), history, myths, fables, folk tales, adventures, and romances. From Bismarck he learned more, Toomer insisted, than from his formal education in school.

After an unsuccessful effort to live in New York with his mother and her second husband, whom he despised, Toomer returned to Washington, to live with Uncle Bismarck. For the first time, the fourteen-year-old experienced life in a "colored" neighborhood, where racial distinctions determined allegiances. Characteristically, even at this age he remained neutral when Blacks and whites confronted each other.

After high school years during which he proved more restless than studious, fell in and out of love, worried about sex, and turned to physical exercise to discipline and strengthen himself, Toomer in the summer of 1914 enrolled at the University of Wisconsin to study agriculture. At that time, Toomer later wrote in an unpublished autobiography, he formulated his views about his racial composition and his racial attitudes. Aware of America's practice of dichotomizing life into Black and white, Toomer resolved to say as little as possible about his race when he entered the predominantly white world of Madison, Wisconsin:

In my body were many bloods, some dark blood, all blended in the fire of six or more generations. I was, then, either a new type of man or the very oldest. In any case I was inescapably myself. . . . If I achieved greatness of human stature, then just to the degree that I did I would justify *all* the blood in me. If I proved worthless, then I would betray all. In my own mind I could not see the dark blood as something quite different and apart. But if people wanted to say this dark blood was Negro blood and if they then wanted to call me a Negro—this was up to them. Fourteen years of my life I had lived in the white group, four years I had lived in the colored group. In my experience there had been no main difference between the two. But if people wanted to isolate and fasten on those four years and to say that therefore I was colored, this too was up to them. . . . I determined what I would do. To my real friends of both groups, I would, at the right time, voluntarily define my position. As for people at large, naturally I would go my way and say nothing unless the question was raised. If raised, I would meet it squarely, going into as much detail as seemed desirable for the occasion. Or again, if it was not the person's business I would either tell him nothing or the first nonsense that came into my head.

Repelled by agricultural studies and alienated from classmates because, anticipating defeat, he had withdrawn from the race for presidency of the freshman class, Toomer left Wisconsin at the close of the fall term. For the student of Toomer's literature, the episode at Wisconsin has significance mainly as the first episode in Toomer's four-year trek through various schools and as a source for an unpublished short story, "Withered Skin of Berries,"[1] the triangle of a young Afro-American woman passing for white, a white male bigot who is courting her, and an athletic, poetic, mystical young man who is sometimes suspected of being an Indian.

After an abortive registration at the Massachusetts College of Agriculture, Toomer, deciding to take advantage of his athletic abilities and his interest in body building, enrolled in the American College of Physical Training in Chicago, a brief but enjoyable experience which furnished the background material later utilized in "Bona and Paul." Reconsidering the desirability of a future as a "mere gym instructor," however, Toomer in the fall of 1916 registered for biology courses at the University of Chicago to prepare for a medical career, but again was diverted from his proposed program. Newly converted to socialism, in which he saw an "intelligible scheme of things" that "evoked and promised to satisfy all in me that had been groping for form amid the disorder and chaos of my personal experience," Toomer discarded friends and studies as he zealously carried the message of socialism to all who would listen. Further inspired by a lecture by Clarence Darrow, whose atheism shattered Toomer's former concept of a religious universe, Toomer, foreshadowing the "teach-ins" of a future generation, secured permission to use a room at the College of Physical Training for evening lectures on socialism, evolution, society, Victor Hugo, the origin of the universe, and the intelligence of women. The lectures ended, he recalled, because his concept of women's intelligence offended female listeners, especially the dean of women.

Just as Toomer's views about race must be examined closely because of the current interest in *Cane* as a presentation of Black life, so his ideas about women must be scrutinized because of the significance of women in that book. The presence of women as the major characters, the most memorable individuals, of *Cane* is not accidental. Throughout his writing and his teaching Toomer emphasized the importance of liberating women from the restrictions imposed by society. Indeed, some of his writing appears to originate from a desire to promulgate that message. One wonders how such a zealous reformer might offend the very group he proposed to assist.

Unfortunately, his autobiographies do not reveal the details of his commentary on the intelligence of women or the bases of their objections, but a reasonable theory may be inferred from other works. In "The Sacred Factory,"[2] an unpublished expressionistic drama, Toomer

---

1. Now published in *The Wayward and the Seeking: A Collection of Writings by Jean Toomer*.

2. Now published in *The Wayward and the Seeking*.

asserts more explicitly than in any other fictional work his thesis that Woman is heart and intuition whereas Man is mind and logic. An appropriate relationship of Man and Woman, therefore, fuses the separate entities into a functioning totality. His thesis obviously suggests women's inferiority in intellectual reasoning and the use of logic; in justice to Toomer, however, one must suspect that he undoubtedly would have been, or was, astonished by the opposition—as he was naively startled later by American reactions to his views about race and about interracial marriages. From his perspective, his view of women was not condescending; in fact, he frequently explained that he did not consider a command of logic sufficient—men need to develop intuition also—and that he considered the female element as essential as the male is. Regardless of Toomer's interpretation, there is little doubt that his theory would provoke opposition then and now. It may, however, constitute a position from which to view the women of *Cane,* who seem motivated by feeling rather than reason.

No longer interested in studies at the University of Chicago or at the American College, Toomer returned to Washington for the now customary winter hibernation. There, a reading of Lester Ward's *Dynamic Sociology,* a desire to earn the Ph.D. degree which he believed prerequisite to the life of a scholar, and perhaps the warmths of spring and of an impatient grandfather rekindled his energies. The following summer, 1917, he enrolled in New York University, where almost immediately he decided that sociology courses were too dull. Equally disillusioned by the slow comprehension of his younger, less mature classmates in history classes at the City College of New York, where he registered that fall, Toomer had begun to speculate about the study of psychology as a fundamental approach to life when the excitement of the First World War and his fear that the draft would interrupt his studies motivated him to withdraw from school near the close of the term. After both the army and the Red Cross rejected him, Toomer, unwilling to return to school, sold Ford automobiles in Chicago, taught briefly as a substitute physical education director in Milwaukee, and finally settled with the Acker, Merrall and Conduit Company in New York City in the spring of 1918.

Soon he was undermined by the characteristic frenzy with which he plunged into new interests. In the hours after work Toomer practiced writing literature. Then, believing music to be a more natural form of expression for him, he began to study it intensively. When he added a physical education job at the University Settlement and many evening lectures to youths of the settlement, the schedule caused a severe breakdown, in late fall of 1918. While recuperating, Toomer experienced a mania for writing, an excitement that seemed to resolve his questions about the appropriate career. After one final chaotic year marked by abrupt, periodic returns to and departures from Washington, interrupted by an abortive effort to teach socialism to shipyard workers, and highlighted by his introduction to a literary circle that included Lola Ridge, Edwin Arlington Robinson, and Waldo Frank, Toomer, now calling himself "Jean," returned to Washington in summer, 1920, to prepare himself for a career as a writer.

For the next two years he studied the literature of Waldo Frank, Sherwood Anderson, Van Wyck Brooks, Robert Frost, Carl Sandburg, and the Imagists. He immersed himself in Buddhist philosophy, Eastern teachings, Christian Scriptures, and occultism. He exhausted himself with his own literary efforts, completing a "trunkful" of essays, articles, poems, stories, reviews—few of them submitted, none published.

Living regularly in an Afro-American world for the first time in six years, Toomer engrossed himself with racial matters while he tried to advise two friends—Harry Kennedy and Mae Wright—who were embittered by the conditions of Black life in the United States. In order to deepen his understanding, he read books on race and the race problem; but he decided that most taught a nonsense that merely reflected the authors' prejudices and preferences. Seeking to clarify and reformulate his own racial attitudes, he wrote essays on the subject. In a poem, "The First American," he introduced his idea that America was transforming the old races into a new race, of which he was the first conscious member—a thesis he expanded later in "The Blue Meridian," a much longer poem. During these years from 1920 to 1922 Toomer probably immersed himself in Afro-American consciousness more deeply than he had during any earlier period, more in fact than he ever would again.

Enervated by his own activities and by the strain of caring for his ailing grandfather, Toomer in late summer of 1921 gratefully accepted an invitation to serve temporarily as the head of an industrial and agricultural school for Negroes while the principal of the school scoured the North for financial support. There, in Sparta, Georgia, Toomer unearthed the substance suitable for the medium he was perfecting, as he later explained in a letter to *The Liberator* magazine:

> From my own point of view I am naturally and inevitably an American. I have strived for a spiritual fusion analogous to the fact of racial intermingling. Without denying a single element in me, with no desire to subdue one to the other, I have sought to let them function as complements. I have tried to let them live in harmony. Within the last two or three years, however, my growing need for artistic expression has pulled me deeper and deeper into the Negro group. And as my powers of receptivity increased, I found myself loving it in a way that I could never love the other. It has stimulated and fertilized whatever creative talent I may contain within me. A visit to Georgia last fall was the starting point of almost everything of worth that I have done. I heard folk-songs come from the lips of Negro peasants. I saw the rich dusk beauty that I had heard many false accents about, and of which til then, I was somewhat skeptical. And a deep part of my nature, a part that I had repressed, sprang suddenly to life and responded to them. Now, I cannot conceive of myself as

aloof and separated. My point of view has not changed; it has deepened, it has widened.

On the train returning to Washington, Toomer began writing sketches, stories, and poems meditating on his experiences in Georgia. Soon after the first of these had been accepted by *The Double Dealer, The Liberator,* and *Broom,* Toomer sent a collection of his best to Waldo Frank. When Frank offered the hoped-for encouragement, Toomer proposed a book of his work:

> Now I wanted a book published as I wanted nothing else. I wanted it because it would be a substantial testament of my achievement, and also because I felt that it would lead me from the cramped conditions of Washington which I had outgrown, into the world of writers and literature. I saw it as my passport to this world.

> But I had not enough for a book. I had at most a hundred typed pages. These were about Georgia. It seemed that I had said all I had to say about it. So what, then? I'd fill out. The middle section of "Cane" was thus manufactured.

Cane is generally adjudged the literary masterpiece of the Harlem or "New Negro" Renaissance, a brief but glittering period during the 1920s when America interested itself in Afro-American art and culture as never before, and when Afro-American artists, proud of their racial identity, saw themselves as a vanguard moving towards full participation in American society. The total significance of *Cane,* however, can be understood only when it is perceived both as a harbinger of that Renaissance and as an illumination of significant psychological and moral concerns of the early 1920s.

The glamour of the Renaissance shines vividly from memories of what F. Scott Fitzgerald called "The Jazz Age." For white America the symbol was jazz, carried from the bordellos of New Orleans' famed Storyville district, first by the Original Dixieland Jass [sic] Band, then by the Black musicians themselves when, after Storyville was closed in 1917, they joined the stream of Blacks migrating north to seek jobs created by wartime needs. Hot, rich, raucous, sensual, alive, redolent with suggestions of emotionalism, primitivism, and savagery, jazz fit the mood of many young, Freudian-inspired Americans shattering the chains of a prim past. Self-conscious couples braved dusky, Prohibition-defying night spots to listen to the music of Joe "King" Oliver, Fletcher Henderson, Louis Armstrong, Duke Ellington, and others. Audiences thronged Broadway theaters for the joyous singing and abandoned dancing of *Shuffle Along* (1921), a musical written, performed, and directed by Blacks—Flournoy Miller, Aubrey Lyles, Eubie Blake, and Noble Sissle. Dancers flung themselves into the acrobatics of the Charleston, popularized by *Running Wild* (1923), a musical by Miller and Lyles. Jazz infiltrated the rhythms of such poets as Vachel Lindsay, Carl Sandburg, and E. E. Cummings; it permeated the consciousness of F. Scott Fitzgerald and his fictional sheiks and flappers; it set tempo to such drama as John Dos Passos's *The Garbage Man* [*The Moon Is a Gong*] (1926); it furnished subject matter for a new talking picture, *The Jazz Singer*. Jazz was not merely sound and rhythm; it was a life-style. And, despite the popularity and the commercial success of white musicians, most devotées knew that jazz was Black.

Black people themselves became themes and subjects of interest for an extraordinary number of white American writers climbing to prominence in the 1920s. With a Black as example, Eugene O'Neill dramatized the power of terror to strip away man's veneer of civilization (*The Emperor Jones*, 1920). Among his explorations of Americans' sexual duels and desires, O'Neill included the conflict within an interracial marriage (*All God's Chillun Got Wings*, 1924). Believing white Americans to be too inhibited, Sherwood Anderson pictured Blacks as innocent, laughing primitives for whom sexual desire is a natural condition of life (*Dark Laughter*, 1925); and William Faulkner contrasted the stolid stability of Blacks with the neurotic sensitivities of whites (*The Sound and the Fury*, 1929). Dubose Heyward (*Porgy*, 1925), Paul Green, and Julia Peterkin described the "primitive" existences of Black peasants in South Carolina, North Carolina, and Virginia. Carl van Vechten titillated readers with the exoticism of Black life in Harlem's nightclubs and soirées (*Nigger Heaven*, 1926). These are only a few of the better-known white American authors who during the 1920s conceived Black Americans as an integral element of their literature.

Explanations of this awakened interest in Black people and Black culture are various. Inferring from the Black jazz, dancing, and singing a corresponding sexual abandon, some Americans undoubtedly presumed that Blacks personified the uninhibited behavior which many whites sought, or professed to seek, for themselves. Other Americans saw in Black peasantry a "noble savage"—simple, close-to-nature, unaffected by the materialism rapidly transforming America from a land of farmers and craftsmen into a society of assembly-line workers. Still others may have looked at Blacks as a group whose needs should be attended to as evidence of America's commitment to the humanitarian sentiments which President Woodrow Wilson had articulated to justify America's participation in World War I.

Obviously, however, the Harlem Renaissance could not have existed without Blacks who shaped and perfected it while regarding it from a different perspective. For many whites the Renaissance was symbolized by the illusion which James Weldon Johnson described in *Black Manhattan* (1930).

> Harlem is known in Europe and the Orient, and it is talked about by natives in the interior of Africa. It is farthest known as being exotic, colourful [sic], and sensuous; a place of laughing, singing, and dancing; a place where life wakes up at night. This phase of Harlem's fame is most widely known because, in addition to being spread by ordinary

agencies, it has been proclaimed in story and song. And certainly this is Harlem's most striking and fascinating aspect. New Yorkers and people visiting New York from the world over go to the night-clubs of Harlem and dance to such jazz music as can be heard nowhere else; and they get an exhilaration impossible to duplicate. Some of these seekers after new sensations go beyond the gay night-clubs; they peep in under the more seamy side of things; they nose down into lower strata of life. A visit to Harlem at night—the principal streets never deserted, gay crowds skipping from one place of amusement to another, lines of taxicabs and limousines standing under the sparkling lights of the entrances to the famous nightclubs, the subway kiosks swallowing the disgorging crowds all night long—gives the impression that Harlem never sleeps and that the inhabitants thereof jazz through existence.

In Black thought, however, the Harlem Renaissance is the decade of the "New Negro," characterized by pride and optimistic anticipation. In Northern industries, Black emigrants were earning more money and enjoying a greater freedom than they had known in the agrarian South. Returning Black servicemen, having received abroad a respect which many had never known in their homeland, were demanding the right to maintain that newfound dignity. In New York City these masses moved into Harlem, which had been opened to Black residents during the first decade of the twentieth century. There they promenaded with the affluent, who had already established their "Strivers Row." They were joined by entertainers (and hustlers and confidence men) moving as usual to where the money seemed to be. They were joined by talented young Blacks who, hearing that something important and exciting was happening, streamed into Harlem to see for themselves. Artists, entertainers, the affluent, the educated, the working classes, the professional classes mingled bodies and ideas in a microcosm of Black America. Despite the cold that seared the newcomers from the South, despite the economic difficulties that compelled "rent parties," despite awareness that neither the North nor Harlem was that Celestial City dreamed of, Afro-Americans, "facing the rising sun of our new day begun," sang "a song full of the hope that the present has taught us." Harlem was the symbol, but Black America knew that the decade was a Renaissance of New Negroes throughout America.

The "New Negro" sentiment was not a mere accident of the times. In part it was meticulously designed and promoted by Afro-American scholars. Since the early years of the twentieth century, such historians as W. E. B. DuBois and Carter G. Woodson had sought to encourage pride by researching Black history in the United States and in Africa to refute the allegations that the African race had bred only slaves and savages incapable of contributing to civilization. In 1915 Woodson founded the Association for the Study of Negro Life and History to encourage scholarly research, and in 1916 he established the *Journal of Negro*

History as an organ to disseminate the results of the research. Literary scholar Benjamin Brawley recounted the cultural achievements of Afro-American writers and musicians in *The Negro in Art and Literature* (1910). Even Toomer himself proposed such encouragement, as he explained in a letter to Sherwood Anderson a few months before *Cane* was published:

> I feel that in time, in its social phase, my art will aid in giving the Negro to himself. In this connection, I have thought of a magazine. A magazine, American, but concentrating on the significant contributions, or possible contributions of the Negro to the western world. A magazine that would consciously hoist, and perhaps at first a trifle over emphasize a negroid ideal. A magazine that would function organically for what I feel to be the budding of the Negro's consciousness. The need is great. People within the race cannot see it. In fact, they are likely to prove to be directly hostile. But with the youth of the race, unguided or misguided as they now are, there is a tragic need. Talent dissipates itself for want of creative channels of expression, and encouragement.

Assistance came also from such associations as The National Association for the Advancement of Colored People and The National Urban League, which committed their energies to improving political, economic, and social conditions for Blacks. Even while it advocated emigration to Africa, Marcus Garvey's Universal Negro Improvement Association strengthened the psychology and the racial pride of Black Americans by emphasizing Africa's identity as a land of Black people and by inspiring Black Americans to develop independent institutions.

Special encouragement was given to the group which W. E. B. Dubois identified as "The Talented Tenth," that educated and talented part of the Afro-American population (or any population) capable of leadership and cultural creativity. Believing that a nation or a race commands respect among the peoples of the world according to its cultural achievements, W. E. B. DuBois used the pages of *The Crisis*, official organ of the NAACP, to stimulate and to provide a showcase for Black educators and writers. Like *The Crisis*, the Urban League's *Opportunity: a Journal of Negro Life* sponsored contests to encourage and publicize Black writers.

Black artists responded enthusiastically to opportunities offered by such periodicals and by white patrons and publishers. An impressive list of new writers of the twenties includes some of the best-remembered, most respected in the annals of Afro-American literature: Jessie Fauset, Langston Hughes, Countée Cullen, Wallace Thurman, Arna Bontemps, Rudolph Fisher, Zora Neale Hurston, Sterling Brown. Reared in diverse regional cultures of the East, the South, and the West, they formed in Harlem the first significant large Black literary community capable of interchanging ideas reflecting the whole of Black America. These Renaissance writers, as Sterling Brown has explained in *Negro*

Poetry and Drama (1937), examined new themes: (1) Africa as a source for race pride, (2) Black heroes and heroic episodes from American history, (3) propaganda of protest, (4) a treatment of Afro-American masses, frequently the folk, with more understanding and less apology, and (5) franker and deeper self-revelation.

If it were no more than an outstanding work of this era, *Cane* would deserve honor. What gives *Cane* even greater significance is that it was one of the first rays of the dawn of that age. When *Cane* was published, Louis Armstrong had been performing with King Oliver's orchestra for only a year, and Duke Ellington was forming his first band. Black musicals had returned to Broadway after more than a decade's absence, but only one or two had appeared. Of the materials now known as the literature of the Renaissance, only one book had been published— Claude McKay's volume of poetry, *Harlem Shadows* (1922). Few white artists of the decade had discovered Black materials. Jazz had not yet attained the national respectability it enjoyed after Paul Whiteman's orchestra featured it in 1924. Among writers of the twenties, only Eugene O'Neill had created a Black protagonist; the "Black" works of Heyward, Anderson, Green, Faulkner, and the rest were still in the future.

No one can fully determine how much *Cane* inspired other Blacks to hope that they too might publish books, or how vividly it suggested to whites the value of Black subject matter. Evidence, however, points to probable influences. Langston Hughes has recalled that the Renaissance writers studied the book assiduously. It affected Sherwood Anderson, who, three years before *Dark Laughter*, voiced his admiration in a letter to Toomer:

> I wanted so much to find and express something clear and beautiful
> I felt coming up out of your race but in the end gave up. . . . And
> then McClure handed me the few things of yours I saw and there
> was the thing I had dreamed of beginning.

Waldo Frank also had read Toomer's materials before he completed his own *Holiday* (1923), a more melodramatic presentation of racial conflicts in the South. No matter how he influenced others, it cannot be denied that Jean Toomer was the first writer of the twenties to delineate Southern Black peasant life perceptively.

To study Toomer's work only in relationship to the New Negro Renaissance, however, is to misjudge its value in the total culture of the twenties. Beneath a superficial gaiety, a stream of conservatism and sobriety flowed through the schizophrenic decade. A conservative, even reactionary force voted for Prohibition and closed down Storyville; promoted riots against Black soldiers who, having fought for democracy abroad, expected to participate in it at home; spread the Ku Klux Klan farther North than ever before and elected a Klansman governor of Indiana. Beneath the superficial gaiety, readers now discern the murmurs of doubt, disillusionment, and insecurity permeating Ernest Hemingway's stories of athletes and expatriates, Sinclair Lewis's ridicule of petty provinciality, the Grotesques cameoed by Edgar Lee Masters and Sherwood Anderson, O'Neill's adumbrations of alienation, the questioning of American values in *What Price Glory?* and *Beggar on Horseback*, and Faulkner's tormented Southerners.

Like these writers Toomer questioned the harmonies and values of his society. *Cane* is no conventional world of Black primitives or exotics. It is a montage: of women "ripened too soon" ("Karintha"), impotized by the moral prescriptions of bourgeois society ("Box Seat"), transfixed into virgins and virgin-mothers by men who do not understand them ("Fern" and "Kabnis"), neuroticized by the tensions between their subconscious physical urges and their conscious conformity to society's strictures against even the possibility of such emotions ("Esther")—women who wail futilely against their society, "Doesnt it make you mad?" *Cane* is a world of men traumatized and destroyed by bigotry ("Becky" and "Blood-Burning Moon"), men bent double by materialism ("Rhobert"), dreamers who cannot rouse themselves to action ("Theater," "Box Seat," "Avey"), men who rationalize their physical desires into idealized abstractions ("Theater," "Bona and Paul"), men who cower in drink and sex to hide their fears ("Kabnis"), men who cannot offer help beyond that of material goods ("Fern"). *Cane* is a society that requires women to be nonphysical ("Carma"), that deludes itself rather than see that people act according to the laws of God as well as those of society ("Becky"), that pretends that innocence has age limits ("Karintha"). In *Cane*, Toomer foreshadowed much of the questioning and criticism of the twenties.

Stylistically too Toomer rode in the vanguard of his generation. His poetry and prose depend upon the clean, impressionistic phrasings of the Imagists. In a decade when American dramatists conspicuously rebelled against the limitations of traditional drama and its stage, he pioneered experiments with dramatic form, in the novelette-drama "Kabnis"; with symbolic uses of dance, language, and characterization, in "Natalie Mann" [1922], an unpublished drama; and with Expressionism, in "The Sacred Factory" [1927], another unpublished drama.[3]

The form of *Cane* has puzzled readers. Some have identified it as a novel—perhaps because it has a thematic and structural unity, or because it faintly resembles Sherwood Anderson's *Winesburg, Ohio* (1919), or because a few literary critics—for reasons of their own—have labeled it a novel, or merely because they have not known what else to call it. No matter what name is given to the book's form, however, Jean Toomer did not conceive *Cane* as a novel. As has been indicated earlier by his letter to Frank, Toomer wanted to publish a volume consisting of "Kabnis" and the stories and poems that are now the first section. When prospective publishers complained that the proposed book was too brief, he added the materials that constitute the second section. Furthermore,

3. "Natalie Mann" and "The Sacred Factory" are now published in *The Wayward and the Seeking*.

a few years later when he sought to satisfy his publisher's request for a novel, he structured a very conventional form in such unpublished novels as "The Gallonwerps" [1927], "Transatlantic" [1929], and "Caromb" [1932].

Except in an effort to understand Toomer's intentions and to perceive his art clearly, the name given to the form of *Cane* probably does not matter. Obviously, the work has a three-part structure: The first section, set in the South (Georgia), focuses on stories about women, particularly women whose behavior or thought contrasts with the expectations and demands of society. The second section, introduced by a lyric description of the major artery of Washington, D.C.'s Black settlement and by a sketch of a property-burdened man, presents men and women in Washington and Chicago whose interrelationships are distorted and disrupted by their conditioning. The third section returns to the South for a grim presentation of a Northern-reared, educated Afro-American who discerns the impotence of the institutionalized education and religion conventionally offered to Blacks, resists the assistance of a messianic figure, derives no meaningful message from his slave heritage, and finds only the anodynes of sex and drink in his journey underground, a Walpurgis-Night experience from which he gathers no truths, only dead coals, which he carries along as he begins his apprenticeship in wagon-making, a trade dying in the new era of the automobile.

Certainly too *Cane* has thematic unity, as might be expected in a series of writings constituting one artist's vision during a single year. Poems link, separate, echo, and introduce the stories with themes of nature's beauty, man's disruption of nature's harmony, work, tributes to Black folksong, love, dreams of escape, false gods and true gods, man's hunger, white woman described through the imagery of the lynching performed in her name, and man's inability and need to harmonize soul, body, and mind. Imagistic, impressionistic, sometimes surrealistic, the poems are redolent with images of nature, Africa, and sensuous appeals to eye and ear.

The sketches and stories—ambiguous, illusive, suggestive—are as rich in imagery as the poems themselves. Visions of pine needles, November cotton flowers, smoke, sugarcane, dusk, flame, and a vari-colored, vari-shaped sun adorn the Southern landscape. The Northern world is pictured as a harsher reality of asphalt streets, alleys, dead or metallic houses, and stone pavements—except when dreams transform the asphalt world into a vision of chestnuts and old leaves and canefields. As the arcs indicate at the beginnings of sections two and three, neither world can form the perfect harmony symbolized by a circle.

As Jean Toomer conceived it, *Cane* was primarily a song for an era that was ending. In an autobiography he described his impressions of Sparta, Georgia:

> The setting was crude in a way, but strangely rich and beautiful. I began feeling its effects despite my state, or, perhaps, just because of

it. There was a valley, the valley of "Cane," with smoke-wreaths during the day and mist at night. A family of back-country Negroes had only recently moved into a shack not too far away. They sang. And this was the first time I'd ever heard the folk-songs and spirituals. They were very rich and sad and joyous and beautiful. But I learned that the Negroes of the town objected to them. They called them "shouting." They had victrolas and player-pianos. So, I realized with deep regret, that the spirituals, meeting ridicule, would be certain to die out. With Negroes also the trend was towards the small town and then towards the city—and industry and commerce and machines. The folk-spirit was walking in to die on the modern desert. That spirit was so beautiful. Its death was so tragic. Just this seemed to sum life for me. And this was the feeling I put into "Cane." "Cane" was a swan-song. It was a song of an end. And why no one had seen and felt that, why people have expected me to write a second and a third and a fourth book like "Cane," is one of the queer misunderstandings of my life.

Ironically, *Cane* sang another song—the end of an era for Jean Toomer. Although he had proposed to write a collection of stories about communistic influences on Afro-American life in Washington, he never again depicted Afro-Americans in literature. Even before *Cane* was published, he had begun to protest against being identified as a Negro. For reasons I have explored in greater detail in another essay (See "Jean Toomer: Exile," *In a Minor Chord* [Carbondale: Southern Illinois University Press, 1971]), he intensified his resistance against such identification until he reached a climactic denial that African blood flowed in his veins. The fallacious assumption, he insisted, derived from Waldo Frank's misunderstanding of his racial position and from Grandfather Pinchback's pretense of Afro-American ancestry in order to gain political advantages during Reconstruction.

Part of Toomer's resistance undoubtedly reflected the internalization of his thesis that America had given birth to a new race, which subsumed all the old identities. Another significant reason, however, was the fear I have mentioned earlier, that the racial identification caused publishers to reject as un-Negro the literature he wanted to create. Yet, a new kind of literature had become vital to Toomer's work; for, soon after *Cane*, he had turned to a new career, a new mission.

As has been shown earlier in this introduction, Toomer's attractions frequently were impulsive, immediate, powerful—whether to ideas, such as socialism, sociology, and Eastern mysticism, or to people, such as Clarence Darrow and Waldo Frank. Rather than distrusting such impulses, Toomer proposed them as the desirable, the true reactions of human beings—kinetic responses which people repress because they fear society's objections. (Notice the attraction of John and Dorris in "Theater" or Lewis and Carrie in "Kabnis," and the mental processes which prevent the consummation of those relationships.)

Toomer experienced just such an instantaneous attraction to Georges Gurdjieff, a spiritual leader whom he met in 1923. Gurdjieff professed to have the ability to help people fuse their fragmented selves into a new and perfect whole—a harmony of mind, body, and soul—through a system of mental and physical exercise emphasizing introspection, meditation, concentration, discipline, and self-liberation. Toomer responded to Gurdjieff totally. In 1930, while he was still a disciple, Toomer wrote, "With certain notable exceptions, every one of my main ideas has a Gurdjieff idea as a parent." Even after disillusionment with Gurdjieff's personal behavior caused Toomer to separate from the group, he continued to praise Gurdjieff's ideas and their influence on his soul.

After a summer's study in 1924 at Gurdjieff's institute in Fontainebleau, France, Toomer returned to America in the fall as a disciple. His earliest efforts to instruct such "New Negro" artists as Wallace Thurman, Dorothy Peterson, Aaron Douglass, and Nella Larsen aborted, according to Langston Hughes, because few Blacks had both the leisure time necessary for the inner observation and the money necessary for the lessons. Toomer achieved greater success with others—primarily the affluent and the artistic; and, for almost a decade, he served as a disciple-teacher-leader, especially among a Chicago group of followers.

It is not surprising that Toomer, who had sought greatness, who had wished to reform others, and who had searched for self-realization, would dedicate himself to such an awe-inspiring mission as his new one. Unfortunately, the effects on his literary career were deleterious. Even in section two of *Cane*, the last written, one sees a shifting of Toomer's artistic approach. Rather than sketching his personae lyrically from a narrator's detached perspective, he more often enters the characters' psyches to describe their thoughts and suggest their psychological motivation. His style too is harsher, more reflective of a sophisticated urban world. Perhaps, therefore, one might suspect that Toomer inevitably would have modified his style and his thought; but Toomer changed them consciously and dramatically to serve his new purposes. Whereas Waldo Frank had once presumed, somewhat mistakenly, that "the fashioning of beauty" was "foremost in . . . Toomer's inspiration," Toomer now asserted that the primary purpose of literature is to teach; and, in order to teach well, he imitated the ponderous style of his master.

For a decade he wrote his messages. In short fiction he psychoanalyzed men who can never realize themselves because they never comprehend the human experience; men who become obsessed by egomania; men who exist in a society which reduces them from personages to faceless beings in a clinic; men who cannot fuse the impulsive, sensitive, artistic self with the domineering, calculating, aggressive self; men who place barriers between emotion and reason. He depicted women who need to grow spiritually, to be liberated by perceptive men. He wrote "Transatlantic," a novel about the lessons that must be learned by an isolated, self-exiled man and a spiritually undeveloped woman. In the guise of novels he wrote autobiographies that describe spiritual experiences or his reactions to nationwide attacks on his first marriage and his moral ideas. In nonfictional essays and books he explained his attitudes about race, his concept of the spiritualization of America, and the significance of a mystic experience which taught him harmony. He prepared thesis poems; and he constructed dramas, which vary in style from an expressionistic presentation of the psychological failure of modern bourgeois man to heavily satiric and symbolic plays ridiculing social types and teaching people the need to liberate the id. But publishers rejected all the books that he wrote. After *Cane* the only book that he published was *Essentials* (1931), a privately printed collection of aphorisms.

Despite what literary scholars sometimes suggest, an author's life does not necessarily end at the time of his final major publication. Jean Toomer lived more than forty years after *Cane*. In 1931, in Portage, Wisconsin, he guided some members of his Chicago group in an experiment in communal living and spiritual growth. One of the members was Margery Latimer, a talented author, whom he married in the same year; she died in 1932 while giving birth to their daughter. In 1934 Toomer married Marjorie Content, who remained with him until his death on March 30, 1967. Through the years following his second marriage, he continued to search for harmony and self-realization in East Indian religions, in the Friends Society, and in psychoanalysis while he continued to lecture, to write, and occasionally to publish in magazines. In the 1940s, abandoning fiction and drama, he restricted his writing to poetry, reviews, philosophical treatises, and autobiographies.

Cane was not Jean Toomer's total life; it was perhaps merely an interlude in his search for understanding. No matter what it may have been for him, *Cane* still sings to readers, not the swan song of an era that was dying, but the morning hymn of a Renaissance that was beginning.

WALDO FRANK

Foreword [to the 1923 Edition of *Cane*]

Reading this book, I had the vision of a land, heretofore sunk in the mists of muteness, suddenly rising up into the eminence of song. Innumerable books have been written about the South; some good books have been written in the South. This book *is* the South. I do not mean that *Cane* covers the South or is the South's full voice. Merely this: a poet has arisen among our American youth who has known how to turn the essences and materials of his Southland into the essences and materials of literature. A poet has arisen in that land who writes, not as a Southerner, not as a rebel against Southerners, not as a Negro, not as apologist or priest or critic: who writes as a *poet*. The fashioning of beauty is ever foremost in his inspiration: not forcedly but simply, and because these ultimate aspects of his world are to him more real than all its specific problems. He has made songs and lovely stories of his land . . . not of its yesterday, but of its immediate life. And that has been enough.

How rare this is will be clear to those who have followed with concern the struggle of the South toward literary expression, and the particular trial of that portion of its folk whose skin is dark. The gifted Negro has been too often thwarted from becoming a poet because his world was forever forcing him to recollect that he was a Negro. The artist must lose such lesser identities in the great well of life. The English poet is not forever protesting and recalling that he is English. It is so natural and easy for him to be English that he can sing as a man. The French novelist is not forever noting: "This is French." It is so atmospheric for him to be French, that he can devote himself to saying: "This is human." This is an imperative condition for the creating of deep art. The whole will and mind of the creator must go below the surfaces of race. And this has been an almost impossible condition for the American Negro to achieve, forced every moment of his life into a specific and superficial plane of consciousness.

The first negative significance of *Cane* is that this so natural and restrictive state of mind is completely lacking. For Toomer, the Southland is not a problem to be solved; it is a field of loveliness to be sung: the Georgia Negro is not a downtrodden soul to be uplifted; he is material for gorgeous painting: the segregated self-conscious brown belt of Washington is not a topic to be discussed and exposed; it is a subject of beauty and of drama, worthy of creation in literary form.

It seems to me, therefore, that this is a first book in more ways than one. It is a harbinger of the South's literary maturity: of its emergence from the obsession put upon its minds by the unending racial crisis— an obsession from which writers have made their indirect escape through sentimentalism, exoticism, polemic, "problem" fiction, and moral melodrama. It marks the dawn of direct and unafraid creation. And, as the initial work of a man of twenty-seven, it is the harbinger of a literary force of whose incalculable future I believe no reader of this book will be in doubt.

How typical is *Cane* of the South's still virgin soil and of its pressing seeds! and the book's chaos of verse, tale, drama, its rhythmic rolling shift from lyrism to narrative, from mystery to intimate pathos! But read the book through and you will see a complex and significant form take substance from its chaos. Part One is the primitive and evanescent black world of Georgia. Part Two is the threshing and suffering brown world of Washington, lifted by opportunity and contact into the anguish of self-conscious struggle. Part Three is Georgia again . . . the invasion into this black womb of the ferment seed: the neurotic, educated, spiritually stirring Negro. As a broad form this is superb, and the very looseness and unexpected waves of the book's parts make *Cane* still more *South*, still more of an aesthetic equivalent of the land.

What a land it is! What an Æschylean beauty to its fateful problem! Those of you who love our South will find here some of your love. Those of you who know it not will perhaps begin to understand what a warm splendor is at last at dawn.

> A feast of moon and men and barking hounds,
> An orgy for some genius of the South
> With bloodshot eyes and cane-lipped scented mouth
> Surprised in making folk-songs. . . .

So, in his still sometimes clumsy stride (for Toomer is finally a poet in prose) the author gives you an inkling of his revelation. An individual force, wise enough to drink humbly at this great spring of his land . . . such is the first impression of Jean Toomer. But beyond this wisdom and this power (which shows itself perhaps most splendidly in his complete freedom from the sense of persecution), there rises a figure more significant: the artist, hard, self-immolating, the artist who is not interested in races, whose domain is Life. The book's final Part is no longer "promise"; it is achievement. It is no mere dawn: it is a bit of the full morning. These materials . . . the ancient black man, mute, inaccessible, and yet so mystically close to the new tumultuous members of his race, the simple slave Past, the shredding Negro Present, the iridescent passionate dream of the To-morrow . . . are made and measured by a craftsman into an unforgettable music. The notes of his counterpoint are particular, the themes are of intimate connection with us Americans. But the result is that abstract and absolute thing called Art.

JEAN TOOMER

[Autobiographical Selection]†

* * *

It was during this spring [1922] that I began feeling dangerously drained of energy. I had used so much in my own work. So much had been used on my grandparents and uncles. I seldom went out. I seldom could go out. Sometimes for weeks my grandmother would be laid up in bed, and by now my grandfather was almost helpless. The apartment seemed to suck my very life. And this is no figure of speech. Everyone has had the experience of being with some person, of leaving this person and feeling bled. He is bled. This person has taken stuff out of him. Just so, only for a protracted period, had my grandfather taken energy from

† From *The Wayward and the Seeking: A Collection of Writings by Jean Toomer*, ed. Darwin T. Turner (Washington D.C.: Howard UP, 1980) 122–27.

me. He was still taking it; and I began to see the situation as a struggle for life between him and myself. It was a question of who would die first.

There was nothing the matter with me organically, though I had contracted a severe case of almost chronic nervous indigestion. Mainly, it was a matter of energy. I felt utterly exhausted. Each morning I was up before nine. I'd try to work, and just simply couldn't. The little force I had gathered during sleep was soon spent, and I'd be in a wretched state. But neither could I rest. To do nothing was even worse than trying to squeeze something out of myself. I drank what whiskey I could get. But when its effects wore off, I was more drained than ever. I didn't know what on earth I was going to do. I had no money even for a short vacation. And even if I had had, I couldn't have left my grandparents alone. A nurse was out of the question.

But, when the heat of summer came on, I got desperate. I felt I would die or murder someone if I stayed in that house another day. Somehow I managed to get enough money for a week's trip to Harper's Ferry. And, luckily, I was able to make arrangements with an old woman to be in the apartment for that time. Grandmother, sensing my state, was glad I was going to have a slight breathing spell. Grandfather, understanding very little other than his own infirmities, was petulant. But I left.

I returned with a small store of force which was soon spent; and I found myself in the same condition as before. The situation was slowly but steadily growing worse. Never in my life before . . . [had I felt] so utterly caught and trapped. It was as if life were a huge snake that had coiled about me—and now it had me at almost my last breath.

Just as this time a man, the head of an industrial and agricultural school for Negroes in Georgia, came to town. He was going to Boston in search of funds and wanted someone to act as principal during his absence. He was sent to me.

My situation was so desperate that any means of getting out of it appeared as a God-send. I accepted his offer. Besides, I had always wanted to see the heart of the South. Here was my chance.

I had grandfather sent to a hospital. I hired a woman to come and stay with grandmother. And off I went.

I arrived in Sparta and took up my duties. I still felt terribly drained, but the shock of the South kept me going.

The school was several miles from the village. All the teachers lived there. I had a little shack off to one side.

The setting was crude in a way, but strangely rich and beautiful. I began feeling its effects despite my state, or, perhaps, just because of it. There was a valley, the valley of "Cane," with smoke-wreaths during the day and mist at night. A family of back-country Negroes had only recently moved into a shack not too far away. They sang. And this was the first time I'd ever heard the folk-songs and spirituals. They were very rich and sad and joyous and beautiful. But I learned that the Negroes of the town objected to them. They called them "shouting." They had victrolas and player-pianos. So, I realized with deep regret, that the spirituals, meeting ridicule, would be certain to die out. With Negroes also the trend was towards the small town and then towards the city— and industry and commerce and machines. The folk-spirit was walking in to die on the modern desert. That spirit was so beautiful. Its death was so tragic. Just this seemed to sum life for me. And this was the feeling I put into *Cane*. *Cane* was a swan-song. It was a song of an end. And why no one has seen and felt that, why people have expected me to write a second and a third and a fourth book like *Cane*, is one of the queer misunderstandings of my life.

I left Georgia in late November of that year, after having been there three months. On the train coming north I began to write the things that later on appeared in that book.

Once again in Washington I had my grandfather brought back from the hospital. His condition there was too pitiable for me to bear. He touched my heart so strongly that I resolved to care for him till the very end. And this I did.

He sank very rapidly. All during December I nursed him; and, at the same time, I wrote the materials of *Cane*. In these last days he seemed to know just what I meant to him. I knew and realized all he had done for me. Our almost life-long struggle and contest was finished, and all my love and gratitude for the once so forceful and dominant but now so broken and tragic man came to the fore. He died the day after I had finished the first draft of "Kabnis," the long semi-dramatic closing-piece of *Cane*.

Walter and I took his body to New Orleans and interred it in the family vault, beside the remains of my mother.

Grandmother bore up remarkably well; and she and I continued living in the apartment.

* * *

I resumed writing.

Some of the pieces were impure and formless. But some, I knew, were really written. These authentic ones I began sending out. The *Double Dealer* of New Orleans was the first to accept. Then the *Liberator* and, later, *Broom*. In these literary magazines I made my mark. Beyond them was Waldo Frank and the possibility of a book.

Now I felt warranted in sending something to Waldo Frank. I sent a batch of the best—and waited his response as if my whole life were at stake.

His words to me fed me as nothing else had done and confirmed my belief.

He too talked about a book. Now I wanted a book published as I wanted nothing else. I wanted it because it would be a substantial tes- tament of my achievement, and also because I felt that it would lead me from the cramped conditions of Washington which I had outgrown, into the world of writers and literature. I saw it as my passport to this world.

But I had not enough for a book. I had at most a hundred typed pages. These were about Georgia. It seemed that I had said all I had to say about it. So what, then? I'd fill out. The middle section of *Cane* was thus manufactured.

I sent the manuscript to Frank. He took it to Horace Liveright. Liveright accepted it, but wanted a foreword written by Frank.

Frank himself had a book to write, based on Negro life.[1] It was arranged that he come to Washington and then both of us would go South.

Frank came. He stayed at the apartment with us. I took this opportunity to convey to him my position in America. I read to him "The First American." I explained my actuality and my ideas to the point where I felt sure he understood them. I did this because I wanted that we understood each other on this point too, and also because he was going to write the foreword to my book and I wanted this introduction of myself to the literary world to be accurate and right.

We went South. We came back. Frank returned to New York. In several of his letters he referred to what he called my "vision," and seemed to feel that it "protected" me. Perhaps it did. But because of the way he used this word "protected," I was mainly concerned with whether or not he understood that it was not a vision, but an actuality. Once or twice I suspected that he, like my colored friend, felt it was words, fine words to be sure, but unrelated to reality. But I argued myself out of the suspicion by reminding myself that Waldo Frank was the author of *Our America*.

One day in the mail his preface to my book came. I read it and had as many mixed feelings as I have ever had. On the one hand, it was a tribute and a send-off as only Waldo Frank could have written it, and my gratitude for his having gotten the book accepted rose to the surface and increased my gratitude for the present piece of work in so far as it affirmed me as a literary artist of great promise. On the other hand, in so far as the racial thing went, it was evasive, or, in any case, indefinite. According to the reader he would have thought I was white or black, or again he may have thought nothing of it. But in any case he certainly would not *know* what I was.

Well, I asked myself, why should the reader know? Why should any such thing be incorporated in a foreword to *this* book? Why should Waldo Frank or any other be my spokesman in this matter? All of this was true enough, and I was more or less reconciled to letting the preface stand as it was, inasmuch as it was so splendid that I could not take issue with it on this, after all, minor point, inasmuch as my need to

1. *Holiday* (1923). It is important to observe that Toomer states that he had completed *Cane* before Frank completed *Holiday*.

have the book published was so great, but my suspicions as to Waldo's Frank's lack of understanding of, or failure to accept, my actuality became active again.

As I found out later from several sources, my doubts were warranted. I have been told that Frank, after seeing me and my family, after hearing my statement, not of words or visions but of facts, returned to New York and told people of the writer who was emerging into the world of American literature. In any event, it was thus through Frank's agency that an erroneous picture of me was put in the minds of certain people in New York before my book came out. Thus was started a misunderstanding in the very world, namely the literary art world, in which I expected to be really understood. I knew none of this at the time. . . .[2]

I saw that it was important for me to be in New York. Grandmother also saw this. Walter had again married. He and his wife had taken a house. Grandmother went to live with them and I took a train for New York [in early summer, 1923]. And thus ended the three-year period of death and birth in Washington.

In New York, I stepped into the library world. Frank, Gorham Munson, Kenneth Burke, Hart Crane, Matthew Josephson, Malcolm Cowley, Paul Rosenfeld, Van Wyck Brooks, Robert Littell—Broom, the Dial, the New Republic and many more. I lived on Gay Street and entered into the swing of it. It was an extraordinary summer.

I wrote reviews, especially for Broom. I worked on the outline of a large complex novel that was to essentialize my experiences with America. I entered the aesthetic-machine-beauty program as sponsored by Munson in Secession and Josephson in Broom. I met and talked with Alfred Stieglitz and saw his photographs. I was invited here and there.

I went up to visit Frank at Darien, Connecticut. And here I met Margaret Naumburg and felt the whole world revolve . .

. . . My birth, and it was truly a birth, came from my experiences with Margaret Naumburg. I do not wish to put these in outline. It is enough here to say that the very deepest centre of my being awoke to consciousness giving me a sense of myself, an awareness of the world and of values, which transcended even my dreams of high experience. All that I had been, all that I had ever done, were as if left behind me in another world.

All the past would have seemed valueless had I not known that it was just this past which had prepared me for these experiences.

["Outline of an Autobiography"]

. . . It was very exciting life and work, giving me a taste and an experience of the literary life such as I had never known before and have never experienced since. There was an excitement in the air. Writing

2. In this part of his autobiography, Toomer asserts that he should not have been identified as "Negro."

was a living thing. We had programs and aims, and we were all caught up in a ferment. These were the last days of *Secession* and *Broom*. But the *Dial* and the *Little Review* were still going, and what was not yet an actuality we had as a glowing potentiality in our minds.

Sometimes I wondered what if anything Frank had said to these other fellows about my race. But it didn't matter much, one way or the other. What they thought of my race was of no more consequence than what I thought of theirs. The life was the thing—and we were having that life.

The first jolt I got was when I received a letter from Horace Liveright asking, in effect, that I feature myself as a Negro for some publicity he was getting out in connection with *Cain* [sic].[3] Now I had seen, talked, lunched with Liveright. Once he had said to me that he had run into prejudice in college, and he asked if I had. I said, "No." That was that. Otherwise, the question of race had not come up even in a vague way. Looking back on it, I can blame myself for not having opened the subject with him. However this may be, I received the request I have just mentioned.

I answered to the effect that, as I was not a Negro, I could not feature myself as one. His reply to this did nothing else than pull my cork. He said he didn't see why I should deny my race. This made me mad, and I was all for going to his office and telling him what was what in no uncertain terms, even at the risk of losing him as my publisher. Friends dissuaded me, and I let the matter drop, but not without having explained to them the facts of my racial actuality.

Cain [sic] came out. The reviews were splendid. It didn't sell well, but it made its literary mark—that was all I asked.

* * *

---

3. I cannot explain the reason for this interesting spelling error in the typed manuscript. Toomer's reference obviously is to *Cane*.

Correspondence†

TOOMER ON HIS WRITING AND REPUTATION

To Katherine Flinn‡

September 20, 1927

* * * What I have done has won me literary recognition and position. And if I wished to devote the time and energy to it, I could now be one of the strongest forces in American literature. * * * But I have in mind becoming something much greater than a literary force, and for this "something" I am deliberately sacrificing certain things in the present. * * *

To Harrison Smith

September 27, 1932

* * * For some years I have been struggling with the autobiography-fiction problem. To date, I have not reached a satisfactory solution. * * *

Heretofore I have held, unconsciously, conflicting attitudes as to details. One part of me has said, "You must convey and incorporate them into the body of your work, else your work will lack body and it will lack relatedness to the very people for whom you are writing. * * * " Another part of me has said, "Detail is uninteresting, and why should anyone bother to put in a book that which our days—even our nights—are already sufficiently full of. * * * " Perhaps a marriage of these attitudes would enable me to produce a book * * * sufficiently projected, sufficiently unusual and essential.

* * * I have repeatedly told myself that my intentions could not be realized in the short time—one, two, to three months—I allowed for each book. Why then have I done as I have done? Partly because I had set myself the task (and I could not have done otherwise) of building a world in literature, and this world, to me . . . was so vast that I felt that only by rapid intensive work could I ever in my lifetime even approach a fulfillment of my aim. (Now, I see, I had my eye too much on the

† Unless otherwise indicated, Toomer's correspondence is reprinted by permission of the Collection of American Literature, The Beinecke Rare Book and Manuscript Library, Yale University.
‡ This letter and the following one are reprinted with permission from Darwin T. Turner, *In a Minor Chord: Three Afro-American Writers and Their Identity* (Carbondale and Edwardsville: Southern Illinois UP, 1971) 46, 51–52.

large structure I had in mind, not enough on the specific book. * * *)
Partly because, in general, I couldn't help it. The pressure of circum-
stance—or something—compelled me to forge ahead and do the best I
could, with the hope that this best would be in some degree worthwhile,
and that it might win a place for the book, and somewhat arrange
conditions so that I could then write a better book, and a better one,
and so on * * * What some people call "leisure for creation," I have
never known. * * * Now, however, I realize I must have time for
ripening and for workmanship. * * *

JEAN TOOMER AND SHERWOOD ANDERSON

To Sherwood Anderson

1341 You Street
Washington
De[cember] 1922

Dear Sherwood Anderson,
    Just before I went down to Georgia I read Winesburg, Ohio. And
while there, living in a cabin whose floorboards permitted the soil to
come up between them, listening to the old folk melodies that Negro
women sang at sun-down, The Triumph of the Egg[1] came to me. The
beauty, and the full sense of life that those books contain are natural
elements, like the rain and sunshine, of my own sprouting. My seed
was planted in the cane- and cotton-fields, and in the souls of black and
white people in the small southern town. My seed was planted in *myself*
down there. Roots have grown and strengthened. They have extended
out. I spring up in Washington. Winesburg, Ohio and The Triumph
of the Egg are elements of my growing. It is hard to think of myself as
maturing without them.
    There is a golden strength about your art that can come from nothing
less than a creative elevation of experience, however bitter or abortive
the experience may have been. Your images are clean, glowing, healthy,
vibrant: sunlight on forks of trees, on mellow piles of pine boards. Your
acute sense of separateness of life could easily have led to a lean pes-
simism in a less abundant soul. Your Yea! to life is one of the clear fine
tones in our medley of harsh discordant sounds. Life is measured by
your own glowing, and you find life, you find its possibilities deeply
hopeful and beautiful. It seems to me that art in our day, other than in
its purely aesthetic phase has a sort of religious function. It is a religion,
a spiritualization of the immediate. And ever since I first touched you,
I have thought of you in this connection. I let a friend of mine, a young
fellow with no literary training but who is sensitive and has had a deep

---

1. *Winesburg, Ohio* (1919) and *The Triumph of the Egg* (1921) are works by Anderson [*Editor*].

experience of life, read Out of Nowhere into Nothing[2] when it first appeared in the Dial. After having finished it he came back to me with face glowing, and said, "When any man can write like that, something wonderful is going to happen." I think that there is. I think that you touch most people that way. And when my own stuff wins a response from you, I feel a linking together within me, a deep joy, and an outward flowing.

Yesterday a letter came from John McClure in which he told me of your stopping past the Double Dealer office, of your reading the things of mine he had on hand. McClure was the real thing, at the *right* time. The impetus I received from him, and from the Double Dealer, has been wonderfully helpful to me. Dec Double Dealer has just come. It features Harvest Song. Good!

Naturally, my impulse was to write you when I first received your note. But at that time I was re-typing my stuff, writing three new pieces, and putting Cane (my book) together. I felt too dry to write. Now, the sap has again started flowing . . .

I am following Many Marriages with deep interest.

Won't you write and tell me more in detail how my stuff strikes you? And at the first opportunity I would certainly like to have a talk with you.

To Sherwood Anderson

1341 You Street, N.W.,
Washington, D.C.,
29 Dec[ember] 1922

Dear Sherwood Anderson,

In your work I have felt you reaching for the beauty that the Negro has in him. As you say, you wanted to write not of the Negro but out of him. "Well I wasn't one. The thing is that it couldn't be truly done." I guess you're right. But this much is certain: an emotional element, a richness from him, from yourself, you have artistically woven into your own material. Notably, in Out of Nowhere into Nothing. Here your Negro, from the stand point of superficial reality, of averages, of surface plausibility, is unreal. My friends who are interested in the "progress" of the Negro would take violent exception to such a statement as, "By educating hismelf he had cut himself off from his own people." And from a strictly social point of view, much that they would say would be true enough. But in these pages you have evoked an emotion, a sense of beauty that is easily more Negro than almost anything I have seen. And I am glad to admit my own indebtedness to you in this connection.

The Negro's curious position in this western civilization invariably forces him into one or the other of two extremes: either he denies Negro entirely (as much as he can) and seeks approximation to an Anglo-Saxon

2. Story by Anderson [*Editor*].

(white) ideal, or, as in the case of your London acquaintance, he overemphasizes what is Negro. Both of these attitudes have their source in a feeling of (a desire not to feel) inferiority. I refer here, of course, to those whose consciousness and condition make them keenly aware of white dominance. The mass of Negroes, the peasants, like the mass of Russians or Jews or Irish or what not, are too instinctive to be anything but themselves. Here and there one finds a high type Negro who shares this virtue with his more primitive brothers. As you can imagine, the resistance against my stuff is marked, excessive. But I feel that in time, in its social phase, my art will aid in giving the Negro to himself. In this connection, I have thought of a magazine. A magazine, American, but concentrating on the significant contributions, or possible contributions of the Negro to the western world. A magazine that would consciously hoist, and perhaps at first a trifle over emphasize a negroid ideal. A magazine that would function organically for what I feel to be the budding of the Negro's consciousness. The need is great. People within the race cannot see it. In fact, they are likely to prove to be directly hostile. But with the youth of the race, unguided or misguided as they now are, there is a tragic need. Talent dissipates itself for want of creative channels of expression, and encouragement. My own means are slim, almost nothing. I have had and am still having a hard pull of it. But as I write these lines there are two young people whom I am barely keeping above surface by the faith and love I have for them. I would deeply appreciate your thoughts in relation to this matter.

My book. Here's how the matter stands. Waldo Frank, whom I met three years ago in New York, has already taken it to Horace Liveright. Liveright has not as yet passed on it. And Waldo is writing the introduction. But as soon as I have definite information, I'll let you know. And I shall always treasure your offer of service at this time.

Do you ever come down this way? For Negro life, its varying shades, its varying phases of consciousness and development there is no better place. I would be glad to share with you whatever I possess.

CANE, SHERWOOD ANDERSON, AND THE NEGRO

To Waldo Frank

[n.d., late 1922 or early 1923]

Brother

* * * There is not another man in the world that I would let touch it [*Cane*]. Any more than I would let someone write Karintha or Kabnis for me. You not only understand CANE; you are *in* it, specifically here and there, mystically because of the spiritual bond there is between us.

* * *

Sherwood Anderson has doubtless had a very deep and beautiful emotion by way of the Negro. Here and there he has succeeded in expressing this. But he is not satisfied. He wants more. He is hungry for it. I come along. I express it. It is natural for him to see me in terms of this expression. I see myself that way. But also I see myself expressing myself, expressing *life*. * * *

There is one thing about the Negro in America. * * * As an entity, the race is loosing [*sic*] its body * * * , race is starkly evident, and racial continuity seems assured. One is even led to believe that the thing we call Negro beauty will always be attributable to a clearly defined physical source. But the fact is, that if anything comes up now, pure Negro, it will be a swansong. Dont let us fool ourselves, brother: the Negro of the folk-song has all but passed away: the Negro of the emotional church is fading. A hundred years from now these Negroes, if they exist at all will live in art. And I believe that a vague sense of this fact is the driving force behind the art movements directed towards them today. (Likewise the Indian.) America needs these elements. They are passing. Let us grab and hold them while there is still time. * * * The supreme fact of mechanical civilization is that you become part of it, or get sloughed off (under). Negroes have no culture to resist it with (and if they had, their position would be identical to the Indians), hence industrialism the more readily transforms them. * * * [I]n those pieces that come nearest to the old Negro, in the spirit saturate with folk-song: Karintha and Fern, the dominant emotion is sadness derived from a sense of feeling, from a knowledge of my futility to check solution. There is nothing about these pieces of the buoyant expression of a new race. The folk songs themselves are of the same order. The deepest of them. "I ain't got long to stay here." Religiously: "I (am going) to cross over into camp ground." Socially: "my position here is transient." * * * When I come up to Seventh Street and Theatre, a wholly new life confronts * * * A life, I am afraid, that Sherwood Anderson would not get his beauty [of the Negro] from. For it is jogged, strident, modern. Seventh Street is the song of crude new life. Of a new people. Negro? Only in the boldness of its expression. In its healthy freedom. American. For the shows that please Seventh Street make their fortunes on Broadway. And both Theatre and Box-Seat, of course, spring from a complex civilization, and are directed to it. And Kabnis is *Me*. * * *

THE MAKING OF CANE

To Waldo Frank

July 25, 1922

* * * Your letters, together with a bit of analysis on my part, have convinced me that the impulse which sprang from Sparta, Georgia last fall has just about fulfilled and spent itself. My book, whether it matures

next month or next year, will place a period. A fresh, and I hope a deeper start will come from our coming venture. * * *[1]

To Waldo Frank

12 Dec[ember] 1922
Washington, D.C.

My brother!

CANE is on its way to you!

For two weeks I haved worked steadily at it. The book is done. From three angles, CANE'S design is a circle. Aesthetically, from simple forms to complex ones, and back to simple forms. Regionally, from the South up into the North, and back into the South again. Or, From the North down into the South, and then a return North. From the point of view of the spiritual entity behind the work, the curve really starts with Bona and Paul (awakening), plunges into Kabnis, emerges in Karintha etc. swings upward into Theatre and Box Seat, and ends (pauses) in Harvest Song.

Whew!

. . . .

You will understand the inscriptions, brother mine: the book to grandma; Kabnis, the spirit and the soil, to you.

I believe that before the work comes out, Little Review, Dial, and Secession will have accepted certain of its pieces. The ones I mention are the certain ones.

Between each of the three sections, a curve. These, to vaguely indicate the design.

I'm wide open to you for criticism and suggestion.

Just these few lines now . . .

love

HOLIDAY?[1]

Waldo Frank to Jean Toomer

[n.d., late 1922 or early 1923]

BROTHER:

Have read Box Seat. Living stuff . . but I think your old form of it with Dan's energy sloughing off in the quarrel with the neighbor and then his disappearing through the alley forgetting all about the man he was to forget is better. I think there is too great a formlessness in Dan's suddenly getting up with his yell, JESUS WAS A LEPER. * * *

lots of love, old soldier,
Waldo

1. A trip to South Carolina to give Frank atmosphere for *Holiday* [*Editor*].

1. The novel on which Frank was working [*Editor*].

To Waldo Frank

[n.d., late 1922 or early 1923]

Brother,

I'm going over Kabnis for Broom. * * *

I'm incorporating the introduction into the body of the work. In this way, two or three pages are cut off. I'm wondering if this form wouldnt be best for the book. I dont believe I lose anything essential. And the piece gains in concentration. As I go over it, new lines etc form. I think I'll have a better Kabnis. * * *

Love . . .

Waldo Frank to Jean Toomer

[n.d., late 1922 or early 1923]

Brother,

* * * Kabnis is big stuff—I don't see its imperfections. It stands. Of course you will do tighter harder bigger ones—but Kabnis is quite perfect as an expression of the man. Some of the shorter sketches are less powerful. Karintha, Avey, Becky, Esther, Calling Jesus, Rhobert, etc. The stories in which you attempted a more complex picture . . Bona & Paul, Box Seat are less perfect. There's a looseness here . . and in much of the imagery a certain lack of inevitability. * * * Theater [*sic*] I find good—& Kabnis is very improved over the version I saw last year—that I wonder if you could tighten up Box Seat & Bona. They pass as they are, but they are not up to the level of your best. There is, in especial, a dissonance between person and background—due to your use of a different method in painting the latter. In Kabnis, the harmony between Georgia & the "folks" is wonderful. * * * "Something is * * * down in Washington," "Tell me," * * * and "Prayer" I consider failures. * * * At best your "lyrics" are your weakest. * * * You are a poet-prose. You are shackled and thwarted in the pure forms. The circles & spheres of drama & story alone can house your * * * song and pure lyricism. * * *

Love
Waldo

To Horace Liveright

1341 You Street NW
Washington, D.C.,
27 Feb[ruary] 1923

Dear Mr. Liveright,

Under separate cover I'm sending CANE.

Waldo's Foreword. [*sic*] is included.

The book is done.
I look at its complacency and wonder where on
earth all my groans and grunts and damns have gone.
It doesn't seem to contain them
And when I look for the power and beauty
I thought I'd caught, they too seem to thin out
and and [*sic*] elude me.
Next time, perhaps . . .

Cordially

Manuel Komroff to Jean Toomer

March 14, 1923

Dear Mr. Toomer,
    The enclosed letter comes from our compositors regarding your book
CANE.[1] Will you kindly answer the questions at once regarding the
apostrophe and also the suspension periods. We believe they should be
consistent throughout the book.
                    Sincerely yours,
                    BONI & LIVERIGHT
                    PER: KOMROFF [Manuel]

Waldo Frank to Jean Toomer

[n.d., summer 1923]

Brother
    Cane proofs have just come, and on the first cursory glance I have
seen SO MANY THINGS WRONG that I hasten to write you, in order
that you may delay their making *plates* until you've had time to make
corrections. If you have already given them your final OK, please wire
to Komroff to hold off. Here is the result of my first glance:
  1. "Foreword by Waldo Frank" is omitted from the title page; it should
     be in smaller type than your name.
  2. In the Foreword, my name should appear not at the end but at
     the beginning under "Foreword," otherwise the reader will think
     he's reading your text till he gets to the bottom, which he should
     not.
  3. I've found several typographical errors in the Foreword.
  4. p. 13; last paragraph of Becky is printed in small type. "Face"
     should go on a page by itself.
  5. Therefore, the entire book requires new pagination.

---

1. There is no record of an enclosure or a response. Contemporary readers puzzled by Toomer's use of apostrophes and suspension periods (ellipsis marks) may be consoled by the fact that even editors and printers at a distinguished publishing house were puzzled [*Editor*].

6. I regret that you printed the verse in smaller type than the prose but I suppose you'll have to let that stand. BUT . . the poetry pages should start a uniform distance from the top of the page, not, as you have it, skipping up and down according to the poem's length.

7. At beginning of Part 2, you have too many blank pages. There should never be a blank oddnumbered [sic] page in the middle of the book. As paginated now, the sign of Part Two should be on p. 67.

(Note: I am not quite certain about point 6 . . perhaps you prefer to have the poem centered, whatever length, rather than have it run over a page. That is for you to decide.)

Waldo

Waldo Frank to Jean Toomer

August 1923

Brother

Herewith, Cane and Holiday. Giving FACE full page will make the pagination for part Two and on, come out right. On thinking it over, leave my name at the end of my foreword, instead of putting it at the beginning . . the thing on the title page is the only change needed.

* * *

Rushing through Cane hurriedly as I have, I am struck quite afresh by its colossal power. Box-Seat strikes me right, now. I dont see how the critics can avoid the immense persuasiveness of Cane . . . but it's always best to realize that they're stupider than we coud [sic] ever dream.

love,
W.F.

Waldo Frank to Jean Toomer

[n.d., summer 1923]

Brother

* * * Doubtless the men who set up your Title page, never saw the MS and did not know about the foreword at all. * * * if they [authors] have any regard for make-up at all, they've got to look sharp . . otherwise there is always something wrong. Dont mind troubling the printers about corrections. That's their job. You are not responsible for their errors. And they are supposed to do WHAT YOU WANT. * * *

love
Waldo

PS The whole tendency nowadays is to make the artist think that he is the favored one . . and it is all bosh. The right attitude to take is that we are the *favoring* ones in the essential.

To Waldo Frank[?]†

[n.d., September 1923?]

Life had had me in a knot, hard and fast. Even in Georgia I was horribly * * * , strained and tense—more so here. The deep releases caused by my experiences there could not liberate and harmonize the sum of me. Cane was a lyric essence forced out with great effort despite my knotted state. People have remarked its simple—easy flowing lyricism, its rich natural poetry; and they may assume that it came to bloom as easily as a flower. In truth, it was born in an agony of internal tightness, conflict, and chaos. It is true that some portions, after I had cleared the way, came forth fluently. Thus Fern came out, not without effort, but with comparative ease soon after I had labored to write Kabnis. But the book as a whole was somehow distilled from the most terrible strain I have ever known. * * * The feelings were in me, deep and mobile enough. But the creations of the forms were very difficult. During its writing, and after it, I left [*sic*] that I had by sheer force emptied myself and given to that book my last blood. I felt drained and dry, with no immediate or prospective source of recreation. Harvest Song, better than any other of the book's content, gives an idea of my state at that time. After finishing Cane, I swore that I would never again write a book at that price. Thus when people—truly moved by Cane and valueing [*sic*] it * * * like it, I have smiled my appreciation of their responses, but have firmly shaken my head. When they, in all good faith have advised me, as Sherwood Anderson did, to keep close to the conditions which produced Cane, I have denied them. Never again in life do I want a repetition of those conditions. And, of equal importance is the fact that Cane is a swan song.

ADVERTISING *CANE*

To Horace Liveright

Box 651
Ellenville, NY
5 Sept[ember] 23

Dear Mr Liveright,

 * * * First, I want to make a general statement from which detailed statements will follow. My racial composition and my position in the world are realities which I alone may determine. Just what these are, I

---

† Toomer wrote this letter on stationery of the Hotel Brevcort. Although the stationery lists the French address for the hotel, Toomer's undated letter is headed "New York." Toomer may have intended this merely as an autobiographical note, but it seems more probable that he wrote it in September 1923, as a draft of a letter to Waldo Frank, whom he would soon visit at Frank's home in Darien, Connecticut [*Editor*].

sketched in for you the day I had lunch with you. As a unit in the social milieu, I expect and demand acceptance of myself on their basis. I do not expect to be told what I should consider myself to be. Nor do I expect you as my publisher, and I hope as my friend, to either directly or indirectly state that this basis contains any element of dodging. In fact, if my relationship with you is what I'd like it to be, I must insist that you never use such a word, such a thought, again. As a Boni and Liveright author, I make the distinction between my fundamental position and the position which your publicity department may wish to establish for me in order that *Cane* reach as large a public as possible. In this connection I have told you, I have told Messrs Tobey and Schneider to make use of whatever racial factors you wish. Feature Negro if you wish, but do not expect me to feature it in advertisements for you. I have sufficiently featured Negro in *Cane.* * * *

Ever,
Toomer

PROJECTS AFTER CANE

To Horace Liveright

March 1923

* * * I have on hand here the crude material for two pieces that approximate Kabnis in length and scope ["Withered Skin of Berries" and "Natalie Mann"]. I have another long story forming in my mind. With these three I'm thinking to make my second volume. The melieu [*sic*] is constantly that of Washington. The characters are dynamic, lyric, complex. I am not quite ready for a novel, but one is forming. As I vaguely glimpse and feel it, it seems tremendous: this whole black and brown world heaving upward against, here and there mixing with the white. The mixture, however, is insufficient to absorb the heaving, hence it but accelerates and fires it. This upward heaving to be symbolic of the proletariat or world upheaval. And it is likewise to be symbolic of the subconscious penetration of the conscious mind. Doubtless, before it is finished, several similar dramas will have been written. At any rate, the horizon for the next three years seems booked and crowded. * * *

TOOMER'S ART

Waldo Frank to Jean Toomer

April 25, 1922

Dear Jean—

* * *

NATALIE MANN

My first impression is that the central drama of Natalie, Merilh, Mertis, Law, etc is smothered by the form of the other stuff . . the teaparties, the talk of the incidental. Then it occurs to me that the trouble is not with the density and amount of this milieu but with the deadness of the texture. If all this were living, the drama would live in it in its correct relation. The thing, therefore, needs rewriting rather than reconstructing. The life is not permeated into the whole thing. In individual scenes, there is a very beautiful colorful glow of life . . as the lovescene of Natalie and Merilh, the two cabaret scenes . . the gorgeous symbolism of the dance with Etty, and the lovely poem ["Karintha"] that M recites in NY.

What is clear is: that you have a vision . . mothered and fathered of true temperament, passion, intellectually well-midwifed . . the start of a true Form, but that the Form is not yet there. Hence the texture drops out of your conception, becomes weak discussive talk. Your whole aim is so new, that the work of formulation must needs be absolutely independent: and to create Form out of chaos, as must all true american artists, takes time time time. Dont lose heart. You are one of the very very, pathetically rare, *real.*

KABNIS

Here the texture is superb, but there is a sacrifice in the bone-structure. You have not yet the strength of pervasion of your own inspiration to give birth to a large form in which bone and stuff stand one and whole. Any bit of this thing is glowing and real, but as a whole it droops and loses its taut sustainedness. I wonder if you would not have done better in a freer form of narrative, in which your dialog, which has no kinship with the theatric, might have thrived more successfully. I felt that the speech of the Ancient at the end was a sudden drop into particulars failing to take along and light with itself the general atmosphere you had built about his relationship with Kabnis. And Kabnis in the only partly formulated organism of the whole never altogether transcends inorganic life . . But here too I feel that there is no true saying for you, save work and fidelity to the wondrously pure vision in you, and the *knowing* that if you nourish it with the best of yourself, like the mystery of all life, you will achieve your form. You have already left far behind you the imitative stage, the stage of acceptance of even the best near to you. You are already on your *own.* You are in that stage most difficult to navigate through when, being ahead of yourself you are temporarily in chaos . . have left home planets and not reached your individual star. In this stage, only the deeply intuitive person can sense where your true form is hardening out of the mists. You háve left behind the monkey crowd who, thinking they can appreciate literature, really love only its stinking afterbirths . . and you have not quite reached that ultimate where you know you are wholly articulately organically yourself. Kabnis has in it the embryon of an expression which America has not had even the faintest inkling of, and which America demands if it is to become a real part of the human adventure. Color, spiritual penetration, counterpoint of human wills, the intuition that they are harmonics of a Unit, the power to convey line and volume in words, intellectual cleansing-capacity . . all here, but not yet fused into the final art. By which I mean that the thing lies in the retrospective mind in its parts, in its details and that in the reading the mind does not catch on to a uniformly moving Life that conveys it whole to the end, but rather steps from piece to piece as if adventuring through the pieces of a still unorganized mosaic. Kabnis is however, very near to its state of fusing. It makes me believe that you are extremely close to your true beginning in this deeply individual genre. Natalie, a more complex organism is a bit farther off.

POEMS

Naturally there are more perfect things among these shorter less organic creations. But although you are a poet, I dont think you'll find your final satisfaction in the mere direct lyric. Something in the way of a free woven narrative that includes the song of Nathan Merilh and gives the texture of the world he springs from will include you all.
Some of the poems are quite perfect. Seventh Street, Becky, Avey, (Daniel less so), Carma are lovely transcripts of a world old in America but new in American expression. The poems Cockswain, Beehive, Evening Song. Marble Faces are another depth . . more metaphysical and yet well pictorialized here. Some of the things are mere statement, not fleshed not living . . like The First American. Some, like Kivalt, are notes for yourself in a rich sensuous garb but still notes that are true in their potential rather than in their kinetic energy.

ON THE WHOLE, my dear Jean Toomer, I am enormously impressed by the power and fulness [*sic*] and fineness of your Say. . . . A man whose spirit is like yours so high and straight a flame does not need to be told that he has enormous gift, and that this means a responsibility beyond the ken and the rules of the masses . . nor does he need anything, one who feels himself his brother and knows that such things need no direct articulation, can send him in a letter. Yet, corroboration from anybody helps. You must go on. You must by whatever ruthless means which will not hurt your spirit, preserve for yourself the freedom, the quiet and the peace in which the spirit may turmoil and seethe and ecstacy to birth.

O if there is one thing I have learned, living in America, knowing my own life and knowing the lives of the many many about me, it is that the artist must have the greater wisdom of fighting for himself, of knowing that only so can the time come when the American world will be a place in which he can live. Today, every rhythm, every will sent through the weave of America is fatal to creation . . and so often not alone economic pressure but the subly [*sic*] insidious Myth of 'the duties of manhood, the need of making ones own way' plunges the delicate artist tissues into a corrodent poisonous bath of American 'reality' which eats them up. Dont think that you will be helping yourself or America in a newspaper office or an advertising agency. If you can keep away, do! Keep to the streets, keep to the quiet of your room . . let that flame burn up clear. And remember that the world which will swallow you, annihilate you today if you take its word and its thought in that very act will be rebuking you who should know not only yourself better, but it better also . . who should know that you must as a part of it prevail against it and so function for it. * * *

your friend and brother,
Waldo Frank

Waldo Frank to Jean Toomer

July 26, 1922

* * * I am probably presumptuous to write about the Negro, and particularly since I know you who are creating a new phase of American literature. (O there's no doubt of that my friend). * * *

Sherwood Anderson to Jean Toomer

December 22, 1922

Your work is of special significance to me because it is the first negro [*sic*] work I have seen that strikes me as being really negro. * * *

Sherwood Anderson to Jean Toomer

[n.d., ca. 1923]

* * * you are the only negro * * * who seems really to have consciously the artist's impulse.

Waldo Frank to Jean Toomer

[n.d., ca. 1923]

* * * The day you write as a Negro, or as an American, or as anything but a human part of *life*, your work will lose a dimension. How typical that is of most recognition: the effort immediately to limit you, to put you in a cubby hole and stick a label underneath. . . . . . the important thing which has at length released you to the creating of literature is that you do not write as a Negro . . . that you take your

race or your races naturally, as a white man takes his. The few talented writers among the Negroes have been ruined because they could not forget. . . . the world would not let them forget. * * *

Allen Tate to Jean Toomer

November 7, 1923

* * * I believe it's the genuine thing—your new technique applied to the material for the first time, and then none of the caricatured pathos of Harris and the others of the southern school of sentimental humors. * * *

Sherwood Anderson to Jean Toomer

January 3, 1924

When I saw your stuff first I was thrilled to the toes. Then I thought "he may let the intense white man get him. They are going to color his style, spoil him."

I guess that isn't true. You'll stay with your own, wont you. * * *

John McClure to Sherwood Anderson

Jan[uary] 22, 1924

Dear Sherwood:

* * * As for Jean Toomer, I am thoroughly convinced that as a piece of literature, of durable writing, Karintha is far superior to Kabnis. I do not think that Toomer can't write short stories. I merely think that his finest work so far is lyrical and that if he ever does supreme work it must be in a lyrical manner. In my opinion he cannot handle dialect. He can do a certain sort of realistic story better than most and can rise to prominence in realism if he wishes to. But the lyrical expression of his own moods he can accomplish, in his own fashion, better probably than nearly anyone. He can be an unusually good short story writer or a supremely fine lyrical rhapsodist, as he pleases. He should mould [sic] his stories into lyrical rhapsodies rather than attempt to present them realistically. I am sure if Toomer attempts realistic fiction as his life-work he will be merely one of a number of men. If he follows that African urge, and rhapsodizes, he will be a commanding and solitary figure. For his own sake, I feel that he ought to do that which he does best. You and I differ, of course, on what he does best. I am sure his dialect is weak. But his English, as he uses it out of his own heart, is founded on a rock.

An honest confession, etc.: Contrary to the opinion of many good critics, I have the same attitude to *your* work. I am sure that the stories in which you have written simply out of your own heart with your own natural intonation of speech are incomparably better than those in which you have constructed the language to fit the character. In other words, I am sure that your genius is lyrical. "I am a Fool" and "I Want to Know Why" (which many people consider among your best) seem to me to be inferior to many things you have done. Not in conception, but in execution. You may disagree with me. I feel the same about Toomer. The moment he attempts to make characters talk in the accents of life he falls from his highest level. He can divine what they think and what they feel but the only way he can express it is in his own language—by stepping into their shoes and then uttering his own words in quotation marks, or else by avoiding altogether and simply telling in his own words, by indirect discourse, what is going on in the other fellow's mind. The lyrical genius is not restricted to poetry. A novel can be lyrical. Realism can be lyrical. * * *

My statement about Toomer is not based, I believe, on a fondness for poetry. "Poetry" as a state of mind does not exist, in my philosophy. Poetry is merely verse, rhythm in speech which reaches the condition of music. The human spirit expresses itself in many ways and verse is only one. Toomer's character seems to me to be lyrical—he is so intensely an individual that it is useless for him to attempt anything other than to express himself. He is not a sponge like Balzac. He is not a dramatist like Shakespeare or even like Eugene O'Neill, for that matter. He is Jean Toomer. Anything he touches will be transmuted into a personal expression. It seems to me he should not try to make his work anything other than an expression of himself, and devote his energies to making it as fine an expression as possible. * * *

Sincerely
Jack McClure

Criticism

Contemporary Criticism

MONTGOMERY GREGORY

[Self-Expression in *Cane*]†

The recent publication of "Cane" marks a distinct departure in southern literature and at the same time introduces a writer of extraordinary power in the person of Jean Toomer. Few books of recent years have greater significance for American letters than this "first" work of a young Negro, the nephew[1] of an acting reconstruction governor of Louisiana. Fate has played another of its freakish pranks in decreeing that southern life should be given its most notable artistic expression by the pen of a native son of Negro descent. * * *

Art is *self-expression*. The artist can only truly express his own soul or the race-soul. Not until Rene Maran, a Negro, had pictured the native life of Africa in "Batouala," did the dark continent find a true exponent of its wrongs and of its resentment against a cruel bondage. The white missionary or itinerant visitor had always described the natives in the light of his own preconceived prejudices.

America has waited for its own counterpart of Maran—for that native son who would avoid the pitfalls of propaganda and moralizing on the one hand and the snares of a false and hollow race pride on the other hand. One whose soul mirrored the soul of his people, yet whose vision was universal.

Jean Toomer, the author of "Cane," is in a remarkable manner the answer to this call. Sprung from the tangy soil of the South, he combines the inheritance of the old Negro and the spirit of the new Negro. His grandfather, P. B. S. Pinchback, was acting governor of Louisiana and later settled in Washington where his grandson, Jean Toomer, was born in 1894. Thus his childhood was spent in a home where dramatic incidents of slavery, of the Civil War and of Reconstruction, were household traditions. The "Song of the Sun," one of the several exquisite lyrics that appear in "Cane," shows the deep affection which young Toomer has for the old South:

> "An everlasting song, a singing tree,
> Caroling softly souls of slavery,
> What they were, and what they are to me,
> Caroling softly souls of slavery."

† From *Opportunity* 1 (December 1923): 374–75.
1. Toomer was the grandson, not nephew, of P. B. S. Pinchback. Gregory corrects it in the fourth paragraph [*Editor*].

A youth rich in wide human experience and marked by a natural love for solitude followed. Later came an opportunity to teach at a small school in Georgia, where he secured the contacts with life in the South which were to give him his final inspirations for the book which is the subject of this criticism. "I felt strange, as I always do in Georgia, particularly at dusk. I felt that things unseen to men were tangibly immediate. I would not have surprised me had I had a vision. . . . When one is on the soil of one's ancestors, most anything can come to one."

"Cane" is not to be classified in terms of the ordinary literary types, for the genius of creation is evident in its form. Verse, fiction, and drama are fused into a spiritual unity, an "aesthetic equivalent" of the Southland. It is not a book to be intellectually understood; it must be emotionally, aesthetically felt. One must approach it with all of his five senses keenly alive if appreciation and enjoyment are to result. No previous writer has been able in any such degree to catch the sensuous beauty of the land or of its people or to fathom the deeper spiritual stirrings of the mass-life of the Negro. "Cane" is not OF the South, it is not OF the Negro; it IS the South, it IS the Negro—as Jean Toomer has experienced them. It may be added that the pictures do not pretend to be the only possible ones in such a vast panorama of life. "The Emperor Jones" was a study of one Negro as Eugene O'Neill saw him. That only. So with "Cane." It cannot be justly criticized because it does not harmonize with your personal conceptions, Mr. Reader!

"Cane" has three main divisions. The first division is laid in the land of cane, cotton and sawdust piles—Georgia. The second part deals with the more sophisticated life of the Negro "world within a world" in Washington. The third section is an intense drama of all the complicated elements of southern life, with its setting also in Georgia.

The writer will be pardoned for expressing his decided preference for the sketches, stories, and poems which comprise part one. Here the matchless beauty of the folk-life of the southern Negro is presented with intriguing charm. It is realism—not of the reportorial type found in "Main Street" writing—but the higher realism of the emotions. Here we have that mysterious, subtle and incomprehensible appeal of the South made all the more interesting because of the discordant and chaotic human elements submerged there. Of course, one is conscious of the protest of those who confuse superficial and transitory political and economic conditions with the underlying eternal elements. Those with an eye for beauty, an ear for music, and a heart for emotion, while abhorring the temporary victimizing of the South by unscrupulous demagogues, must still appreciate the fundamental Beauty which is revealed in "Cane."

The power of portraiture is unmistakable. No effort is made to create ideal characters or to make them conform to any particular standard. Here we have the method of Maran and all great artists. The characters

appear in all of their lovable human qualities. We love them and yet
pity them for human weaknesses for which not they but their ignorance
and environment are largely responsible. It is not a question of morality
but of life.

Toomer appreciates as an artist the surpassing beauty, both physical
and spiritual, of the Negro woman and he has unusual facility of language in describing it. There is "Karintha at twenty, carrying beauty,
perfect as the dusk as the sun goes down." A wayward child of nature
whose tragedy was that "the soul of her was a growing thing ripened too
soon." Of "Carma" it is said, "She does not sing; her body is a song."
I prefer "Fern" to all the other portraits because the author has succeeded
in conveying exquisite physical charm coupled with an almost divine
quality of inarticulate spirituality. Sufficient tribute has never before
been paid to the beauty of the Negro woman's eyes. Visitors from foreign
lands have frequently pointed out this unique glory of our women. Is
it any wonder? For do not their eyes express from mysterious depths the
majesty of lost empires, the pathos of a woman's lot in slavery, and the
spirit of a resurgent race? Fern's eyes. "Face flowed into eyes. Flowed
in soft cream foam and plaintive ripples, in such a way that wherever
your glance may momentarily have rested, it immediately thereafter
wavered in the direction of her eyes. . . . If you have ever heard a Jewish
cantor sing, if he has touched you and made your own sorrow seem
trivial when compared with his, you know my feeling when I followed
the curves of her profile, the mobile rivers, to their common delta."
But her eyes were not of ordinary beauty. "They were strange eyes. In
this, that they sought nothing—that is nothing that was obvious or
tangible or that one could see. . . . Her eyes, unusually weird and open,
held me. Held God. He flowed in as I have seen the countryside."

Mention must also be made of "Blood Burning Moon," a short story
which closes this first section. Its splendid technique and striking theme
are attested by the fact that O'Brien has included it in his collection of
the best short stories of 1923.

A series of impressionistic views of Negro life in Washington, D. C.,
follows in the middle section of "Cane." Again one must be cautioned
that the beauty of the work must be captured thru the senses. Seventh
Street is a "crude boned, soft-skinned wedge of nigger life breathing its
loafer air, jazz songs and love, thrusting unconscious rhythms, black
reddish blood into the white and white-washed wood of Washington."
Thickly scattered thru these pages are unforgettable "purple patches"
which reveal the animate and inanimate life of You Street[2] thru the
sensitive emotional reactions of a poet. It must also be said that the style
is more labored and sometimes puzzling. One feels at times as if the
writer's emotions had out-run his expression. Is it that Mr. Toomer's
highest inspiration is to be found in the folk-life of his beloved Southland
and that his unmistakable distaste for the cramped and strictly conven-

2. "U" Street [*Editor*].

tionalized life of the city Negro restricts his power of clear and forceful language? There is not the same easy rhythmic cadence of expression here as in the first division. There are also a few apparent irrelevancies (for the reader) in the text which add nothing to the total effect and detract from the artistic value of the whole. "Box Seat" which reaches high points of excellence in the portraiture of "Muriel," "Dan," and "Mrs. Pribby," and in its dramatic narrative style, limps at times with obscure writing. The thoughts attributed to "Dan," on page 59, are a case in point and strain the demand of art to the breaking point. The remaining narratives in this division are of great merit but on the whole are not of the same excellence as his chapters of Georgia life.

The drama of "Ralph Kabnis" closes the book and marks a return to Georgia. This is no ordinary drama. It can only be likened to the grimly powerful work of the Russian dramatists. Only Eugene O'Neill in America has written anything to measure up to its colossal conception. One competent critic has stated that only the Moscow Art Theatre could do justice to such a drama. It is to be hoped that a Negro Theatre will immediately arise capable of producing "Kabnis" and other plays sure to follow from Toomer.

"Kabnis" is the fitting climax to a remarkable book. Here are placed upon the stage the outstanding factors in the inner circle of Negro life. The traditional Negro is there—the Negro of the past—mute, blind, motionless, yet a figure of sphinx-like mystery and fascination. There is a type of young Negro, attractive, frivolous, and thoughtless. Then there is Kabnis himself, the talented, highly emotional, educated Negro who goes south to elevate his people but who lacks the strength of mind and character to withstand the pressure of the white South or the temptations within his own group. Finally, there is Lewis. "He is what a stronger Kabnis might have been. . . . His mouth and eyes suggest purpose guided by an adequate intelligence." Yet he does not understand these black people of the South and they do not understand him. In the end he flees from the situation without in any way helping his people who needed his help.

Evidently the author's implication is that there must be a welding into one personality of Kabnis and Lewis: the great emotionalism of the race guided and directed by a great purpose and a super-intelligence.

"Cane" leaves this final message with me. In the South we have a "powerful underground" race with a marvelous emotional power which like Niagara before it was harnessed is wasting itself. Release it into proper channels, direct its course intelligently, and you have possibilities for future achievement that challenge the imagination. The hope of the race is in the great blind forces of the masses properly utilized by capable leaders.

"Dan goes to the wall and places his ear against it. That rumble comes from the earth's core. It is the mutter of powerful and underground races. . . . The next world savior is coming up that way."

ROBERT LITTELL

Cane†

"Reading this book," says Mr. Waldo Frank in his introduction, "I had the vision of a land, heretofore sunk in the mists of muteness, suddenly rising up into the eminence of song. . . . This book *is* the South." Not the South of the chivalrous gentleman, the fair lady, the friendly, decaying mansion, of mammies, cotton and pickaninnies. Nor yet the South of lynchings and hatreds, of the bitter, rebellious young Negro, and of his emigration to the North. Cane does not remotely resemble any of the familiar, superficial views of the South on which we have been brought up. On the contrary, Mr. Toomer's view is unfamiliar and bafflingly subterranean, the vision of a poet far more than the account of things seen by a novelist—lyric, symbolic, oblique, seldom actual.

In many respects Mr. Toomer recalls Waldo Frank. They seem curiously to coincide at their weakest points. Such sentences as these might have been written by either of them: "Dark swaying forms of Negroes are street-songs that woo virginal houses . . . Dan Moore walks southward on Thirteenth Street . . . girl eyes within him widen upward to promised faces . . . Negroes open gates and go indoors, perfectly." Such phrases mean either almost nothing, or a great deal too much. In the case of Mr. Frank they seem to contain, bottled up within them, the very essence of what he wants to say; in the case of Mr. Toomer, they are occasional, accidental, and could be brushed off without damage to the whole. While Mr. Toomer often tries for puzzling and profound effects, he accomplishes fairly well what he sets out to do, and Cane is not seething, like nearly all Mr. Frank's books, with great inexpressible things bursting to be said, and only occasionally arriving, like little bubbles to the surface of a sea of molten tar.

Cane is sharply divided into two parts. The first is a series of sketches, almost poetic in form and feeling, revolving about a character which emerges with very different degrees of clarity. The second half is a longish short story, Kabnis, quite distinct from the sketches, and peculiarly interesting. In this Mr. Toomer shows a genuine gift for character portrayal and dialogue. In the sketches, the poet is uppermost. Many of them begin with three or four lines of verse, and end with the same lines, slightly changed. The construction here is musical, too often a little artificially so. The body of the sketch tends to poetry, and to a pattern which begins to lose its effectiveness as soon as one guesses how it is coming out. The following, which is about a third of one of the sketches, is a fair sample of Mr. Toomer writing at his best:

† From *New Republic* 37 (December 26, 1923): 126.

Her soul is like a little thrust-tailed dog that follows her, whimpering. She is large enough, I know, to find a warm spot for it. But each night when she comes home and closes the big outside storm door, the little dog is left in the vestibule, filled with chills till morning. Some one . . . eoho Jesus . . . soft as a cotton ball brushed against the milk-pod cheek of Christ, will steal in and cover it that it need not shiver, and carry it to her where she sleeps upon clean hay cut in her dreams.

It isn't necessary, to know exactly what this means in order to find pleasure in reading it. Which is one way of defining poetry. And once we begin to regard Mr. Toomer's shorter sketches as poetry, many objections to the obscurer symbolism and obliqueness of them disappear. There remains, however, a strong objection to their staccato beat. The sentences fall like small shot from a high tower. They pass from poetry into prose, and from there into Western Union.

Kabnis, the longest piece in the book, is far the most direct and most living, perhaps because it seems to have grown so much more than been consciously made. There is no pattern in it, and very little effort at poetry. And Mr. Toomer makes his Negroes talk like very real people, almost, in spots, as if he had taken down their words as they came. A strange contrast to the lyric expressionism of the shorter pieces. A real peek into the mind of the South, which, like nearly all such genuinely intimate glimpses, leaves one puzzled, and—fortunately—unable to generalize.

Cane is an interesting, occasionally beautiful and often queer book of exploration into old country and new ways of writing.

W. E. B. Du BOIS

[Sexual Liberation in *Cane*]†

* * * The world of black folk will some day arise and point to Jean Toomer as a writer who first dared to emancipate the colored world from the conventions of sex. It is quite impossible for most Americans to realize how straightlaced and conventional thought is within the Negro World, despite the very unconventional acts of the group. Yet this contradiction is true. And Jean Toomer is the first of our writers to hurl his pen across thè very face of our sex conventionality. In "Cane", one has only to take his women characters *seriatim* to realize this: Here is Karintha, an innocent prostitute; Becky, a fallen white woman; Carma, a tender Amazon of unbridled desire; Fern, an unconscious wanton; Esther, a woman who looks age and bastardy in the face and flees in

† From W. E. B. Du Bois and Alain Locke, "The Younger Literary Movement," *Crisis* 27 (February 1924): 161–63. Reprinted with permission of the Crisis Publishing Co., Inc.

despair; Louise, with a white and black lover; Avey, unfeeling and un-
moral; and Doris, the cheap chorus girl. These are his women, painted
with a frankness that is going to make his black readers shrink and
criticize; and yet they are done with a certain splendid, careless truth.

Toomer does not impress me as one who knows his Georgia but he
does know human beings; and, from the background which he has seen
slightly and heard of all his life through the lips of others, he paints
things that are true, not with Dutch exactness, but rather with an impres-
sionist's sweep of color. He is an artist with words but a conscious artist
who offends often by his apparently undue striving for effect. On the
other hand his powerful book is filled with felicitous phrases—Karintha,
"carrying beauty perfect as the dusk when the sun goes down",—

> "Hair—
> Silver-grey
> Like streams of stars"

Or again, "face flowed into her eyes—flowed in soft creamy foam and
plaintive ripples". His emotion is for the most part entirely objective.
One does not feel that he feels much and yet the fervor of his descriptions
shows that he has felt or knows what feeling is. His art carries much
that is difficult or even impossible to understand. The artist, of course,
has a right deliberately to make his art a puzzle to the interpreter (the
whole world is a puzzle) but on the other hand I am myself unduly
irritated by this sort of thing. I cannot, for the life of me, for instance
see why Toomer could not have made the tragedy of Carma something
that I could understand instead of vaguely guess at; "Box Seat" muddles
me to the last degree and I am not sure that I know what "Kabnis" is
about. All of these essays and stories, even when I do not understand
them, have their strange flashes of power, their numerous messages and
numberless reasons for being. But still for me they are partially spoiled.
Toomer strikes me as a man who has written a powerful book but who
is still watching for the fullness of his strength and for that calm certainty
of his art which will undoubtedly come with years.

* * *

GORHAM B. MUNSON

[Toomer as Artist]†

There can be no question of Jean Toomer's skill as a literary craftsman.
A writer who can combine vowels and liquids to form a cadence like
"she was as innocently lovely as a November cotton flower" has a subtle
command of word-music. And a writer who can break the boundaries
of the sentences, interrupt the placement of a fact with a lyrical cry,

† From "The Significance of Jean Toomer," *Opportunity* 3 (September 1925): 262–63.

and yet hold both his fact and his exclamation to a single welded meaning as in the expression: "A single room held down to earth. . . O fly away to Jesus. . . by a leaning chimney. . .", is assuredly at home in the language and therefore is assuredly free to experiment and invent. Toomer has found his own speech, now swift and clipped for violent narrative action, now languorous and dragging for specific characterizing purposes, and now lean and sinuous for the exposition of ideas, but always cadenced to accord with an unusually sensitive ear.

It is interesting to know that Toomer, before he began to write, thought of becoming a composer. One might have guessed it from the fact that the early sketches in *Cane* (1923) depend fully as much upon a musical unity as upon a literary unity. *Karintha*, for example, opens with a song, presents a theme, breaks into song, develops the theme, sings again, drops back into prose, and dies away in a song. But in it certain narrative functions—one might mention that lying back of the bald statement, "This interest of the male, who wishes to ripen a growing thing too soon, could mean no good to her"—are left undeveloped. Were it not for the songs, the piece could scarcely exist.

But electing to write, Toomer was too canny to try to carry literature further into music than this. *Cane* is, from one point of view, the record of his search for suitable literary forms. We can see him seeking guidance and in several of the stories, notably *Fern* and *Avey*, it is the hand of Sherwood Anderson that he takes hold. But Anderson leads toward formlessness and Toomer shakes him off for Waldo Frank in such pieces as *Theatre* where the design becomes clear and the parts are held in a vital esthetic union. Finally, he breaks through in a free dramatic form of his own, the play *Kabnis* which still awaits production by an American theatre that cries for good native drama and yet lacks the wit to perceive the talent of Toomer.

The form of *Kabnis* is a steep slope downward. In the first scene Ralph Kabnis, a neurotic educated Negro who has returned to Georgia from the North, stands on the top of the slope and delivers a monologue, which reveals his character as that of a frustrated lyricist. In Scene Two he begins to fall in the direction of his weaknesses, in scene three there occurs an opportunity to check his descent, but his momentum carries him straight past it, and in the remaining scenes he lands in a cellar of debauchery. The action of the play then is linear, but what Kabnis falls through is a rich milieu composed of a symbolic ancient Negro who has experienced slavery, an honest craft-loving wheelwright, a bourgeois school supervisor, a clear headed forceful radical black, a couple of prostitutes, a church audience, a minister, and little Carrie K., fresh symbol of a possible future. Toomer's formal achievement is just this: to utilize a milieu and a character, the first as a dense living slope, the second as a swiftly descending point tracing out a line of action upon the first.

It is necessary and important that an artist should be in command of his tools, but if we feel that craftsmanship is only a means to an end, we must proceed to inquire what end Toomer's skill was designed to suit.

Cane is the projection of a vivid personality. What the fundamental motives were that impelled this projection we cannot say, but we can pick out a few probably subsidiary motives that will perhaps indicate Toomer's status at the moment he completed *Cane*. Clearly, he desired to make contact with his hereditary roots in the Southland. One of the poems in *Cane* is an unmistakable recognition of this desire.

> "O land and soil, red soil and sweet-gum tree,
> So scant of grass, so profligate of pines,
> Now just before an epoch's sun declines
> Thy son, in time, I have returned to thee,
> Thy son, I have in time returned to thee."

From this one infers a preceding period of shifting and drifting without settled harborage. Weary of homeless waters, he turns back to the ancestral soil, opens himself to its folk-art and its folk-ways, tries to find his roots, his origins. It is a step toward the definition of himself.

What can we add to this purpose? We can say that Toomer makes a very full response to life, a response that is both robust and sensitive, and we can say, to use the conventional phrase, that he "accepts life." It is plain that he has strong instincts, welling and deep and delicate emotions, and a discriminating and analytical intellect (more fully revealed in his critical work); and these are all keenly aware of life. This life that floods in upon his equipment Toomer finds to be potent and sweet, colorful and singing, interesting and puzzling, pathetic and worthy of respect; he is able to accept it,—perhaps because his survey of it shows it to be beautiful and mysterious. At any rate, the only fully adumbrated attitude in *Cane* is that of the spectatorial artist. But that raises the question, under what circumstances can the artist be a spectator?

* * *

* * * An artist who does not care where the lure and grace that he sheds over the objects led his entranced followers naturally will not inquire very deeply into his purpose for creation. He creates beauty and lets truth and goodness go hang. But an artist who feels that his gifts entail a grave responsibility, who wishes to fight on the side of life abundant rather than for life deficient, must pause and seek the answers to certain questions. What is the function of man? What are the potentials of man and what may he become? What is experience and what is knowledge? What is the world?

The significance of Jean Toomer lies in his strenuous attempt to answer these questions. Shortly after writing *Cane*, he formed two convictions. One was that the modern world is a veritable chaos and the other was that in a disrupted age the first duty of the artist is to unify himself. Having achieved personal wholeness, then perhaps he would possess an attitude that would not be merely a reaction to the circumstances of modernity, merely a reflection of the life about him, but would be an attitude that could act upon modernity, dissolve away the remainder of an old slope of consciousness, and plant the seeds for a new slope.

So he turned to an intensive study of his own psychology. He sifted psycho-analysis for what minute grains of truth it might supply, he underwent the training for "conscious control of the body" prescribed by F. Matthias Alexander, he spent a summer at the Gurdjieff Institute, Fontainebleau, France, where he obtained what he regards as the best method for his quest. We should note that his search is distinguished from that of many other American artists (Sherwood Anderson may be cited as typical) by its positive scientific character. These others work from a disgust or a negation. They cut loose from something they abhor and, unprovided with any method, drift aimlessly in search of a leaven which somewhere, somehow, will heal. Toomer has a method and an aim, and he devotes his whole time and energy to them. In his own words, this is what he is doing: "I am. What I am and what I may become I am trying to find out."

He is a dynamic symbol of what all artists of our time should be doing, if they are to command our trust. He has mastered his craft. Now he seeks a purpose that will convince him that his craft is nobly employed. Obviously, to his search there is no end, but in his search there is bound to occur a fusion of his experience, and it is this fused experience that will give profundity to his later work. His way is not the way of the minor art master, but the way of the major master of art. And that is why his potential literary significance outweighs the actualized literary significance of so many of his contemporaries.

More Recent Criticism

W. EDWARD FARRISON

Jean Toomer's *Cane* Again†

The first edition of Jean Toomer's *Cane* was published by Boni and Liveright in New York in 1923 with a foreword by Waldo Frank. There were a second printing of this edition with Boni and Liveright's imprint in 1927 and a third one in 1967 with the imprint of University Place Press, New York. A paperback edition with an introduction by Arna Bontemps was published by Harper and Row in the same city in 1969. The first two printings, which came early in the Harlem Renaissance, were very small because the demand for the book was very small and continued so for many years. The third printing was occasioned by the current interest in Negro literature, as were the paperback edition and also *The Merrill Studies in Cane* which were compiled by Frank Durham and brought out by Charles E. Merrill Publishing Company of Columbus, Ohio, in 1971. This [University Place] printing seems, however, not to have been generally noticed. Like several others who have recently written about *Cane*, in his research on the work Durham apparently missed seeing this printing. At least his volume just mentioned contains no reference to it.

During the forty-nine years which have passed since its first appearance, *Cane* has repeatedly been a subject of criticism. It has been this not because it has been a popular book, which it has never been, but because it was from the beginning and still is a uniquely interesting work. Its uniqueness consists primarily in the fact that it portrays phases of Negro life in places whence those phases had not previously received authentic, extensive literary treatment. In *Studies in Cane*, Durham brought together and thus made easily available more than twenty representative criticisms of various kinds belonging to the years from 1923 to 1969. "One of the purposes" of his compilation, he said in his preface, "is to bring together the documents which will enable the reader to trace the history of *Cane's* literary reputation" (p. iv).[1] This purpose is indeed commendable, even though some may find its reach beyond the grasp of this small volume. Among the selections in the volume are Frank's foreword (1923), Bontemps' introduction (1969), reviews by Montgomery Gregory (1923), W.E.B. Du Bois (1924), and Robert R. Kerlin,

† From *CLA Journal* 15 (March 1972): 295–302.

1. Page references given thus are to Durham's *Studies in Cane*.

and critical essays by Eugene Holmes (1932), Robert A. Bone, Bontemps (1966), and Durham himself.

In grouping the reviews and essays as he did according to whether their authors were whites or Negroes, Durham fell into what may be considered gross errors, according to who is doing the considering. He included Kerlin among the "Black Reviewers" and Bone among the "Black Critics." Kerlin (1866–1950), whose review Durham quoted from *Opportunity: Journal of Negro Life* for May, 1926, was white; and so is Bone, from whose *The Negro Novel in America* (1958 and 1965) Durham quoted Bone's discussion of Toomer. Anyway it was supererogatory to group the reviews and essays according to the race of their several authors, since the racial identity *per se* of the authors throws little or no light on what they said about Toomer and his book.

Since Durham completed his work, critical comments on *Cane* have continued to appear. The latest one which has come to my attention, and which is an important addition to scholarship on Toomer, is in Darwin T. Turner's *In a Minor Chord*.[2] One of the distinctive features of that work is the amount of biographical information it gives about Toomer—more than has heretofore been readily available.

In his foreword Waldo Frank described *Cane*, perhaps overenthusiastically, as "a harbinger of the South's literary maturity: of its emergence from the obsession put upon its minds by the unending racial crisis," and he further characterized the work as "the harbinger of a literary force of whose incalculable future I believe no reader of this book will be in doubt."

Although Frank's predictions concerning *Cane* can hardly be said to have come true, many have written about the book as if they did. In many of the selections in *Studies in Cane*, notably in the various comments of Montgomery Gregory, Eugene Holmes, and Arna Bontemps, *Cane* is repeatedly said to have influenced greatly the literature written by and about Negroes which has succeeded it. The same thing with some qualifications is said about the book in Durham's preface and in his essay, which is the last one in his compilation. "In 'Cane,' " said Eugene Holmes somewhat ecstatically in 1932, "raving critics and poetasters recognized a naturalism of such a distinctive kind that the applause was deafening," and "It [*Cane*] has also given the necessary influence and impetus to those younger Negro poets who did not know about what to write" (p. 46). In 1966 and again in his introduction 1969, Bontemps said that the reaction to *Cane* of "practically an entire generation of young Negro writers then [in the 1920's] just beginning to emerge" marked the awakening of what came to be called "a Negro Renaissance" (pp. 22 and 78–79). Also in 1966 Bontemps had remarked that "Subsequent writing by Negroes in the United States as well as in the West

2. Carbondale: Southern Illinois University Press, 1971. Chapter 1, "Jean Toomer: Exile." For five other recently published criticisms, see the *CLA Journal*, XIII (September, 1969), 35–50; and XIV (March, 1971), 251–280.

Indies and Africa has continued to reflect its [*Cane's*] mood and often its method, and, one feels, it also has influenced the writing about Negroes by others" (p. 79). In Durham's opinion the influence which *Cane* has had upon Negro writers is the product of Toomer's having learned his craft of writing from such white writers and artists as Sherwood Anderson, Hart Crane, Waldo Frank, and others of their kind (pp. viii–ix).

Interestingly enough it is easier to maximize than to minimize literary influence, and still easier to generalize than to be specific about it. Herein lies the probable reason why the influences by which *Cane* has been said to have been affected and the influence attributed to it have been generally left unexplained as well as overemphasized. Some clarification concerning both of these kinds of influence now seems well in order—in fact overdue.

As to the craft of writing, it is indeed probable that Toomer learned something especially from Anderson and Frank about the effective portrayal of folk life, but it is not improbable that he also learned something about this directly from Edgar Lee Masters' *Spoon River Anthology* (1915). From that work Anderson himself might have learned something about art of portraying what a reviewer of his *Winesburg, Ohio* (1919) called "the inner individual life of a typical American small town." Also, since Frank and Toomer were closely associated while Frank was writing *Holiday* and Toomer was writing *Cane*, they might have influenced each other's writing. Moreover, Toomer, like many other writers, might have learned a great deal independently about writing by constant practice—by trial and error, by studious rewriting.

If Toomer was influenced by Masters, Anderson, Frank, and similar writers, it is at least probable that other Negro writers of his time, like non-Negro writers, were directly influenced by them rather than only indirectly through *Cane*. This probability is strengthened by the fact that *Cane* was never an easily available book until the paperback edition of it was published in 1969.

There seems to be no good reason to believe that *Cane*, which until recently was not widely circulated, could have had the extensive influence which some seem to think it has had. Nor is there any good reason for considering Toomer the father of the Harlem Renaissance, or a pioneering delver into and portrayer of "the soul of the Negro," "the Negro's psyche," "the Negro's spirit," "the race-soul," or "the great emotionalism of the race"—whatever these jargonistic phrases mean. It should be noted, by the way, that in *Cane* Toomer neither philosophized about Negroes nor made any of his characters do so. The Harlem Renaissance evolved from what became known at least as early as 1916 as "The Renaissance of the Negro Race" and also as the "New Negro" movement—long before Toomer's *Cane* or Alain Locke's *The New Negro* (1925) was published. Like other writers, Toomer the writer was as much the creation as the creator of the literary milieu in which he flourished.

Doubtless the Harlem Renaissance helped to make him the writer that he became, and with other writers, probably he in turn helped to some extent, whether great or small, to make some of the writing of his time and afterwards what it became.

Cane has been frequently called a novel, which it certainly is not. It is a collection of thirteen prose sketches, fifteen occasional lyrics interspersed among them, and a closet drama. In addition there are occasional stanzas and fragments of folk verse which serve as headlinks or refrains of the several prose pieces. The subject matter of Cane is the imaginatively treated product of Toomer's actual experiences and observations in Washington, D.C., where he was born and where he made his home until late in the 1920's, in Chicago, where he studied briefly in a school of physical education, and in Sparta, Georgia, where he spent three months as a schoolteacher in the fall of 1921.

The first of the three parts into which the book is divided has its setting in Sempter, a semirural community in northeastern Georgia distinguished by the raising and processing of cane. Hence the title of the book. Sempter, of course, is a fictitious name for Sparta. The six sketches in this part, which are mainly the stories of six different women, reflect various phases of life in the community as Toomer had observed it.

Perhaps the most simply and most effectively written of these sketches, if not all of those in the book, is the one entitled "Fern." Fernie May Rosen, its heroine, who was commonly called Fern, was a "cream-colored solitary girl," whose "face flowed into her eyes," and whose singing reminded one of that of "a Jewish cantor singing with a broken voice." Apparently her singing was more plaintive than beautiful but was still entrancing. Unsophisticated as she was, her personality commanded the interest of all who saw her even casually. Even her naiveté in conversation illustrated by her "yassur or nassur" in reply to whatever was said to her added to the naturalness of her disposition. Hers is a story of a young woman who existed in a narrow zone between hope and frustration.

The first six sketches in the second part of Cane have their setting in Washington early in the 1920's. The scene being incomparably larger and more varied than Sempter, Toomer could not encompass it in such a few sketches as he did the semirural community. What he did was to portray, sometimes effectively and sometimes ineffectively, isolated phases of life in the city.

The most convincing and most interesting of these sketches is "Avey," whose title is the same as the name of its heroine. Like Fern, Avey had sexual experience too early in life and thereafter became indifferent to romantic love. Meanwhile, having been educated and having taught school for a while, she lost her position and eventually degenerated into an "Orphan-woman." Had Avey lived in Sempter, Fern's story might have been Avey's; and had Fern lived in Washington, Avey's story might have been Fern's.

Recently Toomer has been credited with contrasting Washington as the North in the second part of *Cane* with the South in the first part. It is difficult to believe that Toomer would have been naive enough to attempt such a thing, for he certainly knew that Washington in the 1920's was not a part of the North vis-à-vis the South, but was in fact a part of the South. he knew that as far as matters racial were concerned, Washington then had much less in common with New York than with Atlanta, and that Colonel James Crow was as much an habitué of Pennsylvania Avenue as of Peachtree Street. Moreover none of the parts of *Cane* contain anything that suggests such a contrast.

"Bona and Paul," the last sketch in the second part of *Cane*, has its setting in Chicago. More so than any of the preceding sketches, this one is as much a story as a study of characters. It tells of a budding romance between Bona Hale, a Southern white girl, and Paul Johnson, a Southern Negro, who were students in a school of physical education in the city. Before the romance became a full-blown flower, the couple separated because both were too conscious that they were racially different.

The third part of *Cane* is "Kabnis," the closet drama, which, like the first part, has its setting in Sempter. The unifying agent in the drama is Ralph Kabnis, who figures prominently in all six of its scenes. A Northern Negro with a Southern ancestry, Kabnis loses his position as a schoolteacher in Sempter and for no clear reason becomes an apprentice in a local wagon shop, where he becomes a study in frustration. There is a variety of characters of uncertain principles who, along with Kabnis, are involved in much talk and some incidental action, all without very convincing motivation. Because of this fact, although the drama mirrors some phases of the life of the community, it has proved puzzling to many a reader.

Most of the lyrics in the several parts of *Cane* are associationally connected with the locales of the parts. In evidence of ths fact, five of the lyrics in the first part are especially noteworthy. "November Cotton Flower," a sonnet, comments on the ravages of the boll weevil in Georgia during Toomer's sojourn there. "Face" and "Portrait in Georgia," two brief free-verse lyrics, impressionistically yet graphically describe two old women whom Toomer might have seen in Sparta. "Song of the Son," a poem of five stanzas, commemorates the songs which Negroes had learned from their slave forebears and still sang. In its second stanza "thy son" who had returned to Georgia need not be identified as Toomer, but as a persona who had returned there in time to hear these songs before they and their historical significance passed into oblivion. "Georgia Dusk," a slightly longer poem which immediately follows "Song of the Son," also deals with singing by Negroes such as Toomer probably had heard in Sparta. It contemplates the singing of Negro workmen at twilight after their day's work. Incidentally, none of the poems in the second part of the book—the third part contains no original poetry except a folk song—are comparable in thought and lyric qualities with the five just considered.

Cane is an unusually interesting book not only because of its subject matter but also because of the kind of writing it is. A most distinctive feature of the work is its emphasis on the realistic portrayal of characters rather than on action. In some instances, however, the characters are delineated mainly in simple recountings of their actions and their reactions to others and situations, as is true of Fern and Avey. In other instances the method of character revelation employed is a blending of associationism and the stream of consciousness. Both of these literary techniques have long been established. Toomer evinced extraordinary skill in using them notably in the sketches entitled "Esther," "Blood-Burning Moon," "Theater," and "Box Seat," although the last-mentioned sketch leaves the reader somewhat befogged.

Another unusually interesting feature of the work is its gracious plenty of figurative language, much of which is spontaneous and natural and some of which is strained and artificial. All of it serves, nevertheless, to arrest the reader's attention and to keep his interest from flagging, as Toomer presumably intended for it to serve in addition to vivifying and clarifying his ideas. Uniquely interesting work of genius that *Cane* is, it was an auspicious beginning for Toomer's success as a writer of imaginative literature. Unfortunately it also marked the end of that success, for it was his last as well as his first book of creative writing to be published.

ROBERT BONE

[Jean Toomer's *Cane*]†

* * *

In spite of his wide and perhaps primary association with white intellectuals, as an artist Toomer never underestimated the importance of his Negro identity. He attained a universal vision not by ignoring race as a local truth, but by coming face to face with his particular tradition. His pilgrimage to Georgia was a conscious attempt to make contact with his hereditary roots in the Southland. Of Georgia, Toomer wrote: "There one finds soil in the sense that the Russians know it—the soil every art and literature that is to live must be embedded in."[1] This sense of soil is central to *Cane* and to Toomer's artistic vision. "When one is on the soil of one's ancestors," his narrator remarks, "most anything can come to one."

† From *The Negro Novel in America* (1958. New York: Knopf, 1965) 81–88.

1. Quoted in Alain Locke, "Negro Youth Speaks," *The New Negro* (New York, Boni, 1925), p. 51.

What comes to Toomer, in the first section of *Cane,* is a vision of
the parting soul of slavery:

> . . . for though the sun is setting on
> A song-lit race of slaves, it has not set;
> Though late, O soil, it is not too late yet
> To catch thy plaintive soul, leaving, soon gone.

The soul of slavery persists in the "supper-getting-ready songs" of the
black women who live on the Dixie Pike—a road which "has grown
from a goat path in Africa." It persists in "the soft, listless cadence of
Georgia's South," in the hovering spirit of a comforting Jesus, and in
the sudden violence of the Georgia moon. It persists above all in the
people, white and black, who have become Andersonian "grotesques"
by virtue of their slave inheritance. Part I of *Cane* is in fact a kind of
Southern *Winesburg, Ohio.* It consists of the portraits of six women—
all primitives—in which an Andersonian narrator mediates between the
reader and the author's vision of life on the Dixie Pike.

There is Karintha, "she who carries beauty," like a pregnancy, until
her perfect beauty and the impatience of young men beget a fatherless
child. Burying her child in a sawdust pile, she takes her revenge by
becoming a prostitute; "the soul of her was a growing thing ripened too
soon."

In "Becky" Toomer dramatizes the South's conspiracy to ignore mis-
cegenation. Becky is a white woman with two Negro sons. After the
birth of the first, she symbolically disappears from sight into a cabin
constructed by community guilt. After the birth of the second, she is
simply regarded as dead, and no one is surprised when the chimney of
her cabin falls in and buries her. Toward Becky there is no charity from
white or black, but only furtive attempts to conceal her existence.

Carma's tale, "which is the crudest melodrama," hinges not so much
on marital infidelity as on a childish deception. Accused by her husband
of having other men ("No one blames her for that") she becomes hysterical, and running into a canebrake, pretends to shoot herself. "Twice
deceived, and the one deception proved the other." Her husband goes
berserk, slashes a neighbor, and is sent to the chain gang. The tone of
the episode is set by the ironic contrast between Carma's apparent strength
("strong as any man") and her childish behavior.

Fern, whose full name is Fernie May Rosen, combines the suffering
of her Jewish father and her Negro mother: "at first sight of her I felt as
if I heard a Jewish cantor sing. . . . As if his singing rose above the
unheard chorus of a folksong." Unable to find fulfillment, left vacant
by the bestowal of men's bodies, Fern sits listlessly on her porch near
the Dixie Pike. Her eyes desire nothing that man can give her; the
Georgia countryside flows into them, along with something that Toomer's narrator calls God.

"Esther" is a study in sexual repression. The protagonist is a near-white girl whose father is the richest colored man in town. Deprived of normal outlets by her social position, she develops a neurotic life of fantasy which centers upon a virile, black-skinned, itinerant preacher named King Barlo. At sixteen she imagines herself the mother of his immaculately conceived child. At twenty-seven she tries to translate fantasy into reality by offering herself to Barlo. Rebuffed and humiliated, she retreats into lassitude and frigidity.

Louisa, of "Blood-Burning Moon," has two lovers, one white and the other colored. Inflamed by a sexual rivalry deeper than race, they quarrel. One is slashed and the other is lynched. Unlike most Negro writers who have grappled with the subject of lynching, Toomer achieves both form and perspective. He is not primarily concerned with antilynching propaganda, but in capturing a certain atavistic quality in Southern life which defies the restraints of civilized society.

Part II of *Cane* is counterpoint. The scene shifts to Washington, where Seventh Streets thrusts a wedge of vitality, brilliance, and movement into the stale, soggy, whitewashed wood of the city. This contrast is an aspect of Toomer's primitivism. The blacks, in his color scheme, represent a full life; the whites, a denial of it. Washington's Negroes have preserved their vitality because of their roots in the rural South, yet whiteness presses in on them from all sides. The "dickty" Negro, and especially the near-white, who are most nearly assimilated to white civilization, bear the brunt of repression and denial, vacillating constantly between two identities. Out of this general frame of reference grow the central symbols of the novel.

Toomer's symbols reflect the profound humanism which forms the base of his philosophical position. Man's essential goodness, he would contend, his sense of brotherhood, and his creative instincts have been crushed and buried by modern industrial society. Toomer's positive values, therefore, are associated with the soil, the cane, and the harvest; with Christian charity, and with giving oneself in love. On the other side of the equation is a series of burial or confinement symbols (houses, alleys, machines, theaters, nightclubs, newspapers) which limit man's growth and act as barriers to his soul. Words are useless in piercing this barrier; Toomer's intellectualizing males are tragic figures because they value talking above feeling. Songs, dreams, dancing, and love itself (being instinctive in nature) may afford access to "the simple beauty of another's soul." The eyes, in particular, are avenues through which we can discover "the truth that people bury in their hearts."

In the second section of *Cane*, Toomer weaves these symbols into a magnificent design, so that his meaning, elusive in any particular episode, emerges with great impact from the whole. "Rhobert" is an attack on the crucial bourgeois value of home ownership: "Rhobert wears a house, like a monstrous diver's helmet, on his head." Like Thoreau's farmer, who traveled through life pushing a barn and a hundred acre before him, Rhobert is a victim of his own property instinct. As he struggles with the weight of the house, he sinks deeper into the mud:

> Brother, Rhobert is sinking
> Let's open our throats, brother
> Let's sing Deep River when he goes down.

The basic metaphor in "Avey" compares a young girl to the trees planted in boxes along V Street, "the young trees that whinnied like colts impatient to be free." Avey's family wants her to become a school teacher, but her bovine nature causes her to prefer a somewhat older profession. Yet, ironically, it is not she but the narrator who is a failure, who is utterly inadequate in the face of Avey's womanhood.

In "Theatre" Toomer develops his "dickty" theme, through an incident involving a chorus girl and a theater-manager's brother. As John watches a rehearsal, he is impressed by Dorris' spontaneity, in contrast to the contrived movements of the other girls. He momentarily contemplates an affair, but reservations born of social distance prevent him from consummating his desire, except in a dream. Dorris, who hopes fleetingly for home and children from such a man, is left at the end of the episode with only the sordid reality of the theater.

"Calling Jesus" plays a more important role than its length would indicate in unifying the symbolism of the novel. It concerns a woman, urbanized and spiritually intimidated, whose "soul is like a little thrust-tailed dog that follows her, whimpering." At night, when she goes to sleep in her big house, the little dog is left to shiver in the vestibule. "Some one . . . eoho Jesus . . . soft as the bare feet of Christ moving across bales of Southern cotton, will steal in and cover it that it need not shiver, and carry it to her where she sleeps, cradled in dream-fluted cane."

In "Box Seat" Toomer comes closest to realizing his central theme. The episode opens with an invocation: "Houses are shy girls whose eyes shine reticently upon the dusk body of the street. Upon the gleaming limbs and asphalt torso of a dreaming nigger. Shake your curled wool-blossoms, nigger. Open your liver-lips to the lean white spring. Stir the root-life of a withered people. Call them from their houses and teach them to dream."

The thought is that of a young man, whose symbolic role is developed at once: "I am Dan Moore. I was born in a canefield. The hands of Jesus touched me. I am come to a sick world to heal it." Dan, moreover, comes as a representative of "powerful underground races": "The next world-savior is coming up that way. Coming up. A continent sinks down. The new-world Christ will need consummate skill to walk upon the waters where huge bubbles burst." The redemption motif is echoed in Dan's communion with the old slave: "I asked him if he knew what that rumbling is that comes up from the ground." It is picked up again through the portly Negro woman who sits beside Dan in the theater: "A soil-soaked fragrance comes from her. Through the cement floor her strong roots sink down . . . and disappear in blood-lines that waver south."

The feminine lead is played by Muriel, a school teacher inclined toward conventionality. Her landlady, Mrs. Pribby, is constantly with her, being in essence a projection of Muriel's social fears. The box seat which she occupies at the theater, where her every movement is under observation, renders her relationship to society perfectly. Her values are revealed in her query to Dan, "Why don't you get a good job and settle down?" On these terms only can she love him; meanwhile she avoids his company by going to a vaudeville performance with a girl friend.

Dan, a slave to "her still unconquered animalism," follows and watches her from the audience. The main attraction consists of a prize fight between two dwarfs for the "heavy-weight championship"; it symbolizes the ultimate degradation of which a false and shoddy culture is capable. Sparring grotesquely, pounding and bruising each other, the dwarfs suggest the traditional clown symbol of modern art. At the climax of the episode the winner presents a blood-spattered rose to Muriel, who recoils, hesitates, and finally submits. The dwarf's eyes are pleading: "Do not shrink. Do not be afraid of me." Overcome with disgust for Muriel's hypocrisy, Dan completes the dwarf's thought from the audience, rising to shout: "JESUS WAS ONCE A LEPER!" Rushing from the theater, he is free at last of his love for Muriel—free, but at the same time sterile: "He is as cool as a green stem that has just shed its flower."

Coming as an anticlimax after "Box Seat," "Bona and Paul" describes an abortive love affair between two Southern students at the University of Chicago—a white girl and a mulatto boy who is "passing." The main tension, reminiscent of Gertrude Stein's *Melanctha*, is between knowing and loving, set in the framework of Paul's double identity. It is not his race consciousness which terminates the relationship, as one critic has suggested, but precisely his "whiteness," his desire for knowledge, his philosophical bent. If he had been able to assert his Negro self—that which attracted Bona to him in the first place—he might have held her love.

In "Kabnis" rural Georgia once more provides a setting. This is the long episode which comprises the concluding section of *Cane*. By now the symbolic values of Toomer's main characters can be readily assessed. Ralph Kabnis, the protagonist, is a school teacher from the North who cringes in the face of his tradition. A spiritual coward, he cannot contain "the pain and beauty of the South"; cannot embrace the suffering of the past, symbolized by slavery; cannot come to terms with his own bastardy; cannot master his pathological fear of being lynched. Consumed with self-hatred and cut off from any organic connection with the past, he resembles nothing so much as a scarecrow: "Kabnis, a promise of soil-soaked beauty; uprooted, thinning out. Suspended a few feet above the soil whose touch would resurrect him."

Lewis, by way of contrast, is a Christ figure, an extension of Dan Moore. Almost a T. S. Eliot creation ("I'm on a sort of contract with myself"), his function is to shock others into moral awareness. It is Lewis who confronts Kabnis with his moral cowardice: "Can't hold them, can you? Master; slave. Soil; and the overarching heavens. Dusk; dawn. They fight and bastardize you. The sun tint of your cheeks, flame of the great season's multicolored leaves, tarnished, burned. Split, shredded, easily burned.

Halsey, unlike Kabnis, has not been crushed by Southern life, but absorbed into it. Nevertheless, his spiritual degradation is equally thorough. An artisan and small shopkeeper like his father before him, he "belongs" in a sense that Kabnis does not. Yet in order to maintain his place in the community, he must submit to the indignities of Negro life in the South. Like Booker T. Washington, whose point of view he represents, Halsey has settled for something less than manhood. Restless, groping tentatively toward Lewis, he escapes from himself through his craft, and through an occasional debauch with the town prostitute, whom he loved as a youth.

Father John, the old man who lives beneath Halsey's shop, represents a link with the Negro's ancestral past. Concealed by the present generation as an unpleasant memory, the old man is thrust into a cellar which resembles the hold of a slave ship. There he sits, "A mute John the Baptist of a new religion, or a tongue-tied shadow of an old." When he finally speaks, it is to rebuke the white folks for the sin of slavery. The contrast between Lewis and Kabnis is sharpened by their respective reactions to Father John. Through the old slave, Lewis is able to "merge with his source," but Kabnis can only deny: "An' besides, he aint my past. My ancestors were Southern blue-bloods."

In terms of its dramatic movement "Kabnis" is a steep slope downward, approximating the progressive deterioration of the protagonist. Early in the episode Kabnis is reduced to a scarecrow replica of himself by his irrational fears. His failure to stand up to Hanby, an authoritarian school principal, marks a decisive loss in his power of self-direction. Gradually he slips into a childlike dependence, first on Halsey, then on the two prostitutes, and finally on Halsey's little sister, Carrie Kate. In the course of the drunken debauch with which the novel ends, Kabnis becomes a clown, without dignity or manhood, wallowing in the mire of his own self-hatred. The stark tragedy of "Kabnis" is relieved only by the figure of Carrie Kate, the unspoiled child of a new generation, who may yet be redeemed through her ties with Father John.

* * *

ARNA BONTEMPS

[Commentary on Jean Toomer and *Cane*]†

* * *

"In Jean Toomer, the author of *Cane*," [W. S.] Braithwaite wrote in
1925, "we come upon the very first artist of the race, who with all an
artist's passion and sympathy for life, its hurts, its sympathies, its desires,
its joys, its defeats and strange yearnings, can write about the Negro
without the surrender or compromise of the artist's vision. So objective
is it, that we feel that it is a mere accident that birth or association has
thrown him into contact with the life he has written about. He would
write just as well, just as poignantly, just as transmutingly, about the
peasants of Russia, or the peasants of Ireland, had experience brought
him in touch with their existence. *Cane* is a book of gold and bronze,
of dusk and flame, of ecstasy and pain, and Jean Toomer is a bright
morning star of a new day of the race in literature."

Cane was published in 1923 after portions of it had first appeared in
*Broom, The Crisis, Double Dealer, Liberator, Little Review, Modern
Review, Nomad, Prairie and S 4 N*. But *Cane* and Jean Toomer, its
gifted author, presented an enigma—an enigma which has, if anything,
deepened in the forty-three years since its publication. Given such a
problem, perhaps one may be excused for not wishing to separate the
man from his work. Indeed, so separated, Toomer's writing could scarcely
be understood at all, and its significance would escape us now as it has
escaped so many others in the past.

In any case, *Who's Who in Colored America* listed Toomer in 1927
and gave the following vita:

> b. Dec. 26, 1984, Washington, D. C.; s. Nathan and Nina (Pinch-
> back) Toomer; educ. Public Scho., Washington, D. C.; Dunbar,
> High Scho.; Univ. of Wisconsin, 1914–15; taught schools, Sparta,
> Ga., for four months, traveled, worked numerous occupations; auth.
> *Cane*, pub. Boni and Liveright, 1923; Short Stories and Literary
> Criticisms in various magazines; address, c/o Civic Club, 439 W.
> 23rd St., New York, N. Y.

Needless to say, no subsequent listing of Toomer is to be found in
this or any other directory of conspicuous Negro Americans. Judging by
the above, however, Toomer had always been elusive, and the interest
that *Cane* awakened did nothing to change this. Several years later
Toomer faded completely into white obscurity leaving behind a literary

---

† From "The Negro Renaissance: Jean Toomer and the Harlem of the 1920's," *Anger and Beyond: The
Negro Writer in the United States,* ed. Herbert Hill (New York: Harper and Row, 1966) 22–32.

mystery almost as intriguing as the disappearance of Ambrose Bierce into Mexico in 1913.

Why did he do it? What did it mean?

Concerned with writing, as we are, we automatically turn to Toomer's book for clues. This could be difficult, because copies are scarce. *Cane's* two printings were small, and the few people who went quietly mad about the strange book were evidently unable to do much toward enlarging its audience. But among these few was practically the whole generation of young Negro writers then just beginning to appear, and their reaction to Toomer's *Cane* marked an awakening that soon thereafter began to be called a Negro renaissance.

Cane's influence was not limited to the happy band that included Langston Hughes, Countee Cullen, Eric Walrond, Zora Neale Hurston, Wallace Thurman, Rudolph Fisher and their contemporaries of the Twenties. Subsequent writing by Negroes in the United States as well as in the West Indies and Africa has continued to reflect its mood and often its method, and, one feels, it also has influenced the writing about Negroes by others. And certainly no earlier volume of poetry or fiction or both had come close to expressing the ethos of the Negro in the Southern setting as *Cane* did.

There are many odd and provocative things about *Cane,* and not the least is its form. Reviewers who read it in 1923 were generally stumped. Poetry and prose were whipped together in a kind of frappé. Realism was mixed with what they called mysticism, and the result seemed to many of them confusing. Still, one of them could conclude that "*Cane* is an interesting, occasionally beautiful and often queer book of exploration into old country and new ways of writing." Another noted, "Toomer has not interviewed the Negro, has not asked opinions about him, has not drawn conclusions about him from his reactions to outside stimuli, but has made the much more searching, and much more self-forgetting effort of seeing life with him, through him."

Such comment was cautious, however, compared to the trumpetings of Waldo Frank in the Foreword he contributed:

> A poet has arisen among our American youth who has known how to turn the essence and materials of his Southland into the essences and materials of literature. A poet has arisen in that land who writes, not as a Southerner, not as a rebel against Southerners, not as a Negro, not as apologist or priest or critic: who writes as a *poet.* The fashioning of beauty is ever foremost in his inspiration: not forcedly but simply, and because these ultimate aspects of his world are to him more real than all its specific problems. He has made songs and lovely stories of his land. . . .
>
> The gifted Negro has been too often thwarted from becoming a poet because his world was forever forcing him to recollect that he was a Negro. The artist must lose such lesser identities in the great well of life. . . . The whole will and mind of the creator must go

below the surfaces of race. And this has been an almost impossible condition for the American Negro to achieve, forced every moment of his life into a specific and superficial plane of consciousness. . . .

It seems to me, therefore, that this is a first book in more ways than one. It is a harbinger of the South's literary maturity: of its emergence from the obsession put upon its minds by the unending racial crisis. . . . It marks the dawn of direct and unafraid creation. And, as the initial work of a man of twenty-seven, it is the harbinger of a literary force of whose incalculable future I believe no reader of this book will doubt.

It is well to keep in mind the time of these remarks. Of the novels by which T. S. Stribling is remembered, only *Birthright* had been published. Julia Peterkin had not yet published a book. DuBose Heyward's *Porgy* was still two years away. William Faulkner's first novel was three years away. His Mississippi novels were six or more years in the future. Robert Penn Warren, a student at Vanderbilt University, was just beginning his association with the Fugitive poets. His first novel was still more than a decade and a half ahead. Tennessee Williams was just nine years old.

A chronology of Negro writers is equally revealing. James Weldon Johnson had written lyrics for popular songs, some of them minstrel style, and a sort of documentary novel obscurely published under a pseudonym, but *God's Trombones* was a good four years in the offing. Countee Cullen's *Color* was two and Langston Hughes' *The Weary Blues* three years away, though both of these poets had become known to readers of the Negro magazine *Crisis* while still in their teens, and Hughes at twenty-one, the year of *Cane's* publication, could already be called a favorite.

The first fiction of the Negro Renaissance required apologies. It was not first-rate. But it was an anticipation of what was to come later. Even so, it followed *Cane* by a year or two, and Eric Walrond's *Tropic Death* did not come for three. Zora Neale Hurston's first novel was published in 1931[1], eight years after *Cane*. Richard Wright made his bow with *Uncle Tom's Children* in 1938, fifteen years later. *Invisible Man* by Ralph Ellison followed Toomer's *Cane* by just thirty years. James Baldwin was not born when Toomer began to publish.

Waldo Frank's use of "harbinger" as the word for *Cane* becomes both significant and ironic when we recognize the debt most of these individuals owe Toomer. Consciously or unconsciously, one after another they picked up his cue and began making the "more searching" effort to see life *with* the Negro, "through him." *Cane* heralded an awakening of artistic expression by Negroes that brought to light in less than a decade a surprising array of talents, and these in turn made way for others. An equally significant change in the writing about Negroes par-

---

1. Actually 1934 [*Editor*].

alleled this awakening. Strangely, however, *Cane* was not at all the
harbinger Frank seemed to imagine. Despite his promise—a promise
which must impress anyone who puts this first book beside the early
writings of either Faulkner or Hemingway, Toomer's contemporaries—
Jean Toomer rejected his prospects and turned his back on greatness.

The book by which we remember this writer is as hard to classify as
its author. At first glance it appears to consist of assorted sketches, stories
and a novelette interspersed with poems. Some of the prose is poetic,
and often Toomer slips from one form into the other almost impercep-
tibly. The novelette is constructed like a play.

His characters, always evoked with effortless strength, are as recog-
nizable as they are unexpected in the fiction of that period. Fern is a
"creamy brown" beauty so complicated men take her "but get no joy
from it." Becky is a white outcast beside a Georgia road who bears two
Negro children. Layman, a preacher-teacher in the same area, "knows
more than would be good for anyone other than a silent man." The
name character in the novelette *Kabnis* is a languishing idealist finally
redeemed from cynicism and dissipation by the discovery of underlying
strength in his people.

It doesn't take long to discover that *Cane* is not without design, however. A world of black peasantry in Georgia appears in the first section.
The scene changes to the Negro community of Washington, D.C., in
the second. Rural Georgia comes up again in the third. Changes in the
concerns of Toomer's folk are noted as the setting moves from the
Georgia pike to the bustling Negro section in the nation's capital. The
change in the level of awareness that the author discloses is more subtle,
but it is clearly discernible when he returns to the Georgia background.

A young poet-observer moves through the book. Drugged by beauty
"perfect as dusk when the sun goes down," lifted and swayed by folk
song, arrested by eyes that "desired nothing that *you* could give," silenced
by "corn leaves swaying, rusty with talk," he recognized that "the Dixie
Pike has grown from a goat path in Africa." A native richness is here,
he concluded, and the poet embraces it with the passion of love.

This was the sensual power most critics noticed and most readers
remembered about *Cane*. It was the basis for Alfred Kreymborg's remark
in *Our Singing Strength* that "Jean Toomer is *one* of the finest artists
among the dark people, if not *the* finest." The reviewer for the New
York *Herald Tribune* had the rich imagery of *Cane* in mind when he
said, "Here are the high brown and black and half-caste colored folk of
the cane fields, the gin hovel and the brothel realized with a sure touch
of artistry." But there remained much in the book that he could not
understand or appreciate. Speaking of Toomer's "sometimes rather strident reactions to the Negro," he added that "at moments his outbursts
of emotion approach the inarticulately maudlin," though he had to
admit that *Cane* represented "a distinct achievement wholly unlike anything of this sort done before."

Others found "obscurity" and "mysticism" in the novelette which comprises the last third of the book. This is not surprising, for in Toomer's expressed creed "A symbol is as useful to the spirit as a tool is to the hand," and his fiction is full of them. Add to puzzling symbols an itch to find "new ways of writing" that led him to bold experimentation and one may begin to see why Toomer baffled as he pleased readers interested in writing by or about Negroes in the early Twenties.

Kreymborg spoke of Toomer as "a philosopher and a psychologist by temperament" and went on to say that "the Washington writer is now fascinated by the larger, rather than the parochial interest of the human race, and should some day compose a book in the grand manner."

Of course, Toomer didn't, or at least he has not published one up to now, and to this extent Kreymborg has failed as a prophet, but his reference to Toomer as philosopher and psychologist was certainly on the mark, and his rather large estimate of this writer's capacities was significant, considering its date. The "new criticism," as we have come to recognize it, had scarcely been heard from then, and apparently it has still not discovered Toomer, but the chances are it may yet find him challenging. He would have comforted them, I am almost sorry to say, incarnating, as he does, some of their favorite attitudes. But at the same time, he could have served as a healthy corrective for others. Whether or not he would prove less complex or less rewarding than Gertrude Stein or James Joyce, for example, remains to be determined.

Saunders Redding gave *Cane* a close reading fifteen years after its publication and saw it as an unfinished experiment, "the conclusion to which we are fearful of never knowing, for since 1923 Toomer has published practically nothing." He meant, one assumes, that Toomer had published little poetry or fiction, or anything else that seemed closely related to *Cane* or to *Cane*'s author. Toomer had published provocative articles here and there as well as a small book of definitions and aphorisms during that time, and since then he has allowed two of his lectures to be published semi-privately. But Redding must be included in the small group who recognized a problem in *Cane* that has yet to be explained.

To him Toomer was a young writer "fresh from the South," who found a paramount importance in establishing "racial kinship" with Negroes in order to treat them artistically. He was impressed by Toomer's "unashamed and unrestrained" love for the race and for the soil and setting that nourished it. He saw a relationship between the writer's "hot, colorful, primitive" moods and the "naïve hysteria of the spirituals," which he held in contrast to "the sophistic savagery of jazz and the blues." *Cane*, he concluded, "was a lesson in emotional release and freedom."

Chapters about Toomer were included in Paul Rosenfeld's *Men Seen* in 1925 and in Gorham B. Munson's *Destinations* in 1928, and elsewhere there are indications that Toomer continued to write and to experiment for at least a decade after the publication of *Cane*. Long stories by him appeared in the second and third volumes of the *American Caravan.* A thoughtful essay on "Race Problems and Modern Society" became part of a volume devoted to *Problems of Civilization* in Baker Brownell's series on "Man and His World." Seven years later, in the *New Caravan* of 1936, Toomer presented similar ideas in the long poem "Blue Meridian." Meanwhile, contributing a chapter to the book *America & Alfred Stieglitz* in 1934, Toomer was explicit about his own writing as well as several other matters.

The rumor that Toomer had crossed the color line began circulating when his name stopped appearing in print. But a reasonable effort to find out what it was Toomer was trying to say to us subsequently makes it hard to accept "passing" as the skeleton key to the Jean Toomer mystery. He seemed too concerned with truth to masquerade. One wants to believe that Toomer's mind came at last to reject the myth of race as it is fostered in our culture. A man of fair complexion, indistinguishable from the majority of white Americans, he had always had a free choice as to where he would take his place in a color-caste scheme. Having wandered extensively and worked at odd jobs in a variety of cities before he began contributing to little magazines, as he has stated, he could scarcely have escaped being taken at face value by strangers who had no way of knowing that the youth, who looked like Hollywood's conception of an Ivy League basketball star, but who spoke so beautifully, whose very presence was such an influence upon them, was not only a product of the Negro community but a grandson of the man whom the *Dictionary of American Biography* describes as "the typical Negro politician of the Reconstruction."

Men of this kind, such as Walter White of the NAACP or Adam Clayton Powell of the U.S. Congress, sometimes called voluntary Negroes when they elect to remain in the fold, so to speak, have in other circumstances been discovered in strange places in our society—in neofascist organizations in the United States, among big city bosses, on movie screens, in the student body at "Ole Miss"—but seldom if ever before in an organization working "for understanding between people." Yet Jean Toomer's first publication, following the rumors and the silence, was "An Interpretation of Friends Worship," published by the Committee on Religious Education of Friends General Conference, 1515 Cherry Street, Philadelphia, 1947. It was followed two years later by a pamphlet, "The Flavor of Man." The writing is eloquent with commitment. It reflects unhurried reading and contemplation, as was also true of his piece on "Race Problems and Modern Society." Toomer did not fail to remind his readers that certain racial attitudes could not be condoned. He certainly did not speak as a Negro bent on escaping secretly into white society. Jean Toomer, who, like his high-spirited grandfather, had exuberantly published his pride in his Negro heritage, appears to have reached a point in his thinking at which categories in this kind tend to clutter rather than classify. The stand he appears to have taken at first involved nothing more clandestine than the closing of a book or the changing of a subject.

Yet he is on record as having denied later that he was a Negro. That is a story in itself. Nevertheless, at that point, it seems, Jean Toomer stepped out of American letters. Despite the richness of his thought, his gift of expression, he ceased to be a writer and, as I have suggested, turned his back on greatness. His choice, whatever else may be said about it, reflects the human sacrifices in the field of the arts exacted by the racial myth on which so much writing in the United States is based. While he may have escaped its strictures and inconveniences in his personal life, he did not get away from the racial problem in any real sense. His dilemmas and frustrations as a writer are equally the dilemmas and frustrations of the Negro writers who have since emerged. The fact that most of them have not been provided with his invisible cloak makes little difference. He is their representative man. He stands as their prototype.

* * *

B. F. McKEEVER

Cane as Blues†

A pregnant excerpt from Jean Toomer's classic contains this image:

> Oracular
> Redolent of fermenting syrup
> Purple of the dusk
> Deep-rooted cane

To be oracular is to be prophetic, for an oracle is not simply a messenger but a harbinger. The oracle vouchsafes a prediction which is not merely a forecast but a talisman, a way of dealing with the fate foreseen. Cane is oracular, documenting as it does a Southern milieu, naming a certain malaise; but proffering only the alembic of the Experience coupled with the vision of the artist.

Cane is "redolent," indeed, resplendent with the imagery of Georgia, and with the burden of human history that this spiritual/physical region lives.

Georgia is the "blood-burning moon" rising to illuminate "the Dixie Pike (which) has grown from a goat path in Africa." Georgia is also:

> . . . A feast of moon and men and barking hounds,
> An orgy for some genius of the South
> With blood-hot eyes and cane-lipped scented mouth,
> Surprised in making folk-song from soul sounds.

† From Negro American Literature Forum 4 (July 1970): 61–64. Copyright 1970 by B. F. McKeever and Negro American Literature Forum.

And Georgia is the blues, ". . . An everlasting song, a singing tree, / Caroling softly souls of slavery . . ."

The blues is not a state of chronic melancholia but a mood ebony for a condition which can only be described as chaos. This mood, this attitude of mind, signifies man's attempt in the words of Ralph Ellison, "to endow his life's incidents with communicable significance."

Toomer appears to be replete with questions and bereft of answers about the history and destiny of Black humanity. However, the reader is surfeited with symbols which upon examination yield a tacit certainty which is Life—life in all its comedy and tragedy, human and pathos, soul and blues.

For comedy is said to be life viewed at a distance, while tragedy is life seen close at hand; life is supposed to be comedy to the man who thinks, and tragedy to the man who feels. *Cane* is a vision of Life. But Toomer's black exposure gives him a different perspective. For Toomer's *Cane* is the blues.

Ellison explains in *Shadow & Act* that "the blues is an impulse to keep the painful details and episodes of a brutal experience alive in one's aching consciousness, to finger its jagged grain and transcend it, not by the consolation of philosophy but by squeezing from it a near-tragic, near-comic lyricism" (p. 90).

What Ellison says about the blues is an appropriate description of *Cane*, "an autobiographical chronicle of personal catastrophe expressed lyrically." *Cane* is not the autobiography of a man, but rather the chronicle of the fate of an idea, "an idea whose time has come."

Cane is autobiographical because it represents the apotheosis of one man's attempt to bear witness to the reality and the power of an idea. The idea that the Negro is not an apprentice to equality but a journeyman in suffering. The idea that the choice is always and everywhere between freedom and death.

Cane is the oracle of this idea offered in blues. It contains the blues of Karintha, a madonna bereft of a child who engages then imprisons "this interest of the male, who wishes to ripen a growing thing too soon"; the blues of Avey, the "orphan-woman" whose "emotions had overflowed into paths that dissipated them"; the blues of Becky, the outcast white woman who had two Negro sons, and died in a "solitude crowded with loneliness"; and the blues of Carma, a beloved infidel whose primal strength and passion drove her husband to murder and then to the chaingang.

Cane describes the blues of Fern, a veritable black Medusa—one look into whose eyes turned men into slaves who could never fill the loveless void that was her life; and also the blues of Esther, the virgin aged-in-youth whose infatuation for a picaresque/quixotic King Barlo rests upon her like an incubus until his return when she realizes that he can only offer her cheap desire and ersatz satisfaction.

Perhaps the most telltale blues is that of Kabnis, the protagonist in the novella written like a play that climaxes *Cane*. "Kabnis" rehearses the fate of a "dreamed deferred," an inanimate idea held by a weakling idealist, trapped in Hamletesque stasis.

"Kabnis" is the portrait of the artist as a northern Negro teaching school in Georgia. Here is the black artist as educator who can only intellectualize his blues. For example, Kabnis describes his alienation in the South in terms of "loneliness, dumbness, awful, intangible oppression"; and he feels himself to be "an atom of dust in agony on a hillside."

The blues refrain, "sometimes I feel like a motherless child," is reiterated by his calling himself "Earth's child," "Bastardy . . . me"; and by his designating God as "a profligate red-nosed man about town." Kabnis exclaims, "A bastard son has got a right to curse his maker. God." Nevertheless, on the debris of his despair, Kabnis must build phoenix-like his character.

"Through Ramsay (a prototype of the Southern white) the whole white South weighs down upon him." And Kabnis is "burdened with an impotent pain."

Lewis, a prototype of the artist as leader, organizer, activist, who is a colleague of Kabnis, is "a tall wiry copper-colored man, thirty perhaps. His mouth and eyes suggest purpose guided by an adequate intelligence. He is what a stronger Kabnis might have been, and in an odd faint way resembles him."

During a conversation, Lewis turns his eyes to Kabnis:

In the instant of their shifting, a vision of the life they are to meet. Kabnis, a promise of a soil-soaked beauty; uprooted, thinning out. Suspended a few feet above the soil whose touch would resurrect him. Arm's length removed from him whose will to help. . . . There is a swift intuitive interchange of consciousness. Kabnis has a sudden need to rush into the arms of this man. His eyes call, "Brother." And then a savage, cynical twistabout within him mocks his impulse and strengthens him to repulse Lewis.

Kabnis cannot embrace Lewis and, thereby, accept himself. He knows intimately, inescapably what the Black Experience has been; but this knowledge had merely driven him to cynicism and dissipation.

Lewis declares later, "Life has already told him [Kabnis] more than he is capable of knowing. It has given him in excess of what he can receive. I have been offered. Stuff in his stomach curdled, and he vomited me."

Nevertheless, the link between Kabnis and Lewis is represented in the person of Father John, "gray-bearded, gray-haired, prophetic, immobile"; Father John is a blind, deaf black man in the twilight of life. Lewis originally calls John "father," but he is the spiritual and metaphorical father of Kabnis as well. In the dirt basement of an artisan's workshop which is his corner of the world, Father John appears as a "Black Vulcan, a mute John the Baptist of a new religion—or a tongue-tied shadow of an old."

However, Kabnis rejects and denies the old man, insisting that "he aint my past. My ancestors were Southern blue-bloods—" Then he admits, "Aint much difference between black and blue," which is a virtual equation of blackness with the blues.

Lewis supplies the climatic indictment of Kabnis by saying to him:

> . . . Cant hold them, can you? Master; slave. Soil; and the overarching heavens. Dusk; dawn. They fight and bastardize you. The sun tint of your cheeks, flame of the great season's multi-colored leaves, tarnished, burned. Split, shredded: easily burned. No use. . . .

Thus Lewis delivers surrealistically a cryptic commentary on the South's "peculiar institution."

Kabnis confesses in his own defense:

> . . . I've been shapin words after a design that branded here. Know whats here? M soul. Ever heard o that? Th hell y have. Been shapin words t fit m soul. Never told y that before, did I? Thought I couldnt talk. I'll tell y. I've been shapin words; ah, but sometimes theyre beautiful an golden an have a taste that makes them t roll over with y tongue. . . .

> Cant keep a good man down. Those words I was tellin y about, they wont fit int th mold thats branded on m soul. Rhyme, y see? Poet, too. Bad rhyme. Bad poet. Somethin else youve learned tonight. Lewis dont know it all, an I'm atellin y. Ugh. Th form thats burned int my soul is some twisted awful thing that crept in from a dream, a godam nightmare, an wont stay still unless I feed it. An it lives on words. Not beautiful words. God Almighty no. Misshapen, split-gut, tortured, twisted words. . . White folks feed it cause their looks are words. Niggers, black niggers feed it cause theyre evil an their looks are words. Yallar niggers feed it. This whole damn bloated purple country feeds it cause its goin down t hell in a holy avalanche of words. I want to feed th soul—I know what that is; th preachers dont—but I've got to feed it. . . .

He explains, "Mind me, th only sin is whats done against th soul. Th whole world is a conspiracy t sin, especially in America, an against me. I'm th victim of their sin. I'm what sin is." Here we have poignantly presented the datum of the Black Experience: the consciousness of having been more sinned against than sinner.

Kabnis is born into the midst of an oppressed and persecuted people. He is one of them—a part of them and apart from them. He knows the unique experience of being the rejected and despised of men: sometimes one feels like a "motherless child" and other times like a "manchild in the promised land" on the eve of the death of God, when only one's enemies have received the uncovenanted revelation of God's demise.

Thus it is difficult to "sing the Lord's song in a strange land." But he must decide to be or not to be a man. Consequently, Kabnis recognizes that "a soul like mine cant pin itself onto a wagon wheel an satisfy itself in spinnin round."

For he knows and he feels that a man's life is not supposed to be a chronicle of personal catastrophe but rather a celebration: perhaps a poem, a song, a dance, a bacchanalia, a saturnalia, a romantic interlude before the final elegy. However, the difference between the possibility of black life and the reality of black life is the blues. Yet the blues idiom itself celebrates Life; it celebrates the will to endure and the necessity of survival, to "keep on keepin on."

Kabnis does not realize the possibility of saving himself and the opportunity of redeeming his ideal until the Sphinx-like Father John vouchsafes that "the white folks sinned when they made the Bible lie," which is to say that "things are not what they seem."

Perhaps black folks are not the prodigal descendants of Cain; maybe they represent the personae of the "eternal Adam in the new world garden," the only true sons of God. For black folks are the only people, at this time, in this place, who have paid their dues in blues.

JOHN M. REILLY

The Search for Black Redemption: Jean Toomer's Cane†

The migration of southern black people to Northern cities that began at the time of the First World War represents a psychological as well as geographical movement. Leaving the conditions of peasantry black people moved from the highly controlled society of traditional caste relationships to circumstances where imprecise racial restrictions and changed conditions of employment and living impel individuals to become self-conscious and, within the limits of the ghetto, self-determinating. The consequence of the mass migration and the internal transformation of hundreds of thousands of dark-skinned Americans has been a strong racial awareness emerging in the 1920's in the nationalism of Marcus Garvey's United Negro Improvement Association with its black business ventures, a program for an independent state in Africa, and the aim of uniting 400,000,000 colored people in the search for a single destiny.

The counterpart of Garvey's urban nationalism was the cultural movement that came to be known as the Negro Renaissance. It evidenced racial pride in the feeling expressed by writers that they had to create without regard for stereotypical audience expectations if they were to understand the special experience of black America. As Langston Hughes put it in a manifesto of the 1920's: "We younger Negro artists who create

† From Studies in the Novel 2 (Fall 1970): 312–24. Copyright 1970 by North Texas State University. Reprinted by permission.

now intend to express our individual dark-skinned selves without fear or shame. If white people are pleased, we are glad. If they are not, it doesn't matter. . . . If colored people are pleased, we are glad. If they are not, their displeasure doesn't matter either."[1]

Despite their social class and political differences, Garveyites and artists agreed in their devotion to self-discovery. However their programs might differ, first priority for all was enunciation of the inherent meaning of being black. In that respect, of course, the movement begun in the 1920's remains vital in the 1970's, for the dislocation of the black diaspora and the need to come to terms with the effects of a slave past have created a necessity for questions of identity to remain at the core of black literature.

A monument of the early period of self-discovery is Jean Toomer's book *Cane* (1923). Informed by a desire for reclamation of the racial past, *Cane* asserts some of the major values of the Negro Renaissance, so that as the problem of identity remains central to black literature, all attempts to resolve the problem demand our attention.

Cane, however, is a problematic book itself, not the sort to generate direct imitation, nor to be read widely without critical discussion. "There are many odd and provocative things about *Cane*," writes Arna Bontemps, "and not the least is its form. Reviewers who read it in 1923 were generally stumped. Poetry and prose were whipped together in a kind of frappé. Realism was mixed with what they called mysticism, and the result seemed to many of them confusing."[2] Readers of our time may be less confused, but the form of *Cane* still is not patent. In fact it is easy to support the impression that *Cane* is a collection of fragments coincidentally unified by a common binding. For example, there is this external evidence. Toomer published separately some of the sketches he eventually grouped in *Cane*; thus, portions appeared in *Broom, Liberator, Modern Review* and other magazines, while Alain Locke published two sketches from *Cane* in his famous anthology *The New Negro* (1925). Moreover, fragmentary effect is suggested internally by Toomer's use of a large cast of characters appearing individually in different pieces and by the presence in the one volume of two-page sketches and a long short story, impressionistic prose and semi-dramatic narrative. Full appreciation of the book, therefore, depends upon our finding in the apparent "miscellany . . . of fictional portraits and poems of life in the villages of Georgia and Washington, D.C."[3] the basis of unity.

The means of unity may be briefly described. In *Cane* Toomer has dropped from his narrative the conventional dependence upon causal sequence, continuous presence of leading characters, and chronological progression. In their place he has adopted the compressed statement of

1. Quoted in Langston Hughes, "The Twenties: Harlem and Its Negritude," *African Forum*, I (Spring 1966), 20.
2. "The Negro Renaissance: Jean Toomer and the Harlem Writers of the 1920's," *Anger, and Beyond: The Negro Writer in the United States*, ed. Herbert Hill (New York, 1966), p. 25.
3. James A. Emanuel and Theodore L. Gross, eds. *Dark Symphony: Negro Literature in America* (New York, 1968), p. 97.

images linked by their intrinsic associations, and he has represented those imagistic statements becoming synthesized either in the mind of a narrator, in the consciousness and unconsciousness of a character, or in the ambience of locale. Toomer, thus, links his various sketches and lyrics into a poetically structured record of a search for the route to self-expression and consequent redemption for the artist and his race.

Analysis of Toomer's method must begin with two of the poems that appear early in the text. Toomer uses lyrics as epigraphs for his prose pieces and scatters snatches of verse throughout the text as refrains of the characters. Quite often commentary is direct as, for example, in "November Cotton Flower," which follows the prose sketch of Karintha, who is described "as innocently lovely as a November cotton flower." Karintha, who happens to be the subject of the first sketch in *Cane*, is also characterized in a poetic epigraph by "skin like dusk on the eastern horizon." This image then is extensively developed in one of the two thematically determining poems: "Georgia Dusk" and "Song of the Son."

The seven stanzas of "Georgia Dusk" set a rural scene with metonymic images of working life—a saw mill with its smoking sawdust pile, plowed and seeded cotton lands. The richness of the setting is said to offer "An orgy for some genius of the South / . . . Surprised in making folk-songs from soul sounds." The soul is obviously that of the men in a later stanza with "race memories of king and caravan, who go singing through the footpaths of the swamp." These blacks carrying their African identity in their unconscious being sing till the "pine trees are guitars," and the "chorus of the cane / Is caroling a vesper to the stars." Thus, according to Toomer's imagery, the spirit of the workmen animates nature and, at the same time, establishes the metaphor of folk-songs as the expression of fundamental self and an outlet for black soul. Moreover, spontaneous outpouring of soul in folk music is potentially a means of salvation, for the final stanza of "Georgia Dusk" images the songs with power to "give virgin lips to cornfield concubines," and to "Bring dreams of Christ to dusky cane-lipped throngs."

Paired with his lyric celebration of the redemption of the folk through spontaneous expression of their inner selves is Toomer's announcement in "Song of the Son" of a means of redemption for a black poet. The parting souls of the formerly enslaved black people carol softly in folk-song bringing their historical era to a close, and "just before an epoch's sun declines," says the poet, as "Thy son . . . I have returned to thee." Though it is late, there is still time "To catch thy plaintive soul. . . ." In a striking image of fulfillment and rebirth Toomer likens the ex-slaves to "purple ripened plums." One plum saved for him provides a seed that becomes an "everlasting song, a singing tree, / Caroling softly souls of slavery, / What they were, and what they are to me." In image and sensibility the poet is represented in this poem as achieving a unity with his black ancestors, finding inspiration for his song, and glimpsing a place for himself in the spiritual fulfillment of the race.

The operative themes of "Georgia Dusk" and "Song of the Son"—acceptance of the racial past and spontaneous expression—represent the goals of the search for identity throughout *Cane*. The poetic manner of the lyrics is also present, and highly appropriate, throughout *Cane* for two reasons. First is the fact that most of the characters can neither conceptualize nor articulate the goals because they are folk characters, but the second and most important reason is that Toomer conceives of self-discovery as an intuitive experience which must be described or, rather, transmitted in a way that will preserve the content of feeling. The prose in *Cane*, therefore, is impressionistic and non-discursive.

The first discrete section of the book contains six sketches. Each is set in rural Georgia and focuses on a woman's relationship to her instinctual sexual being. The first tells of Karintha. From childhood she is pursued by men in lust, until in time she drops a fatherless child from her womb. Having been forced to ripen too soon, she indulges the men who buy her body but stays spiritually aloof from them "carrying beauty, perfect as dusk when the sun goes down."

Becky of the second sketch is a white woman with two mulatto sons. As a result of her violation of caste prohibitions, Becky must live isolated in an old cabin with her sullen boys until one day she is killed when it collapses on top of her. The narrator and his companion ride by, and to them the scene appears to be a mysterious vindication, but of what they don't know. In confusion they ride frantically into town where folks wait to hear their story. But the story is over. It is all implication.

To impatient male lust and caste taboos Toomer adds jealousy to complicate sexual expression in his third sketch, "Carma." This sketch also amplifies the portrayal of the instinctual woman with imagery that relates her to forces greater than her individual person. In opening the piece the narrator describes the sight of Carma in overalls driving a "Georgia chariot" down the Dixie Pike, which he recognizes "has grown from a goat path in Africa." The scene is heavily sensual. Pine-needles glow in the distance, while "the smell of farmyards" is said to be "the fragrance of the woman." Her body is a song, dancing, it seems, in a forest momentarily African. In these circumstances, replete with imagery of the folk soul and the expressive self, the narrator recounts an episode of the "crudest melodrama." In response to her husband's accusation that she has had other men, Carma runs into the cane and pretends to shoot herself. When he discovers the deceit, her husband in frustration slashes one of his fellows and ends up in the chain gang. This melodrama provides the overt action of the sketch, but the chief effect, as in the other sketches, is conveyed by the imagery relating to feeling and expression.

The significance of the instinctual females climaxes in Toomer's sketch of Fern. Dominating her portrait are her eyes, eyes that attract men, eyes into which the rest of Fern's face and then the whole countryside seem to flow. Like Karintha, Fern by her beauty compels men to desire, but unlike Karintha she carries their attentions to the point where they are deeply devoted to doing things for her. Nothing they do, however, is sufficient to her beauty or notable enough for her to acknowledge. Fern evidently symbolizes natural beauty becoming transformed into spirit. Part black and part Jewish, her appearance affects the narrator as does the sorrowful song of a cantor. Walking up the Dixie Pike almost any time of day one is likely to see her sitting on the railing of her porch, her head tilted slightly forward because of a nail in the post which she won't take the trouble to pull out. If the suggestion of spiritual power seems strained by the possibility that that detail alludes to the Cross of Jesus, it may be enforced more clearly by the narrator's saying that Fern, though she had many men's bodies, "became a virgin." (It will be recalled that the cornfield concubines in "Georgia Dusk" receive virgin lips through the power of folk soul.) As a type of a blessed virgin Fern offers to the narrator salvation through the sensations of mystical uni- fication with his past and people. Walking out with Fern on an evening the narrator felt, as always in Georgia dusk, "that things unseen to men were tangibly immediate." He half expected a vision, for "when one is on the soil of one's ancestors, most anything can come to one." Not he but Fern has the vision. It brings her to her knees crying convulsively about Christ Jesus. Though she speaks unintelligibly through it, Fern's vision gives meaning to the narrator. Passing her house again, this time on a train returning North, he sees Fern's face and eyes with "something that I call God flowing into them. . . ."

For the narrator it appears that redemption is achieved by that insight; yet the cumulative effect of the sketches suggests that spiritual redemption must be continually sought. Even in sensory experience many do not reach a state of soulful expression. For example, the male sexual partners of the women in the sketches of rural Georgia seem not to share spiritual feeling with them. Perhaps they are too sensual, entrapped by lust. Toomer doesn't say, but it is clear that while the way to redemption lies through expression of the spontaneous feeling latent in black people, there are so many obstacles to the way that it must continually be repeated.

The final two sketches in the first part of *Cane* represent two such destructive obstacles to spontaneous feeling. In "Esther" the narrator tells of a near-white middle-class storekeeper's daughter who conceives a love for the black King Barlo upon the occasion when Barlo is possessed of a vision of slave history and subsequent salvation. An old black woman was so inspired by the effect of Barlo's vision of a future redemption of black people that she drew a black Madonna on the courthouse wall. A portrait was also traced in Esther's young mind. In her adolescence it leads her to dream of having a child. "How had she come by it? She thinks of it immaculately." Immaculate conception is not a positive image however, for it omits the sensory experience necessary to black redemption in *Cane*. When Esther is twenty-seven years old, still unmarried and virgin, she hears that Barlo has returned to town, and she goes to claim her fancied love. Apprehensively she enters at midnight into the lowlife joint where he consorts with ordinary people. Almost immediately she is embarrassed by the lower-class women and laughed at by Barlo. To save her pride and the repressive structures in her mind, Esther's consciousness tells her that sex with a drunken man must be sinful. As "jeers and hoots pelter bluntly upon her back," she goes out into the void of her life where "there is no air, no street, and the town has completely disappeared." By negation, therefore, Toomer makes clear that redemption can only come "naturally."

The final sketch in part one, "Blood-Burning Moon," is an explicit treatment of racial caste mores. Here two men, of different race, desire the same black woman. Their jealous rivalry ends in the death of both men, the white by knifing, the black by lynching. The passionate conflict and the deaths occur because the white man presumes that his race gives him special claim to a black girl and exempts him from having to consider her feelings and her lover's. But it is important to see that the social protest also supports Toomer's theme of natural expression by showing that the spontaneous feeling of the characters is diverted by the artificial creations of society, the caste system.

Throughout *Cane* the dynamic force of irrational feeling is the leading motive of action. When it is instinctual, as in sex, the feeling is conveyed by imagery alluding to spiritual redemption and in a representation of environment assimilated to person. The "cane" of the title, like the pine and the soil, thereby derives meaning from the people who work in it and conveys in concrete form the complex of feeling and experience that is the soul of the Georgia blacks. On the other hand, irrational feeling is not always redemptive, for a person can be socially conditioned to repress instinct or to exploit it in others. In these cases Toomer describes motive in images of life-destruction and exploitation. For example, in "Blood-Burning Moon" the burning of Tom Burwell occurs in an ante-bellum cotton factory.

The second discrete part of *Cane* follows the trail of history to portray characters who have migrated from the rural South to Washington, D.C. The whole section displays considerable stylistic experimentation beyond the methods of narration established in Part One and, therefore, also deserves close attention.

The section opens with a highly impressionistic account of a black neighborhood in Washington, D.C. The area is the bastard of Prohibition and the war: "A crude-boned, soft-skinned wedge of nigger life breathing its loafer air, jazz songs and love, thrusting unconscious rhythms, black reddish blood into the white and whitewashed wood of Washington." The first character introduced, in a separate sketch, is Rhobert, the bourgeoisie who "wears a house, like a monstrous diver's helmet, on his head." With Rhobert's appearance in the narrative it is evident that spontaneous black life is threatened in the city by people's increasingly individualistic social ambition. In the succeeding sketch of "Avey" an analytic cast of mind, a correlative of urban self-consciousness, proves to be the obstacle to the flow of feeling.

Avey is described as a sort of Karintha in the North, who goes through life oblivious of the respectable conventions regarding sex and uninterested in bettering her social position in the schoolteacher's job for which she has been educated. Finally, however, it is the articulate, self-conscious narrator who is the complete failure. He longs for Avey but cannot take her. In time he rises above her in social position and then rationalizes his continuing desire for her with the idea that they are destined for an artistic life together. Attempting to tell Avey about his plans for them he puts her to sleep.

A similar point is made by the following sketch, "Theater." This one represents John, the theater manager's brother, fantasizing his desire for Dorris, one of the dancers. Dorris's spontaneous dance expresses her physical and emotional desires in a visible and available way. The entire stage crew and cast are drawn into the orbit of her movement. John is too, until he proceeds to a dream of Dorris where he has the satisfaction of an abstracted and controlled conception of her but of course lacks the sensory gratification that would make fantasy unnecessary. Frustratedly, Dorris rushes from stage crying bitterly, leaving John sitting immobile.

The theme of the first part of Cane is reinforced by the impressionistic style of narration that conveys the sensations of instinctual life as the narrator comes to feel them. With the second part of Cane that style is no longer functional for Toomer, because he believes the urban environment, in contrast to the world of cane and soil and pine, and the changing social experience cut people off from the sources of feeling and vitiate their spirit. Toomer, therefore, needs a style in the second part of Cane that conveys the disintegration of collective and of spontaneous life, and for that reason he introduces, in "Theater," a variety of expressionistic writing that projects subjective states of mind without the intervention of a first person narrator. In this style he uses name tags, as in a playscript, to introduce his characters' thoughts, while their appearances and actions are stated with emphasis on physical appearance and without the evident presence of anyone's consciousness. The thoughts of the characters in this way are opened to the reader, but they are nevertheless the thoughts of people who feel themselves to be, and are in fact, isolated to an extent that cripples them.

"Box Seat" carries the objectification of subjective states to a climax and links the second part of the book to the first by examination of the motif of spiritual redemption in the environment of individualistic urban society. Dan Moore, the leading male, is a redeemer figure much like King Barlo. The hands of Jesus have touched him, he feels, and he can hear through the walls of houses and beneath the asphalt streets the sound of underground races and a world savior struggling to arise. In this society, though, people aren't going to let anything rise from the underground/unconscious. They are pictured as living in metallic, sharp-edged houses keeping cold walls between each other, and when they go to the theater, the site of artistic expression supposedly, they are described sliding like bolts into metal slots that keep them rigidly upright. Dan struggles to bring passion into a relationship with Muriel, to make her yield to feeling, but Muriel gives her attention to a struggle to direct her life by a code of respectability. What she has not yet internalized of its repressive nature is supplied by her landlady, a surrogate mother whose presence intrudes a "cool, thick glass" between Dan and Muriel. Aside from Dan, only an elderly black woman he sits beside in the theater retains the vitality of Southern rural life. Her strong roots appear to sink down beneath the earth disappearing in "blood-lines that waver south." Briefly Dan feels that he can follow those roots with his hands and sense the earth throb against his heart, but only briefly, because others in the theater audience object to Dan's unruly behavior and break his mood of communion. To climax this tale of the redeemer in the city, Toomer brings onto the stage of the Lincoln Theater a pair of dwarfs who delight the audience with a boxing match, followed by a serenade in which one of the fighters offers a rose, bedewed with his blood, to Muriel. Trapped in indecision, Muriel cannot freely accept the debased emblem of love as social pressure demands, nor can she express the revulsion she feels. Reluctantly, she at last reaches for the flower just as Dan rushes from the theater crying scornfully at Muriel's confusion: "Jesus was once a leper!" Failed in his efforts at redemption, Dan walks away, oblivious of a man seeking to pick a fight with him for disturbing the theater audience with his unpredictable behavior.

"Bona and Paul," the final sketch in Part Two of *Cane*, reviews the conflict between spontaneous feeling and reflective thought in an episode between a mulatto boy and a Southern-born white girl. Bona is drawn to Paul by an attraction that overwhelms her caste conditioning. Paul, on the other hand, is reluctant with Bona, as in all his personal relationships, because of his uncertainty about his racial status. When Paul is at last ready to love, he insists upon talking about it to a doorman, assuring him that it is a genuine love. When he turns from this self-conscious apology, Bona is gone.

Lyrics carrying themes from the sketches intersperse the second section as the first. Two are notable. "Her Lips are Copper Wires" has the poet ask in imagery of a city lighting system for an electrifying love. "Harvest Song," anticipating the story of Kabnis in the final section of the book, is the song of a reaper who hungers for some indefinite satisfaction; but rather than seek his hunger's object, he prefers to beat his hands against the stubble, painfully obliterating desire. Contrasting with the lyrics of fulfillment in Part One, these poems emphasize the conversion of the urge for life into a retreat from its sensations.

"Kabnis," the long story making up the third part of *Cane*, returns to rural Georgia for setting and once more concerns a Northerner seeking to relate to the life of black Southerners. This time, however, Toomer objectifies the story with the dramatic tags and descriptions he introduced in the section on Washington. Six scenes move the leading character from an initial mood of anguish in which he inexplicably rejects the beauty of the Georgia night, through an intensified period of guilt marked by a fear of bodily harm, and finally bring him to a condition of self-hate where he despairs of either a personal or a social redemption.

At the opening of the story Ralph Kabnis, who has come South to teach school, finds himself being fired by his pompous principal for somehow setting a bad example to the students. He is inadequate to withstand this change of fortune, because he is already consumed by bitterness that leads him to pray to God to give him "an ugly world. . . . Stinking like unwashed niggers." Do not chain him, he prays, to the hills and valleys "heaving with folk-songs." Then in the twisted logic of his despair Kabnis argues to himself that God "doesn't exist, but nevertheless he is ugly. Hence, what comes from him is ugly." What outrage has turned Kabnis to rejection of the spirit embodied in the Georgia countryside is not clear at first, though gradually his despair becomes concentrated on thoughts of violence and lynching.

Unintentional encouragement in this line of thinking is provided to Kabnis by Halsey, a local blacksmith, and Layman, "by turns teacher and preacher, who has traveled in almost every nook and corner of the state and hence knows more than would be good for anyone other than a silent man." The two of them provide Kabnis knowledge of Southern ways and try to reassure him when he becomes terrified with the thought that he may become a lynch victim. They don't deny violence, but they are matter of fact about the ways it occurs. The gap between their view of lynching and Kabnis' unreasoning terror cannot be bridged, and neither response is finally satisfactory. Without doubt the white society is vicious and shockingly anti-life. This is made clear in the account Layman gives of white folks killing a pregnant woman and then tearing the baby from her belly and pinning it to a tree. On the other hand, Kabnis takes the threat of violence into himself and converts anticipation into a guilt so overwhelming that he is deracinated, becoming, in the imagery of the story, a scarecrow replica of himself.

A stranger named Lewis brings the theme of redemption into Kabnis' story. When Kabnis meets Lewis there is a brief moment of possible union for their intuitive selves before Kabnis rejects the advance. In the description of that moment Toomer reiterates themes that run throughout Cane. "His eyes turn to Kabnis. In the instant of their shifting, a vision of the life they are to meet. Kabnis, a promise of soil-soaked beauty; uprooted, thinning out. Suspended a few feet above the soil whose touch would resurrect him. Arm's length removed from him whose will to help. . . . There is a swift intuitive interchange of consciousness. Kabnis has a sudden need to rush into the arms of this man.

His eyes call 'Brother.' And then a savage, cynical twist-about within him mocks his impulse and strengthens him to repulse Lewis." Like Muriel and others in the world of *Cane*, Kabnis out of fear blocks the flow of spontaneous feeling.

Kabnis' story, thus, is a climax to the volume. In the first section of *Cane* Toomer establishes the need for and the conditions of redemption. The second part of the book, the stories of Washington, D.C., represents increased intuition of spontaneous life. Now the characters become more *self*-repressing because of the mentality they have developed in the city. Where the narrator could respond to a redeemer in the person of Fern in the first part, the characters in the second part reject the means of redemption. Then in "Kabnis" Toomer describes a man who has fully internalized the repressive forces of the environment. In "Blood-Burning Moon" violence came from without. In Kabnis' story the threat is projected from within. Though Kabnis is in the South, which appears to be animated with soul through imagery of song and light, he deliberately closes his senses. Just as deliberately he rejects Lewis, who would stimulate his feeling for the soil and collective humanity.

The final two scenes of "Kabnis" occur in a basement hole beneath Halsey's workshop. Within this hole is an old man "like a bust in black walnut" whom Lewis calls Father John and Kabnis calls Father of Hell. He is a mute presence evidently signifying the slave ancestry, kept hidden from the present but appropriately an inhabitant of the room in which Halsey, Kabnis, and the others put aside constraints to drink and consort with whores. A visit to the room of Father John becomes, therefore, an excursion into the past, an opportunity for sensual release and, for the blacks variously compromising with their social environment, an encounter with the terms of their underlying identity.

Significantly, in this underground/unconscious setting Lewis communes with Father John, wordlessly sensing the vital force present in the soil and its fruit: "Cotton bolls bloom, droop. Black roots twist in a parched red soil beneath a blazing sky. Magnolias, fragrant, a trifle futile, lovely, far off. . . . His eyelids close. A force begins to heave and rise." When Lewis opens his eyes after this momentary communion, his appearance infuriates Kabnis. The old man, Kabnis is driven to say, looks like a black cockroach. "An besides, he aint my past. My ancestors were Southern blue-bloods." Prodded and contradicted by Lewis, Kabnis then raves until he is revealing that a nightmarish form eats into his soul, feeding on the words others speak and driving him to wish, in an image reminiscent of the lynching story he had heard from Layman, that "some lynchin white man ud stick his knife through it an pin it to a tree."

In the context of *Cane*, Ralph Kabnis, so fearful of life, is complementary to characters such as the "I" narrator of Part One who sense the possibility of spontaneous life. for Toomer's book is about life in *black* America. In that realm, violence has always been present as the chief instrument of social control, so that an expedition into the zones of black identity inevitably describes the effect that the threat of violence must have upon personality.

In the final scene of the story the mark of violent oppression is fully revealed as Ralph Kabnis speaks of his death wish directly to Father John. First he taunts and reviles Father John for his impassivity and his ugliness, but the tone of speech makes clear that Kabnis is expressing self-hate. Then Father John speaks. First he says the word "sin," and then the statement that the white folks sinned when they made the Bible lie in a justification of slavery. This too Kabnis reviles, while saying much the same thing in his own words. The only sin is what is done against the soul, Kabnis says, and the world is conspiring to sin against him. "I'm the victim of their sin. I'm what sin is." In this formula Kabnis reveals his condition. He is the victim of racial oppression—a sin—and the consequence is that he has become like the crime, a foe of life.

The bleakness of "Kabnis" is raised briefly by the character of Carrie Kate, Halsey's sister. She too is moved by the appeal of Lewis to feel the possibility of intuitive union. In her case the "sin-bogies of respectable southern colored folks clamor at her" to watch out and she draws back. But in the final scene when Kabnis has been reduced to a groveling wretch, Carrie offers him succor. She draws the fever from his head and comforts him. Then, kneeling before Father John, she murmurs "Jesus, come," while outside the sun "arises from its cradle" and shines down upon the town sending "a birthsong slanting down gray dust streets" to coalesce with Carrie in an image of the continued possibility of spiritual redemption.

In description of his source of artistic inspiration, Jean Toomer wrote: "Georgia opened me. . . . There one finds soil, soil in the sense the Russians know it,—the soil every art and literature that is to live must be imbedded in."[4] The statement suggests how deeply he felt the importance of *Cane*. Toomer himself after all was a man of Southern heritage who went from the city to teach school in Sparta, Georgia. Of course, the personal experience must have contributed greatly to the conception that unites his sketches and lyrics in *Cane*, and in that respect the book is a symbolic record of the sensitive author's attempt to relate to his personal past.

Finally, however, *Cane* is most important to its readers because of its place in Afro-American literary tradition. The point can be made simply by observation of the relationship between *Cane* and that classic of black literature, *The Souls of Black Folk* (1903). Du Bois' book is also a collection of independent pieces recording a Northern observer's understanding of Southern black life. In anticipation of the techniques of *Cane*, Du Bois the social scientist humanized his research findings by a use of narrative style that invites the reader to tour the rural areas, the linking of essays with songs as epigraphs, and animation of the entire

4. Quoted in *The New Negro*, ed. Alain Locke (New York, 1925), p. 51.

book with repeated use of a thematic metaphor—the veil. For his part, Toomer could not have failed to realize that his book repeated the symbolic return to ancestral scenes that grounded *The Souls of Black Folk,* developed Du Bois' theme of a reconciliation between the "Talented Tenth" and the black masses, and imaginatively extended the meanings latent in the image of black folks' souls.

In its own decade *Cane* epitomized the desire among black artists to deal with folk experience in sophisticated literature. Today, when the problem of its form no longer seems so baffling, the relevance of *Cane* has, if anything, been increased, because in its exploration of identity as a process of liberating the spontaneous self in an often oppressive environment we can see how *Cane* established the major terms of the twentieth-century black writer's chief theme—the redemption of personality.

DARWIN T. TURNER

[Contrasts and Limitations in *Cane*]†

* * *

Cane inspires critical rhapsodies rather than analysis. As Robert Bone wrote, "A critical analysis of *Cane* is a frustrating task, for Toomer's art, in which 'outlines are reduced to essences,' is largely destroyed in the process of restoration. No paraphrase can properly convey the aesthetic pleasure derived from a sensitive reading of *Cane.*"[1]

It is not a novel, not even the experimental novel for which Bone pleaded to justify including it in his study of novels by Negroes.[2] It is, instead, a collection of character sketches, short poems, and a play,

† From *In a Minor Chord: Three Afro-American Writers and Their Search for Identity* (Carbondale and Edwardsville: Southern Illinois UP, 1971) 14–30.
1. Robert Bone, *The Negro Novel in America*, rev. ed. (New Haven, Conn., 1965), p. 88.
2. The current debate about *Cane*'s status as a novel seems pointless except as it reveals the willingness of literary historians to cling to their beliefs without regard for facts. Certainly *Cane* can be said to have organization. It also resembles Sherwood Anderson's *Winesburg, Ohio*, which Toomer had read before he went to Sparta, Georgia. Nevertheless, the fact is that Toomer composed the various pieces separately and sent them individually to editors of magazines. By the summer of 1922, as he explained in a letter to Waldo Frank dated July 19, he "had the impulse to collect [his] sketches and poems under the title perhaps of Cane." Anderson, who saw individual pieces as Toomer sent them to the *Double Dealer* and who offered to help secure publication, never referred to the proposed work as a novel. Anderson would have been too

knowledgeable to do so; for, in December 1922, when Toomer first informed him of the proposed book, Toomer stated that he was "writing three new pieces, and putting Cane (my book) together." (No. 43 in Jean Toomer Collection at Fisk University.) In the introduction to *Cane*, Waldo Frank referred to *Cane* only as "a book" even though he emphasized the fact that a reader sees a complex form evolve from the apparent chaos. Most persuasive of all, in addition to the letters in which Toomer describes his organizational preferences to Frank and to his publisher, is the fact that when Toomer proposed a second volume based on black and brown life in Washington, Horace Liveright expressed his regret that Toomer was not yet proposing a novel. (Letter from Liveright to Toomer, March 12, 1923.) It is ironic that while historians bemuse themselves with explanations of their theories that *Cane* is a novel, Toomer suffered during the late twenties and early thirties because publishers insisted on his sending them a novel rather than another book like *Cane*.

which forms one of the distinguished achievements in the writings of Americans. The first section of the book is composed of sketches, stories, and poems based on life—especially the life of Afro-American women—in Georgia. The stories of the second section, located in Washington and Chicago, were written to bring the collection to a length respectable for publication in book form. The third section is a drama set in Georgia.

Toomer's supreme talent in his best prose work is the ability to suggest character lyrically. Restricting his vision to one or two traits of personality, he tells a story intended merely to help the reader perceive the individual.

Six women are the focus of the first section, the most appealing part of *Cane*. One is Karintha, who personifies the physical beauty for which men yearn:

> Men had always wanted her, this Karintha, even as a child, Karintha carrying beauty, perfect as dusk when the sun goes down. . . .

> Karintha, at twelve, was a wild flash that told the other folks just what it was to live. At sunset, when there was no wind, and the pine-smoke from over by the sawmill hugged the earth, and you couldn't see more than a few feet in front, her sudden darting past you was a bit of vivid color, like a black bird that flashes in light. . . . Already, rumors were out about her.

Then,

> Karintha is a woman, and she has had a child. A child fell out of her womb onto a bed of pine-needles in the forest. Pine-needles are smooth and sweet. They are elastic to the feet of rabbits. . . .

> Karintha at twenty, carrying beauty, perfect as dusk when the sun goes down. Karintha. . . .

Five pages. Karintha, a beautiful child whom old men ride hobby horse. Karintha at twelve—beautiful, matured to sexual knowledge, no longer permitting herself to be dandled on the knees of old men. Karintha at twenty—often mated, supported by men, mother of an unwanted child who died unwanted on the pine needles beneath the smoke curling from a sawmill. Karintha—"Men do not know that the soul of her was a growing thing ripened too soon. They will bring their money; they will die not having found it out."

As "Karintha" typifies Toomer's style, so the protagonist typifies his women. Elizabeth Loguen complained about the unreality of his female characters. They all love, she believed, as Toomer thought women should.[3] Perhaps this judgment is accurate. Each in her own way is an elusive beauty, who charitably or indifferently or inquisitively offers her body to men who will never understand her soul. Each portrait haunts

---

3. Letter from Elizabeth Loguen to Toomer, February 14, 1924.

the reader as the woman haunted the narrator, who seeks the soul, the feminine essence of women who in less artistic works would be pitied or castigated as social outcasts.

* * *

Faintly reminiscent of Gertrude Stein, Waldo Frank, and Sherwood Anderson, these portraits, nevertheless, are the work of an artist possessing an individualized style.[4] The style depends upon contrasting images of man and nature: the vivid color of Karintha, a November cotton flower, against the pine-needles and pine smoke; Becky, visible only through her dark children, against the blue-sheen locomotive god; white-skinned Esther against flames and tobacco juice. It depends upon lyric language, deceptively smooth and simple, the language of a poet careful of words.

The dominant contrast between the Georgia section of Cane and the Northern section is between a natural response to sexual drives and a self-conscious, frustrating inability to realize oneself. The women of section one respond naturally and instinctively to their urges, regardless of the attitudes of society. Only near-white Esther experiences frustrating conflicts, and she is the unhappiest of the women. Even in the first part of Cane, Toomer pointed to the tensions and deliberate self-delusions arising in reaction to natural behavior. People refuse to see the wickedness of young Karintha; they tell themselves that Becky must be dead; they transform Fern into The Virgin. Townspeople can accept aberrants only by pretending that there has been no deviation from the socially acceptable. The tragedy resulting from the failure to sustain delusion proves the inability of people to accept the reality of natural sex drives: Carma's husband kills a man when he is forced to realize that Carma has taken lovers in his absence; Bob Stone attacks Tom Burwell when he is forced to realize that Louisa has given herself to a black man.

In Washington and Chicago, delusion becomes reality, will represses action, and natural self-realization becomes impossible. In two of the four stories, conflict arises between a primitive being—instinctively,

4. Knowledge of the friendship between Toomer and Frank has caused some critics to find influences of Frank's Holiday in Cane. Although both books appeared in 1923, and direct correspondence between the two would seem to indicate mutual indebtedness, Toomer had begun writing the stories and sketches of Cane during the winter of 1921–22. By mid-July of 1922, even though he had not yet seen a sketch in print, he had completed most of the sketches. "Box Seat" and "Bona and Paul" were apparently written later.
In July, Frank, who had seen much of Toomer's work, wrote Toomer that he was planning a book about Negroes. During the remainder of the summer, Frank probably developed that idea. In mid-September or, more probably, in October, Toomer and Frank visited South Carolina so that Frank could evaluate the authenticity of the atmosphere for his book. January 16, 1923, Frank wrote Toomer to ask him to review Holiday. Eight days earlier Boni and Liveright had accepted Cane.
This is not intended to imply that Frank did not influence Toomer's style. Sherwood Anderson, who was reading Toomer's manuscripts avidly during the fall of 1922, suspected that he detected such influence in Toomer's changing style. It should not be assumed carelessly, however, that Toomer merely imitated Holiday. In fact, it is as valid to suggest that Toomer was influenced by the style of Sherwood Anderson. In a letter written to Anderson in December 1922, Toomer emphasized the degree to which Anderson's Winesburg, Ohio and The Triumph of the Egg had impressed him. Moreover, while explaining Toomer's lyricism, John McClure, in a letter to Anderson, added his belief that Anderson's talent was the same kind of lyricism.

shamelessly seeking gratification and realization—and a society-sophisticated being—repressed, frustrated, unable to forget the image he seeks to preserve. In the other two, "Bona and Paul" and "Theatre," protagonists are frustrated by their tensions, by the conflict between will and desire.

"Avey" pictures a Northern Karintha. Offered professional opportunities impossible for Fern or Karintha, Avey listlessly, bovinely loses them and accepts, in their stead, her lovers' lust. Unable to understand or approve her aimlessness, the narrator vainly tries first to change her, then to meet her upon her own level. Having failed to mate with her spiritually or physically, he, like a saint, holds her in his arms and meditates about the innocence of the "orphan-woman."

"Box-Seat" tells of Dan Moore, whose dreams of being a militant Messiah fade into his impotence. Frustrated because Muriel, a school teacher, resists his impassioned advances, and infuriated by a world that categorizes people as the accepted or the freaks, Dan challenges the tradition of that world, but forgets that he has offered the challenge.

"Bona and Paul" is located in Chicago, where the two protagonists attend a college of physical education. Paul Johnson is Negro; Bona is white and Southern-bred. After striving to repress their mutual attraction, they yield during ecstatic dancing. Too self-conscious, however, they cannot realize themselves spiritually or physically. Seeing mockery in the eyes of a black doorman, Paul pauses to assure the man that he and Bona are going outside for spiritual rather than physical consummation. By the time Paul reaches the street, Bona has disappeared.

Although both central characters of "Theater" are Afro-American, they stand on different social levels. John is the brother of a theater manager. Dorris is a dancer. Despite their mutual attraction, neither can free himself sufficiently to translate desire into action. Dorris tries to express her feelings by dancing before him. But John's mind is "contained above desire of his body. He wills thought to rid his mind of passion." Fearing that Dorris will ridicule him if he relinquishes this self-control, he dreams of their union, but he does not act.

Longer than the earlier stories of *Cane*, "Theater," "Box-Seat," and "Bona and Paul" reveal the weaknesses that restricted Toomer as a short-story writer and, later, as a novelist. They end vaguely and inconclusively. The perceptively sketched characters act and react; but the narrator then walks away from them. The material remains amorphous—a disappointment to a reader persuaded to expect more than a sketch.

Jean Toomer often transformed his personal experiences into universally meaningful criticisms of life. Like the narrator of "Avey," he had loved a high school girl who had been interested only in college men. He had shuddered when his less sensitive high school friends had described in detail their actual or exaggerated conquests. He too had attended college in Wisconsin, although not as long as the narrator, had hitchhiked to New York, had bruised his vanity in unsuccessful job hunts, had loved a girl at Harper's Ferry, and had tried to change her. Like John, the brother of the theater manager, he had worked in a theater; and even earlier, led by his uncle, he had played stage-door Johnny to older women of the chorus line. Like Paul Johnson, he had attended a school for physical training in Chicago, had writhed before stares of white people whom he imagined to be speculating about his racial identity, and had loved a white girl whose family opposed her relationship with a Negro. These three stories, therefore, contain the truth of imagination based upon reality. They reveal the frustrations of Jean Toomer.

Set against the stories of part one, however, they point to a more universal thought. The educated Toomer, like John, interposed will between desire and action. Consequently, he lived mainly in fantasies and dreams. In contrast, the Beckys and the Karinthas realize themselves by acting according to instinct. These later stories, therefore, express a regret that a male cannot live as instinctively as a female can, and suggest a yearning for a more primitive existence in which desire, not will, can be the ruling force.

If Toomer conceived this existence to be most nearly achieved by Afro-Americans in the South, he saw that even there a restrictive society censured those who obeyed natural urges. Furthermore, unlike Sherwood Anderson and some of the followers of the van Vechten vogue, he noted unhappily that Southern blacks themselves were rapidly losing the innocence of Eden by substituting will and social image for the purity of freedom and naturalness.

"Kabnis" is the longest work in *Cane*.[5] Although Toomer tried to have a revised version produced as a play, Kenneth Macgowan rejected it because it lacked a plot. A producer might be more charitable in these days of the Theatre of the Absurd. Like Samuel Beckett's *Waiting for Godot*, it is a spectacle of futility; like Ionesco's *The Chairs*, it substitutes a meaningless whimper for the anticipated climactic explosion. "Kabnis," however, is not developed as artistically as either of these. Toomer failed to focus the multitudinous rays of light into one clear beam.

The slight plot [of "Kabnis"] sets an inhibited and impotent Northerner among Southerners who have failed to achieve self-realization. Choosing to remain in the South, he becomes an apprentice in a blacksmith shop. Among his people in their ancestral home, he seeks to realize himself; but, because of his moral weakness, he finds only drunkenness, debauchery, and impotence.

Superseding the plot is the theme Toomer attempted to express through allegorical characters. The protagonist Ralph Kabnis represents the contemporary Northern-born, educated Afro-American searching for his identity. Although he has pilgrimaged to the region which he posits for his ancestral home, he cannot fully identify with any of his race who

5. See also Darwin T. Turner, "The Failure of a Playwright," *CLA Journal*, X (June, 1967), 308–18.

live successfully in that region. He cannot merge with uneducated blacks because they discern his cultural dissimilarities. Kabnis despises men of the mold of Hanby, a principal, who represents one type of middle-class Southern Negro. Deferential toward white people, Hanby abuses blacks to compensate for the humiliation which he experiences in relationships with white people. Trained to respect formal education, Kabnis cannot imitate Halsey, who represents the semiskilled worker. Disdaining formal education because it fails to improve lives of Afro-Americans, Halsey derives enjoyment and pride from laboring with his hands. Although he, like Hanby, treats white people deferentially, he considers himself their intellectual equal. Nor can Kabnis assume the indifference of Layman, who represents the intelligent, but untrained clergy of the South. A self-appointed teacher and minister, Layman observes mental and physical indignities inflicted upon the black man, but he preserves his own life by remaining silent. Although he knows the impotence of the primitive religion he teaches, he offers its fervor as a drug to help his race forget the painful reality of their existence.

Because Kabnis is intellectual rather than physical, he cannot mate with Stella, a personification of the sensual female. Stella's mother was abused by white men; she herself has been used by black leaders. Nor can Kabnis do more than dream romantically of union with Halsey's sister Carrie K, the Madonna figure who responds to Lewis but represses her desire. Kabnis must mate with Cora, who is as flat mentally as she is physically. Neither sensual nor intellectual nor spiritual, she imitates and she exists.

Weak, debauched, impotent, betrayed by his faith in education and in religion, Kabnis awaits a message from Father John, symbol of the Afro-American ancestor, the maker of spirituals, the voice of the past. But Father John, aged and infirm, speaks rarely and unintelligibly. When at last he gathers the clarity and force to pronounce a judgment from the past, he merely mutters, "O th sin th white folks 'mitted when they made th Bible lie." As Horatio says, "There needs no ghost . . . come from the grave to tell us this."

The story ends inconclusively but with pessimistically suggestive irony. After a night of debauchery and disappointment, Kabnis, carrying a bucket of dead coals, climbs the stairs to begin his labor as apprentice blacksmith. Behind him, in the cellar, Carrie K kneels before Father John and prays for Jesus to return. The virgin child prays before a deaf, blind, and senile savior. Meanwhile, Kabnis, who is unfit to be a laborer, carries the ashes of dreams into his apprenticeship for a trade which is soon to be obsolete.

The only ray of optimism in the allegory of impotence and nonrealization is Lewis, a Christ figure, who is what a stronger Kabnis might have been. Northern-born, educated, capable of acting according to emotional impulse or of controlling his emotion by will power, Lewis has come South for a month to observe and to communicate with his people. Compassionate and perceptive, he attempts to assist them, but he is driven away when they imbibe the anodynes of sex and alcohol.

* * *

From a vantage point forty years later it is possible to discern limitations in *Cane*. First, Toomer's canvas is limited. Except in "Kabnis," Toomer did not interpret the Southern black. He wrote lyrically about Southern women isolated or destroyed because they have ignored society's restrictions on sexual behavior. In "Natalie Mann" he had argued for such rebellion; in the first part of *Cane*, he described the results with sympathetic awareness that tragedy eventuates as long as society itself erects taboos. Having matured too quickly, Karintha prostitutes herself. Becky is alienated from white and black because she, a white woman, has mated with a black. Children, the natural result of sexual action, are unwanted because they prove the fact which otherwise might be ignored. Unwanted, they are murdered or become murderers. Angered by Carma's adultery and humiliated by her deceit, Carma's husband tries to kill her. Louisa, who took two lovers—one white, one black—loses both. Fern—half-black, half-white—gropes for a spiritual realization which she does not discover in the physical realities of sexual intercourse. Half-white, sex-starved, Esther is forced from her world of sexual fantasies. Both Fern and Esther withdraw from reality—Fern into mystic vision, Esther into Freudian fantasy. Most of Toomer's Northern women know even less happiness than the Southern ones, for they fear to admit their desires.

Toomer could not build a career upon lyric presentations of such women. But he had little else to offer. His male figures are stereotypes, personifications, and reproductions of his satiric, self-pitying, or idealized image of himself. At his best, he did not tell stories; he sang and painted, and his subject was Woman.

An additional weakness appears in the stories located in Washington and Chicago. Toomer shifted from the stance of sympathetic observer or recorder of the tale of folk; he joined in the dance. Lewis replaced Kabnis. The change of point of view was unfortunate. Whereas Toomer could sing of women, he could not write effectively about Jean Toomer. Toomer, the character, is a neurotic, vanity-driven figure, like Paul in "Bona and Paul." Or he is a somewhat pompous, ineffectual reformer of souls, like the nameless narrator of "Avey." Or he is a god, like Nathan Merilh of "Natalie Mann" and like the protagonists of most of the stories Toomer wrote subsequently.

John McClure perceived both Toomer's talent and his potential weakness when he explained to Anderson that Toomer faltered when he tried to write realistic dialogue. As a lyricist, Toomer succeeded only when he expressed the feelings of the characters in his own words either in quotation or in indirect discourse.[6] Toomer's gift was the ability to write

6. Letter from McClure to Anderson, January 2?, 1924. No. 53 in the Jean Toomer Collection at Fisk University.

from within himself, but he could not use that gift effectively when writing about himself. He needed to balance his subjectivity with the objective attempt to create someone other than himself.

The third unheeded warning of impending disaster in *Cane* is Toomer's substitution of satire for sympathy. Part of the reason can be traced to Toomer's contrasting attitudes about his relationship to the characters in the tales. He had identified himself temperamentally with the Southern blacks. As he wrote while he was preparing the lyrics for *Cane*,

> My seed was planted in the cane-and-cotton fields, and in the souls of black and white people in the small southern town. My seed was planted in myself from there.[7]

Although allowance must be made for the characteristic enthusiasm with which Toomer embraced every new interest, whether sociology or the black field hand, much of this feeling was genuine. It is also true, however, that consciously or subconsciously Toomer knew that he, like Lewis, was visiting in the South. Thus, he could write sympathetically as one who feels kinship yet maintains artistic detachment. He desired merely to observe, to sense, and to reflect the milieu, not to change it.

When he wrote of Washington and Chicago, however, he lost his detachment. He wanted to reform the people to rid them of their indolence or their anxieties or their inhibitions. Consequently his tone became sharper, sardonic, satirical. Avey, he lamented, is too much like a cow. She lives by instinct, with few drives and fewer goals. Yet Toomer had not sat in judgment upon Karintha and Fern, who were also creatures of instinct. Jean Toomer, one suspects, expected such behavior from them—they were the Southern blacks, the children of nature. But Avey had been reared in Washington. She had been educated and had had opportunities to improve her economic position. She was of his group. She should have been able to rise above the animal.

Finally, pervading the stories is the sense that human beings need assistance from a superhuman power, a god or a messiah, which will affirm, console, sustain, and guide. Some protagonists in the South, living close to nature, dimly sense and vaguely follow the god of nature, who seems to affirm the actions of Karintha, offer the consolation of Jesus of the pines to Becky, and shelter Fern in a mystic experience. Even in the South, however, the religious power fails to provide what is needed. Becky, a Catholic, must confront the destructive god of the locomotive. Fern's Semitic character cannot flourish. Louisa prays helplessly to a "red nigger moon." Layman offers delusions. Father John mumbles incoherently. And messiahs vanish: Lewis retreats to the North

---

7. Letter from Toomer to Anderson, December, 1922. Walter Pinchback suggests that, in Georgia, Toomer lived near relatives of the Toomers. The authenticity of the report, however, is questionable. There is no reference to such a reunion in any of Toomer's correspondence during the period. The more persuasive possibility is that Walter Pinchback's hazy memory inferred erroneous conclusions from the mere fact that Toomer worked in Georgia, the state from which Nathan Toomer had come and to which he reportedly had returned.

and Barlo retreats into lusts of the flesh. Hope is even dimmer in the North for the urbanized, who cannot turn to religion, cannot even sense it. Southern-born Dan Moore, a would-be messiah, is a madman among the people of the North. There was, Toomer felt, a need for a new kind of salvation; and, as he completed his work on the materials of *Cane*, he became increasingly concerned with helping people discover that new salvation.

In *Cane*, then, although Toomer said that he wrote about a waning way of life, he also wrote unconsciously of the death of an artist. Jean Toomer the lyricist was dying; Jean Toomer the philosopher, psychologist, reformer was coming into being.

PATRICIA WATKINS

Is There a Unifying Theme in *Cane*?†

Two lost and fearful people, crying for help and direction, walk toward each other on a dark and empty street. They stop; they speak—but in different languages—and after fruitless attempts to communicate, to share, to merge, they proceed on their way as before—lost, fearful, unknown, uncomforted, and unloved. This is, I believe, what Toomer is saying throughout *Cane*: that man is a creature alone and apart, unable to share and commit himself with another, and after many abortive attempts to do so, he finds that nothing has happened and nothing has changed. He ends as he began—alone and afraid. Whether the barrier to this interaction is race, as in "Bona and Paul"; or social class, as in "Theater" and "Box Seat"; or lack of will, as in "Blood-Burning Moon"; the barrier is impenetrable.

In "Becky," two strangers—Becky and the community—approach one another. The community builds her cabin, feeds her and her children, prays for her, gives her a strip of land, and bestows a Bible upon her grave. She in turn offers her two sons as the sacrifice for love, makes herself, at the community's demand, invisible and silent. But in this exchange nothing is gained. The community and Becky circle rather than move toward one another. The townspeople attempt to perform acts of kindness, but they are not kind; for they neither understand nor are capable of understanding. At the story's end, the town is unchanged and Becky no better off than if she had been left to starve at its beginning. She was alone when she bore her first child, and she is alone when she dies.

Karintha, Esther, Fern, and Avey are strangers to and in the world they inhabit, which cannot probe beyond their sexuality to reach their souls. Karintha asks for one thing and men offer her another. She knows

† From *CLA Journal* 15 (March 1972): 303–5.

carnality and they insist upon her innocence. Thus, they part—she, full of contempt and they not understanding why she never bared her soul to them. In "Fern," Toomer says that "Men saw Fern's eyes and fooled themselves. Her eyes said one thing but people read another. They begin to leave her, baffled and ashamed . . . for men are apt to idolize or fear that which they do not understand." Esther is alienated as a child and for years she feels that she can only relate to King Barlo, whose blackness, and visions, trances, and reputation as a prophet set him, like herself, alone and apart. She convinces herself that she loves him and she waits. King Barlo returns. "A swift heat sweeps her veins . . . [and] dead dreams are carried upward." They meet, and "her voice is that of a frightened child that calls homeward from miles away." But King Barlo is "slow at understanding." The dream shatters. Esther sees him suddenly as ugly and repulsive, and "draws away, frozen—like a somnambulist." She reverts to loneliness and alienation.

In section two of *Cane*, Toomer changes the locale from rural Georgia to the urban North. But things are no different. Only the methods of loneliness change. As Toomer points out in "Fern," Love is not a thing . . . that can be bettered by changes of town. Could men in Washington, Chicago, or New York, more than the men in Georgia, bring her something left vacant by the bestowal of their bodies? You and I . . . know . . . they could not." Thus, almost all encounter, North or South, ends in a torture and pain so deep that it demands the victim's escape from human interaction. Karintha is contemptuous of everyone who approaches her. Becky dies. Avey escapes into a sleep profound and deep as death. Esther and Louise lose their hold upon reality, and perhaps upon sanity itself. Fern sings her plaintive song, then pounding her head in anguish, faints. Dorris pulls her hair and collapses in tears. And so it goes, through every story. Paul is aloof and inaccessible, and when he finally awakens to self realization, Bona is gone. Dan and Muriel love one another but cannot relate. Muriel is offered a rose and flinches. Dan says "there is no such thing as happiness." Kabnis, a man no longer in tune with his environment, is afraid of everything. He has a compulsion to sit by fires to warm himself; he is always cold. He forfeits his chance to be warmed by Carrie, and sneering bitterly at tousled beds, he grabs the pail of dead coals, substituting death for life and non-commitment for commitment. The same reaction occurs with Lewis who is powerless to help him because Kabnis is "suspended a few feet above the soil whose touch would resurrect him." And Kabnis, who has "a sudden need to rush into the arms of this man" and whose "eyes call, 'Brother,' " repulses Lewis when "a savage, cynical twist . . . mocks his impulse. . . ."

If there is a unifying theme throughout *Cane*, it is the theme of man's inability to communicate and interact with fellow humans; the inability to understand and therefore to love; the inability to quicken another human soul. "Men," says Toomer, "are alone and lonely, and their souls whimper in low, scared voices, lonely and calling out for someone to let them in, to cover them so that they will not shiver." *Cane* is a testament to Toomer's belief that no one can hear these voices, and no one will answer these calls.

SUSAN L. BLAKE

[The Spectatorial Artist in Part One of *Cane*]†

From the men in "Karintha" trying to turn a mysterious woman into a common prostitute, to the poet Kabnis longing to put the terrors of the night world into words, the characters in Jean Toomer's *Cane* are struggling to impose form on a world of chaos. They are all a little bit like Rhobert, the grotesque caricature of a striving homeowner, who "wears a house, like a monstrous diver's helmet on his head" to keep out "life . . . a murky wiggling, microscopic water that compresses him." They fear, with increasing consciousness as the book progresses, that if they do not control chaos it will conquer them, leaving them as disordered and fragmented as the world appears to be. They do not realize that the disorder is within them already—not in the silent, mysterious, paradoxical universe—and that their efforts to impose their idea of order on life only compound their fragmentation. Despite Rhobert's efforts to keep out murky, wiggling, microscopic life, the stuffing in his house is "shredded life-pulp."

Between Jean Toomer and these characters is a creative persona— represented sometimes by a narrator, sometimes simply by the narrative voice—who shares his characters' goals and whose story unifies the book. Like Kabnis, like any artist, he wants to give form to experience, and *Cane* is the record of his attempt. Gorham B. Munson has called this persona the "spectatorial artist,"[1] a term which suggests the artistic process outlined in the book: the persona progresses from a spectator in the first stories to an artist in "Kabnis." His progress is measured by his distance from his characters. Both the spectator and the artist are detached from their material, but the understanding that distinguishes the detached creator of the final story from the detached observer of the first comes from a transitional stage of involvement.

The central conflict in *Cane* is the struggle of the spectatorial artist to involve himself in his material. The characters in the individual stories are engaged in the same conflict. Their "material" is life; involvement for them means acceptance of its chaos. The protagonists in the first stories are unaware of the conflict; the men who try to buy Karintha do not know what they are missing, "do not know that the soul of her was

† From "The Spectatorial Artist and the Structure of *Cane*," *CLA Journal* 17 (June 1974): 516–34.

1. Gorham B. Munson, "The Significance of Jean Toomer," *Opportunity*, 3 (September, 1925), 263.

a growing thing ripened too soon." Kabnis knows; and the sight of "hills
and valleys, heaving with folk-songs, so close to me that I cannot reach
them" drives him mad. For the spectatorial artist, involvement in his
material means identification with his characters and recognition that
the dilemma he is portraying in them is also his dilemma. The characters
become more complex as they become more aware of their experience;
they become more aware as their creator, becoming more involved with
them, puts his own awareness into them. Thus characters and creative
voice develop in parallel in *Cane,* and the book resembles neither a
novel nor a collection of short stories as much as it does a sketchbook—
a record of artistic development.

In the first part of the book, the spectatorial artist maintains the
distance of a reporter. The first four stories are anecdotes, local legends,
related in the past tense from the point of view of an outsider. The
artist's very presence in these stories as a distinct character, the narrator,
emphasizes his emotional distance from the other characters. The struggle to comprehend chaos is represented in these stories as the struggle
of men to possess the women—Karintha, Becky, Carma, Fern—whose
names provide the titles. Superficially the stories are about the women,
but the real interest—the interest developed throughout the book—is in
the men who labor to possess them. They are the active characters, artist
figures with the will to limit, control, define experience. The women—
silent, passive, elusive—represent the experience that the men are trying
to grasp. They embody the beauty, suffer the pain, and above all accept
the domination of the natural chaos. The spectatorial artist remains
aloof from both the men and the women. He sees the mystery in the
women, but intellectually, not sympathetically. He also sees that the
men do not appreciate it and therefore feels superior to them. Only in
the last two stories of Part I, "Esther" and "Blood-Burning Moon," does
the creative voice attempt to enter into the conflict.

"Karintha" dramatizes the essential conflict between the acceptance
and limitation of being. By regarding her as a prostitute, the men who
desire Karintha limit her to an existence defined by the tangible, mea-
surable quantities of body and money. But Karintha is not to be confined
in any way—physically, socially, or conceptually. "Her skin is like dusk
on the eastern horizon," not a texture to be touched or a warmth to be
held, but a quality of light, far off and fleeting. Earth seems not to hold
her down; when she was a child, her running feet did not flop in the
dust like the other children's, "Karintha's running was a whir." Social
and moral laws are suspended for her sake: "even the preacher," the
guardian of public morals, catching her stoning the cows and beating
her dog, finds her "as innocently lovely as a November cotton flower."
Conceptually, Karintha exists outside the normal definition of words.
Though she "has been married many times" and "men will bring their
money," she is not 'a prostitute': "Karintha is a woman. She who carries
beauty, perfect as dusk when the sun goes down." Not only does Toomer

refuse to apply to her a label like 'prostitute,' but the words with which he does describe her have no received meaning apart from the evocation of Karintha. 'Carrying a burden,' for example, is a concept with a restricted, because generally accepted, meaning, but "carrying beauty," the phrase applied to Karintha, is undefined and hence unlimited.

The "interest of the male," however, is the impulse to limit. Men respond to Karintha in the quantitative terms of time and money. First they "count time" until she will be old enough to mate with them; then they run stills and become salesmen and go to college to get money for her. Her attraction for them is of course her sexuality, and it is quite literally her sexual being that they measure in time and money. But Karintha's sexuality is intimately fused with her soul, which is "a growing thing ripened too soon." This metaphor, used in the context of reference to her sexual precocity and to the birth of her child, links her soul to both her sexual potential and its fulfillment, to her reproductive capacity, to her femaleness. The men who try to buy her with money and define her as a prostitute get only half of what should be an indivisible unity of sexuality and soul: "Men do not know that the soul of her was a growing thing ripened too soon. They will bring their money; they will die not having found it out. . . ."

The money the men bring Karintha is only a symbol of the limited and fragmented world in which they try to confine her. They make her a prostitute not so much by bringing her money as by inflicting on her the personal fragmentation that the money implies. Ultimately, however, though Karintha's soul smoulders with her baby in the sawdust pile, it is the men who are left incomplete, who "will die not having found it out." Karintha at the end is still "perfect as dusk"—complete, part of the natural universe—and the men, having failed to know her soul, are still confined in the half-world of time and money.

In the stories of Becky, Carma, and Fern, we begin to see how the conflict dramatized in "Karintha" applies to the spectatorial artist, who functions in these stories as a narrator. There is something about each of these women that other people want to know and never find out. The narrator, experimenting, responds to the unknown in each story with a different pose. In "Becky" he is the bumbling innocent; in "Carma," the detached sophisticate; in "Fern," the earnest and worldly sophomore. His posing reflects his repeatedly unsuccessful attempts to deal with his material. At the end of each of these stories an ironic comment about the limits of knowledge applies to the narrator as well as the other characters.

Becky, the white woman who had two Negro sons, has shattered the laws that the community wants to believe govern social behavior. The townspeople try to deal with the disorder she represents by pretending that she is not part of their world. They redefine her: "Common, God-forsaken, insane white shameless wench, said the white folks' mouths . . . Poor Catholic poor-white crazy woman said the black folks mouths."

They imprison her in a one-room cabin on a narrow strip of ground "islandized between the road and the railroad track." They help her individually and secretly, so they will not have to admit responsibility for her even to themselves. Ultimately, they decide that she does not exist, "that if there was a Becky, that Becky now was dead."

But Becky no more than Karintha will be held down to definitions. First she has a second Negro son; then smoke curling from her chimney proves she is not dead. The conflict between the town's determination to limit and Becky's refusal to be limited is represented stylistically in the interrupted sentence that characterizes this sketch—"A single room held down to earth . . . O fly away to Jesus . . . by a leaning chimney . . ." (ellipses in text). The townspeople's need to define is precisely what prevents them from finding out anything that would satisfy that need: "Taking their words, they filled her, like a bubble rising—then she broke. Mouth setting in a twist that held her eyes, harsh, vacant, staring . . . Who gave it to her? . . . She wouldn't tell." And the chimney by which the townsfolk hold her down to earth is what in the end liberates her to fly away to Jesus.

The narrator in this story allies himself with the townspeople—"our congregation," "we, who had cast out their mother"—and adopts their fears. All he can remember after seeing the rumbling of a ghost train collapse Becky's chimney is "whipping old Dan like fury" to get back to town. "I remember nothing after that—that is, until I reached town and folks crowded round to get the true word of it." That these people who are so dependent on definitions could get the true word, or that this narrator could give it to them, is impossible. Their desire for the true word is as ironic as Barlo's Bible, true Word of the puritanism with which they have cast Becky out, flapping "with an aimless rustle on her mound."

Carma's story, the narrator tells us, is "crudest melodrama"—a term that suggests both sensational events and hollow characters. This story is made melodrama as much by the way the narrator tells it as by the way the characters in it act. Carma's husband, like Becky's persecutors, thinks truth is simple. Either Carma has had other men or she hasn't: "Bane accused her. She denied. He couldn't see that she was becoming hysterical." When he loses his head and slashes his neighbor, he is reacting to the belief that he has been deceived—first by Carma's denial, then by her pretense of suicide, "Twice deceived, and one deception proved the other." His concern with events rather than with Carma implies belief in a universe of fact, where everything may be known and a man has a right to expect not to be deceived.

By calling the story a melodrama, the narrator shows the same lack of sensitivity that characterizes Bane in the story itself. He is detached from Carma: he follows her down the red dust road, but only with his eyes. His interest is that of a storyteller in a bizarre sequence of events, or of a judge in a hypothetical case: "Should she not take others, this

Carma, strong as a man, whose tale as I have told it is the crudest melodrama?" The phrase "as I have told it" suggests, however—at the expense of absolute consistency in point of view—that there may be more to this story than the narrator knows to tell and that by the use of the word 'melodrama' the detached sophisticate shows himself to be as naive as Bane.

The narrator flees from the scene of Becky's destruction, detaches himself from Carma's story, and attempts unsuccessfully to participate in Fern's life. He senses that Fern embodies the mystery of the universe; he sees "the countryside and something that I call God" flow into her eyes, hears the sorrow in her song as of a Jewish cantor singing, feels in her presence the immanence of "things unseen to men." He even half expects to enter into Fern's mystic communion with these things by having a vision. Instead, however, he makes some unconscious, automatic gesture that sends her off into her own world and away from him. She does not come to him on his terms, which are physical, and he does not come to her on hers, which are mystic.

Although the narrator takes Fern's side against the men who are "everlastingly bringing her their bodies," he too brings her something she does not want. He brings his own world—his cosmopolitan experience, his successful friends, his rational approach to life:

> Or, suppose she came up North and married. Even a doctor or a lawyer, say, one who would be sure to get along—that is make money. You and I know, who have had experience in such things. . . .
>
> You and I who know men in these cities will have to say. . . .

By making her a subject for sociological speculation and discussing her in a breezy, intimate, parenthetical tone of voice, the narrator detaches himself from Fern and associates with an audience which is, like himself, not-Southern, not-mystic, and not-Fern. With his final remark—"Her name, against the chance that you might happen down that way, is Fernie May Rosen"—he objectifies Fern's mystic sorrow and defines her in much the same way that the men who bring her money define Karintha. He shows that ultimately he is not trying to enter Fern's world, but to bring her into his. The narrator is not as different as he would like to think from the other men Fern has known. They brought her their bodies, were denied, and left thinking they would like to do something for her. He, too, has brought her something she rejects and leaves thinking, "Something I would do for her. Some fine unnamed thing. . . ." The narrator sees Fern's problem with her admirers, but he doesn't see that he is part of it.

In "Esther" and "Blood-Burning Moon," the spectatorial artist comes a little closer to his characters. Instead of simply relating what has happened to them, he gets inside their thoughts and looks at the world from their point of view. Both of these stories dramatize the personal fragmentation that results from the inability to deal with chaos, and the artist tries to present Esther's and Louisa's mental dislocation from the inside.

In "Esther," the conflict that has been represented so far as a struggle between two distinct groups—men (or, in the case of Becky, the community) and women—takes place within one person. Unlike the women in the first four stories, Esther is an artist figure; like the men, she is seeking personal wholeness through sexual union. But she is a more conscious artist even than the men, for the partner she seeks is largely a creation of her own imagination. Near white and sexually repressed, she decides she is in love with Barlo, who is black—"magnetically so"— and male—"Best man with his fists, best man with dice, with a razor." She imagines that he could fulfill her racial and sexual needs by giving her a coal-black baby. But Esther idealizes both Barlo and sex. She pictures him as she saw him when she was nine—caught up in a religious trance, the embodiment of African spiritualism—and although the imaginary fire from which she rescues her imaginary baby suggests her unacknowledged physical passion, she envisions herself as a sort of madonna with an immaculately conceived baby nibbling at her breast. When she decides, at twenty-seven, to go to Barlo at Nat Bowle's place, it is partly, she rationalizes, to save him from the arms of the loose women there. There is nothing spiritual, however, about either Barlo or Esther's passion for him. Barlo has come back to town "as rich as anyone," worshipping material gods. When Esther sees him he is drunk, hideous. And the loose women who hang around have Esther sized up better than she does herself: " 'So thats how the dictie niggers does it . . . Mus give em credit fo their gall.' " The shattering of her imaginary world leaves Esther with no world at all. When she steps out, "there is no air, no street, and the town has completely disappeared."

The chaos in "Blood-Burning Moon" results from the conflict between natural and social laws. Natural law allows Tom Burwell, black, and Bob Stone, white, to compete for the love of Louisa. Social law, however, prevents a black man from winning a fight with a white man— the white man may not win but the black man must lose. The full moon, a natural deity, shining in the door of the factory, the social center of the community, becomes a symbol for the uneasy balance between the two laws: "The full moon in the great door was an omen. Negro women improvised songs against its spell." Neither of the men can accept the mutual domination of contradictory laws. Bob Stone ignores natural law: "No sir. No nigger had ever been with his girl. He'd like to see one try." Tom Burwell defies social law:

> ". . . white folks ant up t them tricks so much nowadays. Godam better not be. Leastwise not with yo. Cause I wouldnt stand f it. Nassur."
> "What would you do, Tom?"

"Cut him jes like I cut a nigger."
"No, Tom—"

Louisa, caught between the two men, senses the conflict between the
two forces. Her "No, Tom—" may indicate fear for either or both of
her lovers. But Louisa is powerless to prevent the disaster whose immanence she senses rather than sees. Just as there is no way for Louisa
to live, as she would like to, with the love of both Bob and Tom, there
is no concrete way to live between two powerful and conflicting laws.
The people in factory town know this and, admitting the conflict, withdraw from life: "Negroes who had seen the fight slunk into their homes
and blew the lamps out." But Louisa withdraws instead from the knowledge of conflict. When the omen of the full moon shining in the factory
door is fulfilled in the yell of the lynch mob slipping out the door, Louisa
has lost both her lovers and all hold on objective reality. She still thinks
Tom Burwell might come out to hear her sing to the moon. She cannot
accept the reality of contradiction.

Though Esther is active and Louisa passive, both women experience
the dilemma of living within a disordered world. In the previous stories,
the narrator had observed the dilemma without suggesting that the characters feel it. The men are obtuse, the women inert. By locating the
basic conflict of the book within a single character, the spectatorial artist
not only gives the character, a shade of complexity—which indicates a
step in his artistic development—but also acknowledges that the conflict
he observes is individual, psychological. By giving his characters some
of the sensibility that so far has been his alone, he acknowledges their
kinship with him, the artist; by putting himself imaginatively into their
fragmented minds, he acknowledges his kinship with them. * * *

* * *

BERNARD W. BELL

[The Poems of *Cane*]†

* * *   On the surface, *Cane* is a pastoral work, contrasting the values
of uninhibited, unlettered Black rustics with those of the educated, class-
conscious Black bourgeoisie. On this level, Toomer draws on the Afro-
American tradition of music as a major structural device. The melan-
cholic fragments of spirituals and work songs that appear throughout the
sketches create a flowing rhythm and intricate pattern of Gothic images
that unify the dissimilar Christian and non-Christian elements of the
book. While in Georgia, Toomer was deeply moved by the beauty of
the folk songs he heard and saddened by the belief that the industrialization of the South would soon make them relics of the past. Adapting

† From "Portrait of the Artist as High Priest of Soul: Jean Toomer's *Cane*," *Black World* (September
1974): 13–16.

the conventions of the pastoral to his subject, he therefore employs folk songs as symbols of the folk spirit of Black Americans and, by extension, of the eternal soul of man.

* * *

In addition to their striking imagery, all 10 poems in Part One are functional. They serve to elucidate or to set the stage or to provide a transition between the sketches. "Reapers" and "November Cotton Flower," for example, are companion poems to the first sketch. They reinforce the haunting appeal and religious core of Karintha by their emblematic representation of death as a timeless source of tension in life. By their allusion to death as a spiritual release from physical suffering, "Face" and "Cotton Song" extend the religious symbolism of "Becky." Portraying the "channeled muscles" of a woman's face as "cluster grapes of sorrow / purple in the evening sun / nearly ripe for worms," "Face" draws on the traditional typology of the suffering and sacrifice of Christ. "Cotton Song" complements this image of the Crucifixion with a subtle reference to the Resurrection as Black stevedores call for strength to roll a bale of cotton aboard ship. In the refrains "Come, brother, roll roll!" and "We ain't agwine to wait until the judgment Day," the exhortative mood of the poem reaches its zenith, conveying not only the harmonizing of physical and spiritual energy but the will to act now in their own behalf and not wait passively for salvation.

"Song of the Son" and "Georgia Dusk" expand on the regional imagery and metaphysical meaning of "Carma." The opening stanza of "Song of the Son" picks up the "sad strong song" of the girl in "Carma":

> Pour O pour that parting soul in song,
> O pour it in the sawdust glow of night,
> Into the velvet pine-smoke air to-night,
> And let the valley carry it along.
> And let the valley carry it along.

In the plaintive cry of these lines we discover Toomer turning to the blood and soil of his ancestors for inspiration:

> O land and soil, red soil and sweet-gum tree,
> So scant of grass, so profligate of pines,
> Now just before an epoch's sun declines
> Thy son, in time, I have returned to thee,
> Thy son, I have in time returned to thee.

The juxtaposition of antithetical ideas further underscores the metaphysical nature of the narrator's quest.

The key to the irony and yoking together of disparate elements in the poem is found in the play on "son" in the last two lines. The pun is a subtle allusion to the Son of God, which in the context of the rapid association of images in the poem, stresses the Christian paradox that in death is life. This is particularly true of the slaves and their songs:

O Negro slaves, dark purple ripened plums,
Squeezed, and bursting in the pine-wood air,
Passing, before they stripped the old tree bare
One plum was saved for me, one seed becomes

An everlasting son, a singing tree,
Caroling softly souls of slavery,
What they were, and what they are to me,
Caroling softly souls of slavery.

For Toomer the spirituals were the "one seed" of the past that enabled the slaves to transcend the grim hardships of bondage. And since these songs embody the spirit of the many thousand gone, they—like the mythical Tree of Life—possess the power to awaken the eternal soul of man. The impulse for art and religion, in short, has a common root.

As stated earlier, Toomer viewed his experiences as a school administrator in Georgia as a return to his ancestral roots. "My seed was planted in the cane-and-cotton fields," he wrote, "and in the souls of black and white people in the small southern town. My seed was planted in myself down there." And in a letter to *The Liberator,* he stated:

A visit to Georgia last fall was the starting point of almost everything of worth that I have done. I heard folk-songs come from the lips of Negro peasants. I saw the rich dusk beauty that I had heard many false accents about, and of which till then, I was somewhat skeptical. And a deep part of my nature, a part that I had repressed, sprang suddenly to life and responded to them.

The lyrical expression of this regenerating experience is found in "Georgia Dusk," another salute to the South and the tradition of Afro-American music. Toomer's vision of the primeval unity of life is communicated in his symbolic association of a Southern barbecue with a Bacchanalian feast.

The sky, lazily disdaining to pursue
    The setting sun, too indolent to hold
    A lengthened tournament for flashing gold,
Passively darkens for night's barbecue,

A feast of moon and men and barking hounds,
    An orgy for some genius of the South
    With blood-shot eyes and cane-lipped scented mouth,
Surprised in making folk-songs from soul sounds.

The word that stands out in these stanzas is "genius." Stirred by the organic forces of this ritualistic feast, the first Black genius of the South fused the sights and sounds of his African past with his bitter-sweet slave experience into soulful music.

The images of the final three stanzas of "Georgia Dusk" are equally exquisite in their ancestralism:

Meanwhile, the men, with vestiges of pomp,
    Race memories of king and caravan,
    High-priests, an ostrich, and a juju-man,
Go singing through the footpaths of the swamp.

Their voices rise . . . the pine trees are guitars,
    Strumming, pine-needles fall like sheets of rain . . .
    Their voices rise . . . the chorus of the cane
Is caroling a vesper to the stars . . .

O singers, resinous and soft your songs
    Above the sacred whisper of the pines,
    Give virgin lips to cornfield concubines,
Bring dreams of Christ to dusky cane-lipped throngs.

Like the magical potency of pre-colonial African rituals and ceremonies, the voices of a transplanted race blend with the rhythmic vibrations of the New World and become mystical agents of transformation.

Two cryptic nature poems follow "Fern." "Nullo" gives an aura of wonder and mystery to the commonplace phenomenon of "A spray of pine-needles, / Dipped in western gold" falling in the quiet forest. "Rabbits knew not of their falling, / Nor did the forest catch aflame." In "Evening Song," the metaphysical forces of life are represented by the image of a pastoral character "curled like the sleepy waters where the moon waves start," dreaming with her "Lips pressed against my heart." Dusk and dawn, moon and sun are naturally complementary. While the sun symbolizes death and rebirth, Toomer uses the waxing and waning of the moon as a symbol of creative energy, its changing phases influencing the cycle of fertility in plant, animal, and man.

Like the other poems in Part One, "Conversion" and "Portrait in Georgia" are closely related to the themes and imagery of the sketches they connect. "Conversion" heightens the meaning of the parable in Barlo's sermon by exposing the Christian deception of substituting "a white-faced sardonic god" for the "African Guardian of the Soul." The grim image of a woman in "Portrait in Georgia" forcefully establishes the sexual link between the Southern ritual of lynching and the myths of white purity and Black bestiality.

In contrast to the 10 poems in Part One, there are only five in Part Two. However, they are characterized by the same dramatic tensions between either the spirit, emotions, and intellect or man and modern social conventions. In an intricate cosmic conceit, "Beehive" depicts man's failure to develop his intellectual and spiritual potential by associating the mechanical activity of human life with that of bees. "Storm Ending" captures the insensitivity of man to the awesome beauty of Nature, while "Her Lips are Copper Wire" focuses on the lips, the breath, and the tongue as transmitters of the electrical current of the soul. "Prayer" continues this theme with the plea: "O Spirits of who my soul is but a little finger, / Direct it to the lid of its flesh-eye." In

"Harvest Song," the last of the poems, the image of a reaper overpowering the knowledge of his hunger by beating the palm of his hand against a stubble of grain communicates the delicate balance between the emotions, will, and soul of man. Indeed, the primary focus of Part Two is on the perversion of the will and emotions when they are enslaved by the genteel mores of society. When freely and fully realized, the mind and body function as a spiritual unit. Spirituals, folk-songs, jazz, poetry and dance are Toomer's symbols for the attainment of this goal.

* * *

MICHAEL KRASNY

The Aesthetic Structure of Jean Toomer's *Cane*†

In the fall of 1922 Toomer published the poems "Storm Ending," "Georgia Dusk," "Harvest Song," and "Song of the Son," as well as the stories "Fern," "Carma," and "Becky" and the poetic prose pieces "Nora" and "Seventh Street."[1] With the publication of the latter piece, Toomer began to write more about Negroes in the North. These pieces were included in *Cane* in contrast to the poems and prose portraits which resulted from his Georgia experiences. All of the sketches, poems, and stories of *Cane*, as well as the revised version of the culminating dramatic novella "Kabnis," were composed by the end of the year.

To further clarify the conception one merely needs to consider the arcs printed on separate pages in *Cane*, one preceding both "Karintha" and "Seventh Street," and two preceding "Kabnis." The arcs represent the basic design of *Cane*, which, like a circle, moves from the simple forms of life in the South to the more complex forms in the North and back to the South in "Kabnis." Thematically, the structure of the book begins with a lyrical response to the beauty and natural impulses of six primitive women who live close to the soil and, to varying degrees, act outside conventional Christian morality. It then moves to a consideration of the Northern Negro, a transplanted Southerner who has become the victim of technology and white mores. Finally, the book deals with Kabnis, an urbanized Northern Black who returns to the ancestral soil

† From *Negro American Literature Forum* 9.2 (1975): 42–43. Copyright 1975 by Michael Krasny and *Negro American Literature Forum*.
1. "Storm Ending," "Harvest Song" and "Nora" (later changed to "Calling Jesus" in *Cane*) were all published, with the aid of Waldo Frank, in 1922 issues of *The Double Dealer*; "Fern" in *The Little Review* (Autumn 1922, Vol. IX, No. 3), "Carma," "Becky" and "Georgia Dusk" in *The Liberator* (Sept. 1922, Vol. V, No. 9, p. 13 and Oct. 1922, Vol. V, No. X, pp. 25 and 30); "Song of the Son" in *Crisis*; and "Seventh Street" in *Broom* (Dec. 1922).

In August 1923 the revised version of "Kabnis" appeared in *Broom* and before *Cane* was published, "Karintha" was also published in *Broom* (Jan. 1923). Other poems were published in early 1923 such as "November Cotton Flower," which appeared in *Nomad*, and "Her Lips are Copper Wire" which appeared in *S4N* (issue 26, May, 1933) [actually 1923—*Editor*].

For a more detailed analysis of Frank's aesthetic theory the reader is referred to *Waldo Frank* by Gorham Munson (New York: Boni and Liveright, 1923).

in an abortive attempt to discover meaning and acceptance in his heritage.

The discovery and acceptance of heritage is implicit in the first section, embodied in the point of view of the poem "Song of the Son." Though Toomer believed that the folk-spirit and spontaneity of the Southern Negro were dying, he tried to capture vestiges in the portraits of the book's first section. The gallery of Southern women and the poetry of this section bear out the nostalgia the poet feels in "Song of the Son" and emphasize physicality, natural impulse, and the soil. The section moves toward the sexual repression of "Esther"—a result of the infiltration of white morality—and the symbolic murder of Black vitality by white culture in the poem "Portrait in Georgia" and the short story "Blood-Burning Moon."

The next section, or the book's second arc, is concerned with the pervasive effects of white culture upon the Black man of the North. The Northern Negro has undergone a spiritual death not unlike the physical one of Tom Burwell in "Blood-Burning Moon." In counterpoint to the first section of Cane there is thus an emphasis upon exclusion from the soil, natural impulses, and the soul. Exclusion is most clear, for example, in the poetic prose piece "Calling Jesus." The second section begins after two pieces of related poetic prose, with "Avey," the portrait of a Northern Black woman who retains, despite the wishes of the story's narrator, the natural and sensual impulses associated with the emotional South. The movement of the section then focuses on the repression of these impulses in the characters of John in "Theater," and of Muriel and the Southern Black man Dan Moore in "Box Seat." In "Bona and Paul" there is an awakening of Paul's consciousness to the natural and racial beauty of the first section, brought about as a result of his need to gather petals and to comprehend why he was unable to hold the sensual though domineering Bona. In this story, which ends the book's second section, or arc, there is a basic counterpoint between Bona, the Southern white woman, and Louisa of "Blood-Burning Moon." Instead of the moon and blood associated with the latter story, there is sunburst and the Crimson Gardens, forces which act in concert with the story's crimson-uniformed Black doorman to activate Paul's consciousness into understanding his confused, i.e., "moony," racial identity.

The two arcs which precede the last section of Cane, "Kabnis," represent the neuroticized Black consciousness of the North in quest of its uprooted spirituality and racial identity by means of a return to the moon-filled Southland of "moon-children." "Kabnis" thus incorporates the significance of the previous two arcs: the artistic need for lyrical beauty and the discovery of terror of the first section; the stifled spirit and awakening consciousness of the second. The "Kabnis" section of Cane ends, in contrast with the fading past associated with the setting sun in the book's first section, with the sun, a "Gold-glowing child," arising and sending forth "a birth-song," the everlasting song of the

"Deep-rooted Cane." The overall design of *Cane* apparently became clear in Toomer's mind by the time he was writing the second section of the book.

Both of the last two sections of *Cane* deal with the effects upon Black people of the fading of the beautiful and ancestrally linked folk culture, symbolically completed by the impending death of Father John in "Kabnis." Aesthetically, however, the consciousness of Kabnis is able to discover the forms which it seeks in the portraits of the book's first section. The arcs unite in a circle, and this form remains fluid by means of the organic unity and metaphor of the artist's imagination. Like the mystical South of "High-Priests . . . and a juju-man" the book transcends temporal dimensions.

LUCINDA H. MacKETHAN

Jean Toomer's *Cane*: A Pastoral Problem†

"Rhobert wears a house, like a monstrous diver's helmet, on his head." He is suffocating under the weight of it. Like Thoreau's farmer, who has become the tool of his tools, Rhobert is a victim of a system of values. He is no longer a man, but only a housekeeper. "The best works of art," Thoreau says, "are the expression of man's struggle to free himself from this condition. . . ." Jean Toomer writes, as Rhobert sinks into the mud, "Lets open our throats, brother, and sing 'Deep River' when he goes down."

Jean Toomer's *Cane* can be read as an expression of one man's struggle to free himself from the condition of America's Rhoberts—robots of an industrial society who have forgotten how to live. Examined in this light, the book is seen to employ a pastoral design, moving from a lyrical delight in a primitive world, to a recognition of the forces that are destroying that world, and on to a consideration of alternatives: can any sort of pastoral ideal be affirmed in the face of modern realities? Toomer's work is organized around the traditional pastoral motif of a journey away from society, toward nature, though he recognizes, as good pastoral must, that the sojourn is temporary, his Arcadia is being, as Thoreau would say, "whirled past and away." "Though late, O soil, it is not too late yet, / " he says, "To catch thy plaintive soul, leaving, soon gone."

Cane, however, represents more than simply a pastoral eulogy to a fading myth of rural paradise. For Rhobert is a black man—the world that he attempts to uphold is not just a sterile, industrial world; it is, more significantly, the white man's world. The house that enslaves him is made of the "white and whitewashed wood of Washington."

And the Arcadia that is eulogized by a black poet-narrator in Section

† First published in *Mississippi Quarterly* 35 (Fall 1975): 423–34.

One is the South, land not only of red soil, cane-field and folk-song, but also land of lynching and prejudice, primitive violence as well as pastoral peace. And the hero who makes his pilgrimage to Georgia in Section Three does so without essential faith or hope. In response to the "pain and beauty" of the South he prays, "Give me an ugly world. . . . Stinking like unwashed niggers."

Thus irony informs every aspect of Toomer's version of pastoral. The struggle to get free from the conditions which were "bastardizing" the educated, city-bred Negro of the 20's took Toomer south in search of his "roots"; seemingly triumphant, he could write, "Georgia opened me . . . for no other section of the country has so stirred me."[1] Yet locating his roots in the red soil of Georgia provided Toomer not with an escape but only with a new confrontation, for there were disturbing moral ambiguities in this landscape, too.

Cane therefore becomes a work expressive of both the joy of discovery and the frustrations of loss, and Toomer's conclusion leaves only the ambiguities clear: the potential Savior flees, his cowardly antithesis ascends at dawn carrying a bucket of dead coals. It is *Cane*'s pastoral design which provides a certain measure of stability for the complex and often contradictory urges reflected in Toomer's work as he confronts the world that he, as both black man and modern man, must negotiate.

Toomer's trip to Georgia in 1921 was only one of a series of journeys oriented around his need to escape the conditions of his life as well as his determination to find an adequate concept of self. When he finished high school, Toomer signed up for the agriculture curriculum at the University of Wisconsin. There followed a physical training college in Chiago, a history course at the City College of N.Y., and much more.

Little wonder that Toomer wrote of the years before *Cane*, "Personally my life has been tortuous and dispersed."[2] The acceptance of a job as temporary superintendent of a small Negro industrial school in Georgia provided, for a time, relief and restoration. Toomer would say, of this part of his life, that seeing the Negro, "not as a pseudo-urbanized and vulgarized, a semi-Americanized product, but the Negro peasant, strong with the tang of fields and the soil," had the effect on him of giving "birth to a whole new life."[3]

The image of birth, which Toomer used s often to describe his experience in Georgia, is one of the most important symbols in *Cane*. It is an ironic one too, particularly when used by Toomer to define his feelings about his discovery of relation with the Southern Negro. Recognizing that his "roots" were in the Southern black man's world was what made him an artist, according to a letter he wrote to Claude McKay

1. Quoted in Alain Locke, "Negro Youth Speaks," *The New Negro* (New York: Albert and Charles Boni, 1925), p. 51.
2. Quoted in Arna Bontemps, "Introduction" to *Cane* (New York: Harper and Row, 1969), p. viii.
3. Mabel Dillard, "Behind the Veil: Jean Toomer's Esthetic," in *Studies in Cane*, ed. Frank Durham (Columbus, Ohio: Charles E. Merrill, 1971), p. 5.

not long after his venture had borne fruit in several poems and stories. His need for "artistic expression" had pulled him "deeper and deeper into the Negro group," he said.[4] Toomer, seemingly, had found himself and a way to express himself through his association with the black people of a Southland still unspoiled by modern civilization.

Thus the first section of *Cane* records, on one level, Toomer's excitement and newfound sense of belonging. Yet it records, too, on a different level, his separateness and also his awareness that the special environment to which he was witness was fast disappearing. For in yet another letter of this period he wrote that "the Negro is in solution, in the process of solution. As an entity, the race is losing its body. . . ."[5] The question, the implications of which Toomer at the time did not seem fully to recognize, was this: if the "song-lit race of slaves" with whom he associated his artistic being were passing into oblivion, what of his future as artist? He wrote that "if anything comes up now, pure Negro, it will be a swan song."[6] So, while his birth as an artist is celebrated in *Cane*, the book also acknowledges the passing of his primary source of inspiration. "In those pieces that come nearest to the old Negro," he said in his own analysis of *Cane*, "the dominant emotion is a sadness derived from a sense of fading. . . ."[7] Thus while *Cane* represents an awakening in Toomer's life, we now know that he expected to go on to other things, other concerns. In *Cane*, his concern was for the black man in the modern world; it is a concern which caused him to mold his book into a version of Southern pastoral perceived with the black man's double vision of deep belonging and forced alienation.

The Negro artist, Alain Locke once wrote, had an advantage over the white artist in that through his art he could fashion "a return to nature, not by way of the forced and worn formula of Romanticism, but through the closeness of an imagination that has never broken kinship with nature."[8] *Cane* contains in its first part the open exuberance of Toomer's discovery of himself as artist; too, it boasts of his kinship with the land that he found so rich in inspirational value. In the stories and poems of this section, it is the presence of the soil which dominates. The black Southern women of the stories are defined in terms that bind them closely to the fertile land they live on. Carma has a "mangrove-gloomed, yellow flower face"; Louisa's skin is "the color of oak leaves on young trees in fall"; the countryside "flows" into Fern's eyes. Yet it is significant that no one ever possesses the sexually disturbing women; men feel their mystery and promise but cannot reach them by taking their bodies. The imagery of Part One thus gives a sense of fresh and primitive joy, but at the same time the end result of the stories themselves is, as Toomer himself pointed out, "a sense of fading." Karintha, in the first sketch, is a "growing thing ripened too soon." In her story we have the first of

---

4. Bontemps, pp. viii–ix.
5. Dillard, p. 3.
6. Ibid.

7. Ibid.
8. Locke, p. 52.

many births that end immediately, violently in death—"A child fell out of her womb onto a bed of pine-needles in the forest. . . . Weeks after Karintha returned home the smoke was so heavy you tasted it in water." There is imagery of life and birth in most of the poems and sketches of the first section, but most often it is overpowered by imagery of death. The poem "November Cotton Flower" is an example; full of "Beauty so sudden for that time of year," the bloom appears in late autumn during a drought.

Part One thus exhibits two opposite moods; on the one hand, Toomer approaches a kind of hysterical rapture as he displays the vitality of the "song-lit" race of blacks and the Southland they inhabit. But there is also an objectivity born of distance. The poet who records the black man's energetic re-casting of the white man's Christianity in the poem entitled "Conversion" must also record the inroads that white man's civilization has made into the black's more primitive, more poetic world. In "Blood-Burning Moon" Toomer tells of Louisa, who gives herself freely to both a black man and a white man. Uninhibited, completely natural, she represents the liberated soul of the South. Yet given the terms of the actual world she inhabits, her situation is impossible. The black lover kills the white one, and is burned alive by the white lover's friends. Toomer describes the lynching party as it moves toward Louisa's home: "The moving body of their silence preceded them over the crest of the hill into factory town. It flattened the Negroes beneath it." Too strong to be resisted, the white man's world, Toomer believed, would soon either destroy or absorb the more vigorous but also more vulnerable black man's world.

Part One of *Cane* thus shows the black Southerner in his twilight hour, his strength and beauty still discernible against the complementary background of Georgia pine forest and cane field, but his future definitely in jeopardy. In Part Two the background changes, becoming now the streets and "white-walled" buildings of Northern cities. Here the black man stands out against his surroundings instead of merging as with his source; here "nigger life," like a wedge, thrusts "unconscious rhythms, black reddish blood into the white and whitewashed wood of Washington." In Leo Marx's terms, here we have the counterforce essential to literary pastoral, the real world that qualifies and forces an ironic slant on the poet's vision of Arcadia.[9]

The central images of Part One carry over into the second section with significant alterations, all of which suggest sterility and corruption. Footpaths are now busy streets; tall pines that "are guitars" became trees planted in boxes, "whinny[ing] like colts impatient to be let free." The changed regard for the element of sexuality marks the most dramatic difference between the two sections. "That the sexes were made to mate is the practice of the South," Toomer's narrator observes in Part One.

9. Leo Marx, *The Machine in the Garden* (New York: Oxford Univ. Press, 1964), p. 70.

In Part Two, a black man feebly rationalizes his inability to make love to a girl he desires: "Her suspicion would be stronger than her passion. It wouldnt work."

The black women in Part Two are afraid of their sexuality, and men are afraid to approach them. Civilization stifles them; the pressure to conform makes them impotent. Symbolic of the frigidity that the city's social taboos produce is the woman in "Calling Jesus" who locks herself in her house at night, shutting out her soul which is "a little thrust-tailed dog that follows her, whimpering." Toomer equates soul and sex in the image of the dog, who symbolizes the essence of the Southern Negro and what he has lost in the city. Only when the dog's mistress forgets in sleep "the streets and alleys, and the large house where she goes to bed of nights," is she receptive to the soul of her Negro heritage. As she dreams "her eyes carry to where builders find no need for vestibules, for swinging on iron hinges, storm doors."

Houses represent the white world's confinement and inhibition in Part Two. In "Box Seat" a Negro savior-figure comes to his "withered people" in the city to "call them from their houses and teach them to dream." Dan Moore appears as a sort of fertility symbol from the South who has come to "stir the root-life" of a people so afraid of what he is that they hide indoors when they hear him coming. The kind of freedom he offers from "zoo-restrictions and keeper-taboos" is too strong for them. Yet Dan saves no one. Seeing his philosophy rejected, he grows incoherent and impotent, "cool as a green stem that has just shed its flower."

In Part One the fate of all Toomer's women demonstrates finally the violent consequences of life lived according to nature. If failure to abide by society's standards results in such tragedies, is not the self-denial practiced by the characters of the second section preferable; are not their fears of sex, in particular, well-grounded? The answer lies in the desperate attempts to conform that the section dramatizes, in Dorris's futile effort to break out of the mold society has cast for her, in Bona's hypocrisy, and Avey's resignation. The overt violence of the sketches of Part One is replaced in the city stories by repression; physical damage, like physical fulfillment, is thus avoided, but we witness instead the deterioration of potentially valuable personalities. In Part One the women are shown experiencing all of life. In Part Two they experience only frustration.

The point of view also changes in the second section so that we have no longer one calm, reflective vision of life, but many fragmented pictures seen through the consciousness of several male protagonists. The change is functional in pastoral and psychological terms. The narrator of Part One accepts almost subconsciously the primitive side of his nature as a vital part of his personality, and his poetic response to his world reflects his sense of release. In Part Two on the other hand we see the conscious mind of the black man at work in Toomer's characterizations of men who are paralyzed by thought; they think instead of acting, so their actions are self-conscious, artificial as in a play. The theater itself is thus a telling image for Toomer. Watching a group of black chorus girls as they relax, the stage manager's brother thinks. "Soon the director will herd you, my full-lipped, distant beauties, and tame you, and blunt your sharp thrusts in loosely suggestive movements, appropriate to Broadway. (O dance!) Soon the audience will paint your dusk faces white, and call you beautiful."

This man recognizes the artificiality of his world and its incapacities. Yet he himself is trapped by the same diseased mentality. "John's body is separate from the thoughts that pack his mind," says Toomer, and the chorus girl who dances out her longing for him, when looking for approval in his face, finds only "a dead thing in the shadow which is his dream."

In the sketch, "Bona and Paul," a black man living a white man's life in Chicago dreams of a Southern Negro woman giving birth to a son: "She weans it, and sends it, curiously weaving, among lush melodies of cane and corn." The message of the song is drowned out by music of a city nightclub, and so we have another aborted birth which leads the way into Part Three, in which a black man from a Northern city dreams of and denies, like Paul, the pastoral song of the South.

In the third and final section of *Cane* Toomer dramatizes the coming to Georgia of a man who is very different from the narrator of Part One. Ralph Kabnis travels south as a man who has long since "broken kinship" with nature. He can only wish and then deny the possibility that "If I, the dream (not what is weak and afraid in me) could become the face of the South. How my lips would sing for it, my songs being the lips of its soul."

Toomer in Part Three draws together the opposing strains of the first two sections into a dramatic enactment of the concerns of the book as a whole. Though *Cane* was not written as a novel with the novel's sort of unity, Part Three gives the book a unified design, which is pastoral, and a major theme, which might be called Resurrection. Each section has its savior figure, with Lewis in Part Three achieving an amalgamation of Barlo and Dan Moore. Each section also follows a symbolic pattern of light fading into darkness while the third section ends with a significant sunrise. In each section, too, there is a preoccupation with birth, and with pastoral images like the November cotton flower or the trees in boxes which hold in tension the forces of life and death. The third section dramatizes two symbolic birth/death situations.

For the black American, the return in imagination to the rural South involves not just a desire to regain the peace of the simpler world, but it also demands an acceptance of black heritage, rooted in soil, savagery, and slavery. Ralph Kabnis is described as being "suspended a few feet above the soil whose touch would resurrect him." As in Part One, there is here the pastoral suggestion that the soil possesses regenerative force for man. However, in the last section the struggle to become "rooted" is complicated by the fact that the characters involved here have been over-exposed to the debilitating pressures of the white man's artificial, mechanical civilization.

Ralph Kabnis is portrayed as "a promise of soil-soaked beauty; up-rooted, thinning out." He cannot accept the capacity for joy and suffering that characterizes the Southern black folk. The folk songs, revival hymns, and church shouts, forming a constant background music in this section, alternately irritate and frighten him: "We dont have that sort of thing up North," he says. He has come to Georgia seemingly to find himself, but only feels more "cut off" in the South because he is so close to the answers that he is unable or unwilling to understand. "Things are so immediate in Georgia," he complains.

In direct contrast to Kabnis is Lewis, a Northern Negro who "lets the pain and beauty of the South meet him there." Like Kabnis he has come to Georgia "on a contract" with himself, but unlike Kabnis he resembles the narrator of the first section, who is fully receptive to the land and the people around him.

Lewis is a Savior figure, though of a different type than King Barlo or Dan Moore, both of whom exhort their people to "look unto the heavens." Their religion is thus a religion of escape, while Lewis's seems rather one of confrontation. He asks those he meets to forget the "sin-bogies" that artificial conventions have forced them to fear. To Kabnis, for instance, he says: "Can't hold them, can you? Master; slave. Soil; and the overarching heavens. Dusk; dawn. They fight and bastardize you." Here Lewis defines the basic problem of the black man who lives in a white man's world; he has a need to belong to the land of his ancestors, to define himself in terms of his racial inheritance, but also a need to transcend the indignities of the past that the Southland still suggests.

Lewis would seem to offer an answer, a way through. He has Kabnis' poetic vision coupled with a strengthening sense of mission that Kabnis lacks. He is able to see the significance of Father John, who for Kabnis represents only the ignominies and bigotry that the black man is made to bear. To Lewis, on the other hand, Father John is potentially a "mute John the Baptist of a new religion" as well as "a tongue-tied shadow of an old." Lewis recognizes that the past is part of the future, and it is this knowledge which frees him from Kabnis' rootless soul-searching.

Yet Lewis, like Dan Moore, ends up fleeing a scene which suggests things too painful for him. Looking at Father John, Lewis manages to "merge with his source" and to accept both the pain and beauty of the South. But later in the night, when he watches Halsey, a black craftsman, and Kabnis carry on meaningless affairs with two prostitutes, the lone-liness of his deeper understanding of the black man's needs becomes too chilling, and he rushes out: "Their pain is too intense. He cannot stand it."

What it is that Lewis understands about the South and what plan he has to offer for its salvation are matters never clearly defined. His responsiveness and directness seem to indicate a productive way to meet and transcend the dilemma of the Southern black man facing "solution." Yet like the other Negroes of the Southern town, he too seems to become "burdened with an impotent pain." His meeting with Carrie Kate is the only positive scene involving him in the role of savior, and even here he is denied complete power.

Carrie Kate seems to be an extension of the women-figures who dominate Part One. When Lewis draws her attention, she impulsively gives herself to him: "The sun-burst from her eyes floods up and haloes him." Yet there is something else in Carrie Kate that is foreign to her inclinations, and it prohibits her from yielding to Lewis. As she is about to make a commitment to him, she recalls the conventions of her society: "The sin-bogies of respectable southern colored folks clamor at her: 'Look out! Be a *good* girl. A *good* girl. Look out!' "

Carrie represents the Negro's spirit, emphasizing soil and primitive past. Lewis is the modern black man, educated and involved in the present. The possibility of the union of the two, combining the best of North and South, past and present as influences on the black race, symbolizes perhaps a hope for the Negro's future. Yet it is only a possibility, cast in doubt by Carrie Kate's fear of social recriminations. The symbolic potential of Carrie Kate's role is complicated even more by the last scene in "Kabnis," during which she functions as food-bringer, healer, mother, Madonna, and mid-wife.

Early in the drama, Kabnis was told the story of a pregnant black woman killed by a white mob in the street of a Southern town. As she died her child was born living, but a white man took it, "jabbed his knife in it an stuck it t a tree." Kabnis, deeply impressed by the story, later makes the wish that some "lynchin white man" would take his soul and "stick his knife through it an pin it to a tree." This death-wish shows Kabnis' essential need to associate himself with the life of his people, but also indicates his sense of despair concerning his, as their, future.

Yet in the final scene, there is another birth; in symbolic terms it is the rebirth of Kabnis himself. Left alone in Halsey's basement after a night of joyless debauchery, Kabnis curses Father John, representative of his own debased past. Then Carrie Kate appears, "lovely in her fresh energy of the morning." Father John speaks of the sin of the "white folks"; Kabnis is contemptuous. Yet all this time the dark basement is slowly being lighted by the first rays of a "new-sun." Carrie's palms draw the fever out of Kabnis, and she helps him to take off a robe that he had worn during the night to mock himself and his race. The basement, dark and clammy, is like a womb, and Kabnis, now disrobed, goes up the stairs to sunlight.

Is Kabnis a new man? The drama does not tell us. What he meets as he takes up his life again at the end may be the same violence that ended the life of the black baby. Or he may continue simply to fade, in "impotent pain." There are no clear signs from his own actions that he has found the necessary compassion or perception, other than the fact that he "trudges upstairs to the workshop."

Yet in terms of the book's symbolic design, the sunrise described in the last paragraph is highly significant. It is the book's only dramatic description of a true dawn: "The sun arises. Gold-glowing child, it steps into the sky and sends a birth-song slanting down gray dust streets and sleepy windows of the southern town." *Cane* begins with sunset scenes. There is, then, from the very beginning, a realization that the life represented in the Southern scenes is a dying thing which might be captured in art but not preserved as an escape from or a cure for modern ills. The sunrise at the end of *Cane*, then, is a symbol of hope, but not hope based on the simpler rural existence that is given lyrical treatment throughout the book. Rather, because of the sunrise we are able to hope for a sort of reconnection or rerooting process through which Kabnis, a modern black man, might find renewal through an acceptance of the land and the past that have molded his racial identity. We see Kabnis first in the dead of night, waiting for daylight. At the end he is bathed in sunlight, after a night which presents a dramatic possibility of catharsis.

Cane's conclusion points to possibilities through the inclusion of symbols of rebirth and sunrise. The resolution provided is aesthetic, then, not actual, which is as it must be in pastoral art. Toomer takes the idea of restoration through connection with a pastoral world and applies it to the condition of the modern Negro, who he felt was in the process of having racial identity "dissolved." Yet he recognized that a return to the simpler, more vital world was possible only in the artistic sense, which is the sense that he affirms through the pastoral design of *Cane*.

NELLIE Y. McKAY

[Structure, Theme, and Imagery in *Cane*]†

On the train from Georgia to Washington, D.C., in November 1921, Jean Toomer began to write the sketches that became the first section of *Cane*. He had been unprepared for what he saw and heard in the South, and he was incapable of holding back his creative responses to the experience. By Christmas of that year the first draft of those first sketches and of "Kabnis" were done. Through most of 1922 he worked at his writing with zest. His friend, Waldo Frank, suggested that he put the pieces together for a book, and so, in order to form a book-length manuscript, he added to his southern narratives selections based on the

† From *Jean Toomer, Artist: A Study of His Literary Life and Work, 1894–1936.* Copyright 1984 The University of North Carolina Press. Reprinted with permission of the publisher, the Marjorie Content Toomer Estate, and the Jean Toomer Special Collection, Fisk University.

black urban experience. Frank wrote an introduction to the completed manusript and recommended it to Boni and Liveright, who accepted it for publication in 1923.

When he was done he wrote, in wonder, "My words had become a book. . . . I had actually finished something."[1] It was the moment for which he had waited a very long time. Now he felt he had arrived and that, in the company of his literary friends, he was in the "upswing of natural culture" with a "function in the regenerative life that transcended national boundaries and quickened people."[2] He saw himself as part of a living world of promise. He and such men as Waldo Frank, Hart Crane, and Gorham Munson were "men of mission, pioneering up a new slope of consciousness."[3] He was ecstatic. The feeling gave him a sense of experiencing new life. He felt the mystery in being. He wrote: "I gave with abandon the flow of myself. And as I gave I was given to myself. My soul was resurrected and we were joined. . . . There was holy union. And I, united in myself, found myself thereby joined to people and the whole of life, in love. . . . In my soul I found new life. There I discovered what I had sought elsewhere, without finding."[4]

Toomer took great pains in *Cane* to make sure that the structure of the book reflected the relationship of the individual parts to the whole. The design is a circle, he said. Aesthetically, *Cane* builds from simple to complex forms; regionally, it moves from the South to the North and then back to the South; and spiritually, it begins with "Bona and Paul," grows through the Georgia narratives, and ends in "Harvest Song."[5] The first section is about the life of the southern folk culture; the second section is about the urban life of Washington, D.C.; and the third section is about the racial conflicts experienced by a northern black person in the South.

In the original edition of *Cane*, there was a set of arcs on the blank pages before each section, symbols of the book's internal unity. For unexplained reasons, either oversight or intent, the arc preceding the first section has been left off all subsequent editions. On the dust jacket of the original edition, Toomer tells us that the work is a "vaudeville out of the South," with its acts made up of sketches, poems, and a single drama. He notes that although no consistent movement or central plot is present, the sensitive reader can find a beginning, a progression, a complication, and an end.[6]

When the first euphoria over its completion had passed, even before it was published, Jean Toomer saw *Cane* as less of a splendid beginning to his writing career than he had hoped to make. "The book is done," he wrote, but "when I look for the power and beauty I thought I'd

1. Jean Toomer, "Why I Joined the Gurdjieff Work," unpublished manuscript, Fisk University Archives.
2. Ibid.
3. Ibid.
4. Ibid.
5. Letter from Toomer to Frank [1922], Fisk University Archives.
6. From the dust jacket of the first printing of *Cane* (New York, 1923).

caught, they thin out and elude me."[7] In particular, he thought the
Georgia sketches lacked complexity and described them as "too damn
simple for me." Of "Fern," he wrote in a letter to Sherwood Anderson,
the "story-teller style had too much waste and made too many appeals
to the reader." He noted that he could rework it, only he did not think
it sufficiently important to spend more time on it.[8]

He liked Section 2 better. These narratives had the unrestrained energy
that black people brought with them from the South to the North, an
energy that was the source of their spiritual strength. He saw possibilities
for greater development of this energy, which he thought he had especially demonstrated in "Theater" and "Box Seat." Of John and Dorris
in "Theater," he noted that the barrier of class separated them—"stage
folk are not respectable, audiences are."[9] Dorris attempts to break through
the arbitrary social division by using her art—the dance—to try to win
John. But he, a slave to conventions, is unable to respond to the challenge she raises, and she perceives his inadequacy as willful rejection
of her, and it humiliates her.[1]

In "Box Seat" the raw energy belongs to Dan Moore. Toomer describes
it as "ragged, dynamic, perhaps vicious." Dan attempts to save the
woman he loves from the suffocation of oppressive social conventions.
But like Dorris of "Theater" he does not succeed—in this case because
the woman is already trapped and unable to break from her world.
Toomer had doubts about the plausibility of the ending of this sketch.
He questioned Waldo Frank on whether Dan's energy would allow him
to walk away from the fight he initiated: "Would the ego and consciousness of the new Dan permit such an ending?"[2]

Toomer placed himseslf at the center of "Kabnis." He completed this
section after he had made a second trip to the South, and he said that
it stood as his immediate response to the dilemma of Afro-America as
he saw it when he discovered the folk culture. In a letter to Frank, he
points out that he is the source of both Lewis and Kabnis, Lewis with
"the sense of direction and intelligent grip on things that Kabnis lacks,
Kabnis with the sensitivity and emotion Lewis does not have."[3]

When the manuscript was completed, Jean Toomer appeared happy
to his friends. In a letter to Waldo Frank, he intimated that he was in
full agreement with Frank's introduction. In February 1923, in response
to a letter from Horace Liveright he noted that nothing short of being
hit by a "street car" would keep him from having more manuscripts for
publication in the near future. He had two pieces in mind, each about
the length of "Kabnis," and another long story; these were to be the
three pieces for his second book. "[T]he mileau [*sic*] is . . . Washington

7. Toomer, "Outline of An Autobiography."
8. Letter from Toomer to Sherwood Anderson
[1922], Fisk University Archives.
9. Letter from Toomer to Gorham Munson [1922],
Fisk University Archives.

1. Ibid.
2. Letter from Toomer to Frank [1922], Fisk University Archives.
3. Letter from Toomer to Frank [1922], Fisk University Archives.

. . . the characters dynamic, lyric, complex."[4] His autobiographical writings suggest that *Natalie Mann* was one of the works intended for this book. In his letter to Liveright, he mentioned that he did not feel confident to tackle writing a novel yet but nevertheless had one in mind. "At any rate, the horizon for the next three years seems packed and crowded," he concluded.[5] During that time he joined the Poetry Society of South Carolina because he believed the South was in an upswing and ready to provide the material for a new literature.[6] He was full of enthusiasm and confidence in his ability to become an important writer.

Cane was published in September 1923, and immediately took on a life of its own. His family welcomed his achievement. His grandmother was overjoyed and regretted only that his grandfather had not lived to see it happen. His uncle, Bismarck Pinchback, had many good things to say about it. He found the stories and sketches familiar to him, but he was especially pleased with the "beauty and interest in [Toomer's] wonderful descriptions, and in the strength and vigor of [his] language generally."[7]

Among Toomer's friends who praised the book were Hart Crane, Alfred Stieglitz, Georgia O'Keeffe, and Allen Tate. Tate pointed out that one of its strengths was the absence of the "pathos of Harris and others of the southern school of sentimental humor."[8] Black writers and critics immediately gave it high praise. W. E. B. Du Bois and Alain Locke, Countee Cullen and Claude McKay were among those who wrote Toomer their personal feelings. Du Bois called him the "writer who first dared to emancipate the colored world from the conventions of sex."[9] Locke praised his writing and thought process;[1] Cullen called it "a real contribution, a classical portrayal of things as they are";[2] and McKay was equally generous in his compliments. Aside from the personal responses, the book was widely reviewed in newspapers, magazines, and journals. Although it received some negative comments, most of those who read it found it praiseworthy. A large number of people saw it as the dawn of a new day for Afro-American literature and writing. Many people called Jean Toomer a new Negro writer of great promise.

Cane and Jean Toomer have now been talked about and written about for close to six decades, yet they remain among the most intriguing and tantalizing American literary topics of this century. As a work of art,

4. Letter from Toomer to Horace Liveright, March 1923, Fisk University Archives.
5. Ibid.
6. In 1923 Toomer joined the Poetry Society of South Carolina as a non-resident member. Founded in 1920, the society had no written rules against admitting non-Caucasians as members but evidently had not expected such a situation. The discovery that one of its members, Jean Toomer, was the author of a book about Negroes that was advertized as having been written by a Negro created consternation among the members. See Durham's

Studies in Cane for further information.
7. Letter from Bismarck Pinchback to Jean Toomer (September 28, 1923), Fisk University Archives.
8. Letter from Allen Tate to Jean Toomer [1923], Fisk University Archives.
9. W. E. B. Du Bois and Alain Locke, "The Younger Literary Movement," *Crisis*, 27, (February, 1924), p. 161.
1. Letter from Alain Locke to Toomer [1923], Fisk University Archives.
2. Letter from Countee Cullen to Toomer [1923], Fisk University Archives.

the book has been subject to numerous critical interpretations and doubt-less will continue to stimulate interest among new generations of scholars for a long time to come. Toomer's disappearance—by free will or force, by caprice or from feelings of compulsion—from the world of letters shortly after the book was published and at the moment when his success in literature seemed almost assured, has piqued the curiosity of a great many people and has led to various speculations on its causes and meaning.

In addition, for more than a decade, critics and scholars, captivated by *Cane*, have explored Toomer's subsequent writings for further glimpses of the genius who wrote that book. All agree that his most important, most powerful, and best writing is in *Cane*, which differs significantly even from those things he wrote during the same period. Why then did he turn his back on the possibilities that art in literature held for him, especially after all of those years of searching for his own voice? Why was *Cane* a swan song, not only, as he believed, for the folk culture but also for Jean Toomer's writing career, which he never understood or accepted?

These are questions that have not been definitively resolved in the minds of many who admire *Cane* and Toomer's art in this book. While the issues of race and society are undoubtedly of the utmost significance to his decision, the "facts" do not constitute the whole answer. Those who continue to pursue Toomer studies are themselves in search of the meaning in his motivation, a meaning that he consciously sought to understand for most of his life. In the discussion to follow, my aim is to discover a nexus between some of the tangled threads of conscious and unconscious thought that propelled him away from the people and ideas that culminated in *Cane* and to demystify his actions by attempting to understand the complicated emotions from which they originated. Toomer's relationship to *Cane*—and how that differs in observable ways from his relationship to some of his other works of that period—is what this particular inquiry seeks to clarify.

Balo, Natalie Mann, and *Cane* were projects that engaged Toomer in 1922. In my examination of the plays, I noted that Toomer wrote them in the process of experimenting with dramatic forms in an attempt to analyze particular aspects of the American experience. What is most important about them in terms of the relationship between the author and his work is Toomer's conscious use of artifice—of forms then still very new to American literature—to gain his ends. In other words, Toomer's relationship to the plays has to do with the way in which he uses language and form, just as the relationship between a sculptor and his work has to do with the way he uses clay or wood or marble. He molds and carves them to fit the particular contours of his imagination.

On the other hand, *Cane* comes from a separate frame of reference. From its multiplicity of literary forms that have been a source of con-fusion, frustration, and/or admiration for many readers to the realistic details that can be understood even through its maze of impressionism, there is an intricate and intimate relationship between Toomer and *Cane*, which differs from that between him and his other works. In this connection, the book claims close ties of lineage with the stream of consciousness writing that first gained wide attention in James Joyce's *Ulysses* [1922], a year before *Cane* was published, and that William Faulkner would make popular in American literature later in that decade. If we believe Toomer's account of the inception of the work, and we have no reason to doubt it, in writing *Cane* he gave expression to feelings that overwhelmed him concerning the southern experience. He created in art, from those feelings, his own consciousness and reality as he confronted the history of black and white America—the pain, oppression, and strength of the past, the complications he saw in the present, and the ambivalences they all raised in him. Recalling his feelings while he was in Georgia, he wrote that "at times I identified with the whole scene so intensely that I lost my own identity."[3] Indeed, *Cane* is the outcome of the process of writing *out* of himself, out of the identity he discovered and recovered in the experiences he had in the South in the fall of 1921.

The epigraph on the title page of the book establishes the relationship of black Americans to its subject:

> Redolent of fermenting syrup,
> Purple of the dusk,
> Deep-rooted cane.

It is the metaphor for the experience of a people's connection to the land and soil that made them what they are. The symbol appears repeatedly in Sections 1 and 3 of the book, which are set in the South, but only rarely in Section 2, which represents aspects of the urban world.

Karintha's purple-dusk beauty opens the Georgia narratives, which, in part, take place against a background of the grinding of cane and the boiling and stirring of the sweet syrup. At the end of the day, black men gather around David Georgia's stove with its hot mellow glow that rose and "spread fan-wise into the low-hanging heavens" at the edge of the forest, and they are drenched in the heavy fragrance that exudes from the copper cauldron. In the final section, Kabnis's nightmare in the canebrake culminates in the sun's rising on the treetops of the forest. The tenacity to survive the harshness of black American reality is mirrored in the hard and grinding work from which the sweet cane syrup comes.

The most immediately striking feature of *Cane* is its language, which Toomer uses masterfully to create tones and atmospheres. Section 1, the Georgia stories, embodies a good deal of nature imagery, which makes it the most vivid, mystical and sensuous part of the book. At the

---

3. Toomer, "Outline of An Autobiography."

same time, as the section develops, the lyricism gives way to dissonance, sarcasm, and irony, all of which lead up to a bloody finale. The imagery in Section 2, set in Washington, D.C., and Chicago, reflects the industrialization and mechanization of the urban environment. The dominant themes are concerned with man's alienation in a repressive society. There is no canebrake in Section 2, no lyric or mystical language, but there is energy that comes from the tension between free will and arbitrary restraints. In Section 3, the action moves back to Georgia but the language does not incorporate all of the lyric qualities of the first section. However, the nature imagery restores a sense of contact with the earth. The predominant themes of Section 3 are ambivalence and fear, and the sensuousness and elusiveness of the women of Section 1 are replaced by the impotence and uncertainty that Kabnis experiences in the land of his forefathers. Only at the end is there a sign of hope for healing, and it comes from expectations that the voice and the pen of the artist will help to make it possible.

Toomer uses two modes of presentation for the sketches in Section 1 and Section 2 of *Cane*; in one, the narrator is the detached observer, and in the other, he is a character in his own story. In both sections, the narrator's mood ranges from disengaged pathos to subjective involvement. The narrator as persona also goes through stages of development. An important difference between Sections 1 and 2, aside from those of language and tone, is the fact that although the narrator has a degree of identification with the people and the region in Section 1, he never fully becomes integrated into either the richness or the pain of Georgia. In Section 2, however, one instinctively feels that he belongs to this world of the city and shares intimately in its shortcomings and its failings. In both sections, Toomer explores positive and negative aspects of each culture and shows how they reflect meaning in the lives and experiences of the people.

Section 3, a single dramatic piece, is less a presentation of experience than an opportunity for the reader to share the experiences of the artist— to observe his intentions and note the sources of his despair and his hopes. Neither an observer nor merely a character in the drama, he is the central figure around whom the action revolves. Ralph Kabnis is in search of his identity. He is a northerner, but he is also a southerner. He despises his southern history, which he cannot disregard, and he despises himself because he finds that history so painful. It challenges his weakness, and he is afraid to claim his heritage. He moves from painful resistance to painful acknowledgment of his history, and readers share his expectations for full, positive self-acceptance in the future.

* * *

Selected Bibliography

BOOKS OF WRITINGS BY JEAN TOOMER

Cane. New York: Boni and Liveright, 1923. Reprinted, 1927. Reprinted, New York: University Place Press, 1967. Reprinted with introduction by Arna Bontemps, New York: Harper, 1969. Reprinted with introduction by Darwin T. Turner, New York: Liveright, 1975.

Essentials: Definitions and Aphorisms. Privately printed by H. Dupee's Lakeside Press. Chicago: 1931.

The Wayward and the Seeking: A Collection of Writings by Jean Toomer. Ed. Darwin T. Turner. Washington: Howard UP, 1980.

BIBLIOGRAPHIES

Griffin, John C. "Jean Toomer: A Bibliography." *The South Carolina Review* 7.2 (April 1975): 61–64.

Reilly, John M. "Jean Toomer: An Annotated Checklist of Criticism." *Resources for American Literary Study* 4 (Spring 1974): 27–56.

BIOGRAPHY AND CRITICISM

Ackley, Donald G. "Theme and Vision in Jean Toomer's *Cane.*" *Studies in Black Literature* 1 (Spring 1970): 45–65.

Armstrong, John. "The Real Negro." *New York Tribune* 14 Oct. 1923: 26.

Baker, Houston. "Journey toward Black Art: Jean Toomer's *Cane. Singers at Daybreak.* Washington: Howard UP, 1974.

Bell, Bernard W. "Jean Toomer's 'Blue Meridian': The Poet as Prophet of a New Order of Man." *Black American Literature Forum* 14 (Summer 1980): 77–80.

———. "A Key to the Poems in *Cane.*" *CLA Journal* 14 (March 1971): 251–58.

Benson, Brian, and Mabel Dillard. *Jean Toomer.* Boston: Twayne, 1980.

Blackwell, Louise. "Jean Toomer's *Cane* and Biblical Myth." *CLA Journal* 17 (June 1974): 535–42.

Bowen, Barbara. "Untroubled Voice: Call-and-Response in *Cane.*" *Black American Literature Forum* 16 (Spring 1982): 12–18.

Braithwaite, William Stanley. "The Negro in American Literature." *Crisis* 28 (September 1924): 204–10.

Chase, Patricia. "The Women in *Cane.*" *CLA Journal* 14.3 (March 1971): 259–73.

Clark, J. Michael. "Frustrated Redemption: Jean Toomer's Women in *Cane,* Part One." *CLA Journal* 22.4 (June 1979): 319–34.

Davis, Charles T. "Jean Toomer and the South: Region and Race as Elements within a Literary Imagination." *Studies in the Literary Imagination* 28 (1975): 423–34.

Dillard, Mabel. "Jean Toomer: Herald of the Negro Renaissance." *DA* 28 (1967): 3178A–79A. Ohio U.

———. "Jean Toomer: The Veil Replaced." *CLA Journal* 17 (June 1974): 468–73.

Duncan, Bowie. "Jean Toomer's *Cane:* A Modern Black Oracle." *CLA Journal* 15 (March 1972): 323–33.

Durham, Frank, comp. *The Merrill Studies in Cane.* Columbus: Charles E. Merrill, 1971.

Eldridge, Richard. "The Unifying Images in Part One of Jean Toomer's *Cane.*" *CLA Journal* 22.3 (March 1979): 187–214.

Faulkner, Howard. "The Buried Life: Jean Toomer's *Cane.*" *Studies in Black Literature* 7.1 (Winter 1976): 1–5.

Fisher, Alice P. "The Influence of Ouspensky's *Tertium Organum* upon Jean Toomer's *Cane.*" *CLA Journal* 17.3 (June 1974): 504–15.

Fullinwider, S. P. "Jean Toomer: Lost Generation or Negro Renaissance?" *Phylon* 27.4 (Winter 1966): 396–403.

Gloster, Hugh M. *Negro Voices in American Fiction.* Chapel Hill: U of North Carolina P, 1948.

Gross, Theodore, L. *The Heroic Ideal in American Literature.* New York: Free Press, 1971.

Helbling, Mark. "Jean Toomer and Waldo Frank." *Phylon* 41.2 (June 1980): 167–78.

Holmes, Eugene. "Jean Toomer—Apostle of Beauty." *Opportunity* 10 (August 1932): 252–54, 260.

Huggins, Nathan I. *The Harlem Renaissance.* New York: Oxford UP, 1971.

Hughes, Langston. "Gurdjieff in Harlem." *The Big Sea.* New York: Knopf, 1940. 241–43.

Innes, Catherine L. "The Unity of Jean Toomer's *Cane.*" *CLA Journal* (March 1972): 306–22.

Jung, Udo O. H. " 'Nora' Is 'Calling Jesus': A Nineteenth-Century European Dilemma in an Afro-American Garb." *CLA Journal* 21.2 (December 1977): 251–55.

Kerlin, Robert T. "Singers of New Songs." *Opportunity* (May 1926): 162.

Kerman, Cynthia Earl and Richard Eldridge. *The Lives of Jean Toomer: / A Hunger for Wholeness.* Baton Rouge: Louisiana State UP, 1987.

Kousaleos, Peter G. "A Study of the Language: Structure and Symbolism in Jean Toomer's *Cane* and N. Scott Momaday's *House Made of Dawn.*" *DAI* 34 (1973): 2631A. Ohio U.

Kramer, Victor. "The Mid-Kingdom of Crane's 'Black Tambourine' and Jean Toomer's *Cane.*" *CLA Journal* 17.4 (June 1974): 486–97.

Krasny, Michael J. "Jean Toomer and the Quest for Consciousness." *DAI* 32 (1972): 6982-A. University of Wisconsin.

———. "Jean Toomer's Life Prior to *Cane*: A Brief Sketch of the Emergence of a Black Writer. *Negro American Literature Forum* 9.2 (1975): 40–41.

Lewis, David L. *When Harlem Was in Vogue.* New York: Knopf, 1981.

Lieber, Todd. "Design and Movement in *Cane.*" *CLA Journal* 13.1 (September 1969): 35–50.

Locke, Alain. "From *Native Son* to *Invisible Man*: A Review of the Literature for 1952." *Phylon* 14.1 (1953): 34–44.

Martin, Odette C. "*Cane*: Method and Myth." *Obsidian* 2.1 (Spring 1976): 5–20.

Mason, Clifford. "Jean Toomer's Black Authenticity." *Black World* 20.1 (November 1970): 70–76.

Munson, Gorham. "The Significance of Jean Toomer." *Destinations: A Canvass of American Literature since 1900.* New York: J. H. Sears, 1928. 178–86.

Perry, Margaret. "Two Outcasts." *Silence to the Drums.* Westport: Greenwood Press, 1976. 27–44.

Redmond, Eugene. "A Long Ways from Home." *Drumvoices.* Garden City: Anchor/Doubleday, 1976. 137–293.

Redding, [J.] Saunders. "American Negro Literature." *American Scholar* 18 (Spring 1949): 137–48.

———. "The Emergence of the New Negro." *To Make a Poet Black.* Chapel Hill: U of North Carolina P, 1939. 104–6.

Riley, Roberta. "Search for Identity and Artistry." *CLA Journal* 17.4 (June 1974): 480–85.

Rosenfeld, Paul. "Jean Toomer." *Men Seen: Twenty-four Modern Authors.* New York: Dial, 1925. 227–33.

Schultz, Elizabeth. "Jean Toomer's 'Box Seat': The Possibility for Constructive Crisises." *Black American Literature Forum* 13.1 (Spring 1978): 7–12.

Scruggs, Charles. "Jean Toomer: Fugitive." *American Literature* 47.1 (March 1975): 84–96.

———. "The Mark of Cain and the Redemption of Art: A Study in Theme and Structure of Jean Toomer's *Cane.*" *American Literature* 44.2 (May 1972): 276–91.

Sergeant, Elizabeth S. "The New Negro." *New Republic* 44 (1926): 371–72.

Shockley, Anne A., ed. *Banc!* 2.2 (1972). Fisk U Library. Special issue about Toomer.

Spofford, William K. "The Unity of Part One of Jean Toomer's *Cane.*" *Markham Review* 3 (1972): 58–60.

Starke, Catherine J. *Black Portraiture in American Fiction: Stock Characters, Archetypes, and Individuals.* New York: Basic Books, 1971.

Taylor, Carolyn. " 'Blend Us with Thy Being': Jean Toomer's Mill House Poems." Diss. Boston College, 1977.

Turner, Darwin T. "And Another Passing." *Negro American Literature Forum* 1.1 (Fall 1967): 3–4.

———. "Jean Toomer's *Cane*: A Critical Analysis." *Negro Digest* 18 (January 1969): 54–61.

Thompson, Larry E. "Jean Toomer: As Modern Man." *The Harlem Renaissance Remembered.* Ed. Arna Bontemps. New York: Dodd, Mead, 1972. 51–62.

Turpin, Waters E. "Four Short Fiction Writers of the Harlem Renaissance—Their Legacy of Achievement." *CLA Journal* 11.1 (September 1967): 59–72.

Twombly, Robert. "A Disciple's Odyssey: Jean Toomer's Gurdjieffian Career." *Prospects: Annual of American Cultural Studies* 2. New York: Burt Franklin, 1976. 437–62.

Wagner, Jean. *Black Poets of the United States. From Paul Lawrence Dunbar to Langston Hughes.* Trans. Kenneth Douglas. Urbana: U of Illinois P, 1973.